Praise for *Pragmatic AI*

"[This is] a sweeping guide that bridges the gap between the promise of AI and solutions to the gritty problems that must be solved to deploy real-world projects. Clear and usable, *Pragmatic* AI covers much more than just Python and AI algorithms."

—**Christopher Brousseau**, founder and CEO of Surface Owl, the Enterprise AI platform

"A fantastic addition for any technology enthusiast! There is so much you can say about this book! Noah Gift really made this a practical guide for anyone involved with machine learning in the industry. Not only does it explain how one can apply machine learning on large data sets, it provides a valuable perspective on technology feedback loops. This book will benefit many data science and development teams so they can create and maintain their applications efficiently right from the beginning."

—**Nivas Durairaj**, technical account manager, AWS (Certified Professional Architect AWS)

"A great read if you want insights into building production-quality ML pipelines and tools that truly help your data engineering, data science, or data DevOps team. Even experienced developers often find themselves spinning their wheels on low-productivity tasks. Oftentimes, software books and university classes don't explain the steps needed to go into production. Noah has a gift for finding pragmatic approaches to software deployments that can really accelerate the development and delivery process. He has a focus and passion for enabling rapid software solutions that is very unique.

"The key to building production-quality ML pipelines is automation. Tasks and steps, which engineers may do manually during the research or prototype phase, must be automated and scaled in order to create a production system. This book is full of practical and fun exercises that will help any Python developer automate and extend their pipelines into the cloud.

"I'm currently working with big data, ML pipelines, Python, AWS, Google cloud, and Azure at Roofstock.com, an online real estate company. Our analytics database is approaching 500 million rows! Within this book I found many practical tips and exercises that will immediately improve my own productivity. Recommended!"

—**Michael Vierling**, lead engineer, Roofstock

Pragmatic AI

Pragmatic AI

An Introduction to Cloud-Based Machine Learning

Noah Gift

✦Addison-Wesley

Boston • Columbus • New York • San Francisco • Amsterdam • Cape Town
Dubai • London • Madrid • Milan • Munich • Paris • Montreal • Toronto • Delhi • Mexico City
São Paulo • Sydney • Hong Kong • Seoul • Singapore • Taipei • Tokyo

Library of Congress Control Number: 2018939834

ISBN-13: 978-0-13-486386-3
ISBN-10: 0-13-486386-0

1 18

❖

*This book is dedicated to my family and extended family,
who have always been there for me: my wife, Leah Gift;
my mom, Shari Gift; my son, Liam Gift; and my mentor,
Dr. Joseph Bogen*

❖

Contents

Preface

About twenty years ago I was working at Caltech in Pasadena and I dreamed of someday working with AI on a daily basis. At the time, in the early 2000s, it was not a popular time to be interested in AI. Despite that, here we are, and this book culminates a lifelong obsession with AI and science fiction. I feel very lucky to have rubbed elbows with some of top people in AI while at Caltech, and undoubtedly this experience led me down the road to writing this book.

Beyond just AI, however, I have also had an obsession with both automation and pragmatism. This book incorporates those themes as well. As a seasoned, experienced manager, consistently shipping products and surviving terrible, horrible, no-good technology has made me practical. If it isn't deployed into production, it doesn't count. If it isn't automated, it is broken. Hopefully this book will inspire others to share my point of view.

Who Should Read This Book

This book is for anyone interested in AI, Machine Learning, the cloud, and any combination of those topics. Programmers and non-programmers alike should be able to find useful nuggets of knowledge. Many students with whom I have interacted in workshops at NASA, PayPal, or the University of California, Davis, have been able to assimilate these notebooks and ideas with limited or no prior programming experience. Python is used heavily in this book, and it is one of the most ideal languages to pick up if you are new to programming.

At the same time, there are many advanced topics covered like using cloud computing platforms (i.e., AWS, GCP, and Azure) and doing ML and AI programming. For advanced technologists who are fluent in Python, the cloud, and Machine Learning, there are many useful ideas that can be immediately transplanted into current work.

How This Book Is Organized

This book is divided into three sections: Part I: Introduction to Pragmatic AI, Part II: AI in the Cloud, and Part III: Creating Practical AI Applications from Scratch. In Part I, Chapters 1–3 cover introductory material.

- Chapter 1, "Introduction to Pragmatic AI," includes an overview of the goals of this book and a rapid-fire tutorial of Python, with just enough background to allow a user to understand other uses of Python in the book.

- Chapter 2, "AI and ML Toolchain," covers the lifecycle of build systems, command line, and Jupyter Notebooks in a data science project.

- Chapter 3, "Spartan AI Lifecycle," incorporates the pragmatic production feedback loop into projects. Tools and frameworks like Docker, AWS SageMaker, and TensorFlow Processing Units (TPUs) are covered.

In Part II, Chapters 4 and 5 cover AWS and Google Cloud.

- Chapter 4, "Cloud AI Development with Google Cloud Platform," goes into the GCP platform and some of the unique, developer-friendly offerings it provides. Services like TPUs, Colaboratory, and Datalab are covered.

- Chapter 5, "Cloud AI Development with Amazon Web Services," dives into workflows on AWS like Spot instances, CodePipeline, using and testing Boto, and a high-level overview of services.

In Part III, Chapters 6–11 cover practical AI applications and examples.

- Chapter 6, "Predicting Social-Media Influence in the NBA," is a chapter that is based on work at a startup, several articles, and a Strata talk. Topics include: What drives the valuation of teams? Does winning bring more fans to games? Does salary correlate with social-media performance?

- Chapter 7, "Creating an Intelligent Slackbot on AWS," covers creating a serverless chat bot that scrapes web sites and provides summarized information back to the mothership on Slack.

- Chapter 8, "Finding Project Management Insights from a GitHub Organization," investigates a common source of behavior data, GitHub metadata. Pandas, Jupyter Notebook, and the command-line tool *click* are used to mine for Behavioral Data Gold.

- Chapter 9, "Dynamically Optimizing EC2 Instances on AWS," turns AWS signals into an opportunity to use Machine Learning techniques to optimize price.

- Chapter 10, "Real Estate," explores national and local home prices using Machine Learning and interactive plotting.

- Chapter 11, "Production AI for User-Generated Content," explores how to use AI to interact with user-generated content. Topics such as sentiment analysis and recommendation engines are covered.

- Appendix A, "AI Accelerators," discusses hardware chips that are specifically designed to run AI workloads. An example of an AI accelerator is a TPU from Google.

- Appendix B, "Deciding on Cluster Size," discusses this activity as more art than science, although there are some techniques to make the decision process more clear.

Example Code

Throughout the book, each chapter has a companion Jupyter Notebook or set of Jupyter Notebooks. These notebooks have been developed throughout the last couple of years as the result of articles, workshops, or courses I have taught.

Note

All of the source code for book can be found in the form of Jupyter Notebooks here: https://github.com/noahgift/pragmaticai.

Many examples also include Makefiles like the one below.

```
setup:
        python3 -m venv ~/.pragai

install:
        pip install -r requirements.txt

test:
        cd chapter7; py.test --nbval-lax notebooks/*.ipynb

lint:
        pylint --disable=W,R,C *.py

lint-warnings:
        pylint --disable=R,C *.py
```

Makefiles are a great way to orchestrate the different aspects of a data science project in Python or R. Notably, they are useful at setting up an environment, linting source code, running tests, and deploying code. Additionally, isolated environments like virtualenv do eliminate a whole class of problems. It is amazing how many students I encounter that have exactly the same issue: they installed something to one Python interpreter but use another. Or they cannot get something to work because two packages conflict with each other.

In general, the answer to this is to use a virtual environment for each project and to be judicious about always selecting that environment when you work on that project. A little bit of project planning goes a long way toward preventing issues in the future. Including Makefiles, linting, Jupyter Notebook tests, SaaS build systems, and unit tests are best practices that should be replicated and encouraged.

Conventions Used in This Book

The following typographical conventions are used in this book.

- In [2]: shows IPython terminal output. Often this is similar to the supplied Jupyter Notebook examples available in GitHub.

Acknowledgments

I am grateful to Laura Lewin who gave me the opportunity to publish this book with Pearson, as well as the rest of the team: Malobika Chakraborty and Sheri Replin. I would also like to thank the technical reviewers: Chao-Hsuan Shen (https://www.linkedin.com/in/lucashsuan/), Kennedy Behrman (https://www.linkedin.com/in/kennedybehrman/), and Guy Ernest (https://www.linkedin.com/in/guyernest/) from Amazon. They played an important role in getting the book into tip-top shape.

In general, I would like to acknowledge Caltech. My interest in AI was formed when I worked at Caltech during the AI winter of the early 2000s. I remember one professor at Caltech telling me that AI was a waste of time, but I remember thinking I wanted to do it anyway. I then set a goal for myself that I would be doing significant AI programming by the time I was in my early 40s, and that I would be fluent in several programming languages—and this actually happened. Telling me I cannot do something has always been a huge motivator for me, so thank you to that professor!

I also met some really influential people there including Dr. Joseph Bogen, a neurophysiologist who was an expert in theories of consciousness. We would have dinner conversations about neural networks, the origins of consciousness, calculus, and work he was doing in Christof Koch's lab. To say he had an influence on my life is understatement, and I am proud to say that I am actually working on neural networks today partially because of dinner conversations we had 18 years ago.

There were other people I met at Caltech that I didn't interact with as much but who still had an impact on me: Dr. David Baltimore (whom I worked for), Dr. David Goodstein (whom I worked for), Dr. Fei-Fei Li, and Dr. Titus Brown (who got me hooked on Python).

Sports and athletic training have always played a huge role in my life. At one point I was serious about playing professional basketball, track, and even Ultimate Frisbee. I ran into Sheldon Blockburger, an Olympic Decathlete, at Cal Poly, San Luis Obispo, and he taught me how to run 8 × 200-m intervals in under 27 seconds and 300-m intervals until I puked. I still remember him saying that "less than 1 percent of the population has the discipline to do this workout." This training in self-discipline has played a huge role in my development as a software engineer.

I have always gravitated toward being around world-class athletes because of their intensity, positive outlook, and willingness to win. In the last several years, I accidently discovered Brazilian jiu-jitsu (BJJ) by working out at Empower in San Francisco, California. The coaches there—Tareq Azim, Yossef Azim, and Josh McDonald—have all played a huge role in getting me thinking like a fighter. In particular, Josh McDonald, a world-class athlete in multiple sports, has been an inspiration to me, and his workouts have played a huge role in me getting through this book. I cannot recommend this gym or these coaches enough to technical professionals in the Bay Area.

These initial contacts have led to meeting more people in the martial arts community, like NorCal Fight Alliance in Santa Rosa, run by Dave Terrell. I train with Dave Terrell, Jacob Hardgrove, Collin Hart, Justin Sommer, and others, and they selflessly share their knowledge and thoughts on martial arts. There is nothing more challenging that I have experienced yet in life than having a 240-pound black belt squeeze the life out of me over and over again, day after day. Knowing that I can withstand that has been helpful in withstanding the pressures of writing this book. I am very fortunate to be able to train at this gym, and I highly recommend it for technology professionals in the Bay Area.

The last acknowledgment, on the BJJ front, I have to also thank Maui Jiu Jitsu, in Haiku, Maui, for serving as a muse to writing this book. I took a break last year to figure out what I wanted to do next and trained with Professor Luis Heredia and Joel Bouhey. They were both incredible teachers, and that experience was very helpful in deciding to write this book.

Thanks to Zak Stone, the Product Manager for TensorFlow, for early access to TPUs and help with GCP. Thanks also to Guy Ernest at AWS for advice on AWS services. Thanks to Paul Shealy from Microsoft for advice on Azure cloud.

Another institution I need to thank is UC Davis. I received my MBA in 2013, and it had a big impact on my life. I was able to meet some incredible professors like Dr. David Woodruff, who let me program in Python for the Optimization class and helped write a really powerful library called Pyomo. I must also thank Professor Dickson Louie, who has been a great mentor to me, and Dr. Hemant Bhargava, who gave me the opportunity to teach Machine Learning at UC Davis. Dr. Norm Matloff has also selflessly helped me get better at Machine Learning and Statistics, and I am very grateful to him. I am also thankful to the students in my course BAX-452, who got to try out some of this material, and the MSBA staff: Amy Russell and Shachi Govil. Another friend to thank is Mario Izquierdo (https://github.com/marioizquierdo), who is a brilliant developer and has been a great person to throw programming ideas around about real world deployment.

Lastly, I would like to thank a couple of my friends from my startup days: Jerry Castro (https://www.linkedin.com/in/jerry-castro-4bbb631/) and Kennedy Behrman (https://www .linkedin.com/in/kennedybehrman/), who are as reliable, hard-working, and resilient as they come. Much of the material for this book was developed while we worked side by side in the trenches at a startup that ultimately failed. It is experiences like this that reveal the true character of individuals, and I am honored to have been their coworker and friend.

About the Author

Noah Gift is lecturer and consultant at UC Davis Graduate School of Management in the MSBA program. He is teaching graduate Machine Learning and consulting on Machine Learning and Cloud Architecture for students and faculty. He has published close to 100 technical publications including two books, on subjects ranging from Cloud Machine Learning to DevOps. He is a certified AWS Solutions Architect, and Subject Matter Expert on Machine Learning for AWS, and has helped created the AWS Machine Learning certification. He also has an MBA from UC Davis, a MS in Computer Information Systems from Cal State Los Angeles, and a BS in Nutritional Science from Cal Poly, San Luis Obispo.

Professionally, Noah has approximately 20 years' experience programming in Python and is a Python Software Foundation Fellow. He has worked in roles ranging from CTO, General Manager, Consulting CTO, and Cloud Architect. This experience has been with a wide variety of companies including ABC, Caltech, Sony Imageworks, Disney Feature Animation, Weta Digital, AT&T, Turner Studios, and Linden Lab. In the last 10 years, he has been responsible for shipping many new products at multiple companies that generated millions of dollars of revenue and had global scale. Currently he is consulting in startups and other companies on Machine Learning, Cloud Architecture, and CTO-level consulting as the Founder of Pragmatic AI Labs.

You can find more about Noah by following him on GitHub https://github.com/noahgift/, visiting his company Pragmatic AI Labs, https://paiml.com, visiting his personal site http://noahgift.com, or connecting with him on Linkedin https://www.linkedin.com/in/noahgift/.

Introduction to Pragmatic AI

Introduction to Pragmatic AI

Don't mistake activity with achievement.

John Wooden

If you are picking up this book, you are probably curious about pragmatic AI. There are no shortage of books, courses, and webinars on the latest machine learning and deep learning technique. The shortage lies in how to get a project to the place where it is even possible to use advanced techniques. This is why this book exists—to bridge the gap between theory and the real-world issues with implementing artificial intelligence (AI) projects.

In many cases, it may not be feasible to train your own model because the project in which you are involved may not have some combination of time, resources, or skills to implement it. There is a better solution than to continue on a path where failure is almost certain. A pragmatic AI practitioner will use the appropriate technique for the situation. In some cases, this may mean calling an application programming interface (API) that has a pretrained model. Another pragmatic AI technique may be creating a model that is intentionally less effective because it is simpler to understand and to deploy to production.

In 2009, Netflix had a famous competition in which it awarded $1 million to a team that increased the accuracy of the company's recommendations by 10 percent. The contest was exciting and before its time in making data science mainstream. What few people know, though, is that the algorithm that won the contest was never implemented because of engineering costs (https://www.wired.com/2012/04/netflix-prize-costs/). Instead, some of the algorithms from a team that had "only" an 8.43 percent improvement were used. This is a great example of how pragmatism is really the goal of many AI problems, not perfection.

This book focuses on being the second-place team that actually ships its solution to production. This common thread ties this book together. Shipping code to production is the goal of this book—not being the best solution that never made it into the product.

Functional Introduction to Python

Python is a fascinating language because it is good enough at so many things. There is an argument to be made that Python is not exceptional at anything, but good enough at most things. The real strength of the language is this intentional lack of complexity. Python can be programmed in many different styles as well. It is completely possible to use Python to literally execute statements in a procedural way, line by line. Python can also be used as a complex object-oriented language with advanced features like metaclasses and multiple inheritance.

When learning Python, especially in the context of data science, parts of the language are less important to focus on. An argument could even be made that many parts of the language, mainly heavy object-oriented programming, may never need to be used in the course of writing Jupyter Notebooks. Instead, an alternative approach would be to focus on functions. This section briefly introduces Python, which can be thought of as the new Microsoft Excel.

One of my recent graduate students told me before he took my machine learning course he was worried about how complex the code looked. After spending a few months using Jupyter Notebook and Python, he mentioned he felt very comfortable using Python to solve data science problems. It is my strong belief, based on evidence I have seen while teaching, that all users of Excel can become users of Jupyter Notebook at Python.

It is worth pointing out that in deploying code to production, Jupyter may or may not be the delivery mechanism. There is a lot of traction with new frameworks like Databricks, SageMaker, and Datalab that allow for Jupyter-based production deployments, but often the purpose of Jupyter is to do experiments.

Procedural Statements

The following examples assume the installation of at least Python 3.6. You can download the latest version of Python at https://www.python.org/downloads/. Procedural statements are literally statements that can be issued one line at a time. Below are types of procedural statements. These statements can be run in.

- Jupyter Notebook
- IPython shell
- Python interpreter
- Python scripts

Printing

Python has one of the simplest forms of printing. Print is a function that accepts input and sends it to the console.

```
In [1]: print("Hello world")
   ...:
Hello world
```

Create Variable and Use Variable

Variables are created by assignment. This example both assigns a variable and then prints it by combining two statements with a semicolon. This semicolon style is common in Jupyter Notebooks but is typically frowned upon for production code and libraries.

```
In [2]: variable = "armbar"; print(variable)
armbar
```

Multiple Procedural Statements

Complete solutions to a problem can be created by writing straight procedural code as shown. This style is reasonable for Jupyter Notebooks but is uncommon for production code.

```
In [3]: attack_one = "kimura"
   ...: attack_two = "arm triangle"
   ...: print("In Brazilian jiu-jitsu a common attack is a:", attack_one)
   ...: print("Another common attack is a:", attack_two)
   ...:
In Brazilian jiu-jitsu a common attack is a: kimura
Another common attack is a: arm triangle
```

Adding Numbers

Python can also be used as a calculator. This is a great way to get comfortable with the language; start using it instead of Microsoft Excel or a calculator app.

```
In [4]: 1+1
   ...:
Out[4]: 2
```

Adding Phrases

Strings can be added together.

```
In [6]: "arm" + "bar"
   ...:
Out[6]: 'armbar'
```

Complex Statements

More complex statements can be created that use data structures like the belts variable, which is a list.

```
In [7]: belts = ["white", "blue", "purple", "brown", "black"]
   ...: for belt in belts:
   ...:     if "black" in belt:
   ...:         print("The belt I want to earn is:", belt)
   ...:     else:
   ...:         print("This is not the belt I want to end up with:", belt)
   ...:
```

```
This is not the belt I want to end up with: white
This is not the belt I want to end up with: blue
This is not the belt I want to end up with: purple
This is not the belt I want to end up with: brown
The belt I want to earn is: black
```

Strings and String Formatting

Strings are a sequence of characters and they are often programmatically formatted. Almost all Python programs have strings because they can send messages to users of the program. However, there are a few core concepts to understand.

- Strings can be created with the single, double, and triple/double quotes.

- Strings can be formatted.

- One complication of strings is they can be encoded in several formats, including Unicode.

- Many methods are available to operate on strings. In an editor or IPython shell, you can see these methods by tab completion.

```
In [8]: basic_string = ""

In [9]: basic_string.
            capitalize()   encode()        format()
        isalpha()       islower()       istitle()      lower()
            casefold()   ` endswith()     format_map()
isdecimal()    isnumeric()    isupper()       lstrip()
            center()        expandtabs()    index()
isdigit()       isprintable()  join()          maketrans()   >
            count()         find()          isalnum()
isidentifier() isspace()     ljust()         partition()
```

Basic String

The most basic string is a variable that is assigned to a phrase with quotes. The quotes can be triple quotes, double quotes, or single quotes.

```
In [10]: basic_string = "Brazilian jiu-jitsu"
```

Splitting String

Turn a string in a list by splitting on spaces or some other thing.

```
In [11]: #split on spaces (default)
    ...: basic_string.split()
Out[11]: ['Brazilian', 'jiu-jitsu']

In [12]: #split on hyphen
    ...: string_with_hyphen = "Brazilian-jiu-jitsu"
    ...: string_with_hyphen.split("-")
    ...:
Out[12]: ['Brazilian', 'jiu-jitsu']
```

All Capital Letters

Python has many useful built-in methods for changing strings. This is how a string is converted to all caps.

```
In [13]: basic_string.upper()
Out[13]: 'BRAZILIAN JIU JITSU'
```

Slicing Strings

Strings can be referenced by length and sliced.

```
In [14]: #Get first two characters
    ...: basic_string[:2]
Out[14]: 'Br'
In [15]: #Get length of string
    ...: len(basic_string)
Out[15]: 19
```

Adding Strings Together

Strings can be added together both by concatenating two strings or by assigning a variable to a string and then building up longer sentences. This style is reasonable and intuitive for Jupyter Notebooks, but for performance reasons it is better to use f-strings in production code.

```
In [16]: basic_string + " is my favorite Martial Art"
Out[16]: 'Brazilian jiu-jitsu is my favorite Martial Art'
```

Formatting Strings in Complex Ways

One of the best ways to format a string in modern Python 3 is to use f-strings.

```
¶ In [17]: f'I love practicing my favorite Martial Art,
        {basic_string}'
    ...:
Out[17]: 'I love practicing my favorite Martial Art,
        Brazilian jiu-jitsu'
```

Strings Can Use Triple Quotes to Wrap

It is useful to take a snippet of text and assign it to a variable. An easy way to do this in Python is by using triple quotes to wrap up the phrase.

```
In [18]: f"""
    ...: This phrase is multiple sentences long.
    ...: The phrase can be formatted like simpler sentences,
    ...: for example, I can still talk about my favorite
        Martial Art {basic_string}
    ...: """
Out[18]: '\nThis phrase is multiple sentences long.\nThe phrase
can be formatted like simpler sentences,\nfor example,
I can still talk about
my favorite Martial Art Brazilian jiu-jitsu\n'
```

Line Breaks Can Be Removed with Replace

The last long line contained line breaks, which are the **\n** character, and they can be removed by using the replace method.

```
In [19]: f"""
    ...: This phrase is multiple sentences long.
    ...: The phrase can be formatted like simpler sentences,
    ...: for example, I can still talk about my favorite
         Martial Art {basic_string}
    ...: """.replace("\n", "")
Out[19]: 'This phrase is multiple sentences long.The phrase can be
formatted like simpler sentences,for example, I can still talk about
my favorite Martial Art Brazilian jiu-jitsu'
```

Numbers and Arithmetic Operations

Python is also a built-in calculator. Without installing any additional libraries, it can do many simple and complex arithmetic operations.

Adding and Subtracting Numbers

The Python language is also flexible in that it allows f-string–based formatting of a phrase.

```
In [20]: steps = (1+1)-1
    ...: print(f"Two Steps Forward:  One Step Back = {steps}")
    ...:
Two Steps Forward:  One Step Back = 1
```

Multiplication with Decimals

Decimal support is also included in the language, making it straightforward to create word problems.

```
In [21]:
    ...: body_fat_percentage = 0.10
    ...: weight = 200
    ...: fat_total = body_fat_percentage * weight
    ...: print(f"I weight 200lbs, and {fat_total}lbs of that is fat")
    ...:
I weight 200lbs, and 20.0lbs of that is fat
```

Using Exponents

Using the math library, it is straightforward to call 2 to the 3rd power, as shown.

```
In [22]: import math
    ...: math.pow(2,3)
Out[22]: 8.0
```

An alternative method would be

```
>>> 2**3
8
```

Converting Between Different Numerical Types

Be aware of many numerical forms in Python. A couple of the most common are

- Integers
- Floats

```
In [23]: number = 100
    ...: num_type = type(number).__name__
    ...: print(f"{number} is type [{num_type}]")
    ...:
100 is type [int]
In [24]: number = float(100)
    ...: num_type = type(number).__name__
    ...: print(f"{number} is type [{num_type}]")
    ...:
100.0 is type [float]
```

Rounding Numbers

A decimal with many digits can be rounded to just two decimals, as shown.

```
In [26]: too_many_decimals = 1.912345897
    ...: round(too_many_decimals, 2)
Out[26]: 1.91
```

Data Structures

Python has a couple of core data structures that are used frequently.

- Lists
- Dictionaries

Dictionaries and lists are the real workhorses of Python, but there are also other data structures like tuples, sets, counters, etc., that are worth exploring too.

Dictionaries

Dictionaries are good at solving many problems, much like Python. In the following example, a list of Brazilian jiu-jitsu attacks are put into a dictionary. The "key" is the attack, and the "value" is the half of the body on which the attack is made.

```
In [27]: submissions = {"armbar": "upper_body",
    ...:                 "arm_triangle": "upper_body",
    ...:                 "heel_hook": "lower_body",
    ...:                 "knee_bar": "lower_body"}
    ...:
```

A common dictionary pattern is to iterate on a dictionary by using the items method. In this example, the key and the value are printed.

```
In [28]: for submission, body_part in submissions.items():
    ...:     print(f"The {submission} is an attack \
             on the {body_part}")
    ...:
The armbar is an attack on the upper_body
The arm_triangle is an attack on the upper_body
The heel_hook is an attack on the lower_body
The knee_bar is an attack on the lower_body
```

Dictionaries can also be used to filter. In the example below, only the submission attacks on the upper body are displayed.

```
In [29]: print(f"These are upper_body submission attacks\
 in Brazilian jiu-jitsu:")
    ...: for submission, body_part in submissions.items():
    ...:     if body_part == "upper_body":
    ...:         print(submission)
    ...:
These are upper_body submission attacks in Brazilian jiu-jitsu:
armbar
arm_triangle
```

Dictionary keys and values can also be selected:

```
In [30]: print(f"These are keys: {submissions.keys()}")
    ...: print(f"These are values: {submissions.values()}")
    ...:
These are keys: dict_keys(['armbar', 'arm_triangle',
        'heel_hook', 'knee_bar'])
These are values: dict_values(['upper_body', 'upper_body',
        'lower_body', 'lower_body'])
```

Lists

Lists are commonly used in Python. They allow for sequential collections. Lists can hold dictionaries, just as dictionaries can hold lists.

```
In [31]: list_of_bjj_positions = ["mount", "full-guard",
                                  "half-guard", "turtle",
                                  "side-control", "rear-mount",
                                  "knee-on-belly", "north-south",
                                  "open-guard"]
    ...:
```

```
In [32]: for position in list_of_bjj_positions:
   ...:       if "guard" in position:
   ...:            print(position)
   ...:
full-guard
half-guard
open-guard
```

Lists can also be used to select elements by slicing.

```
In [35]: print(f'First position: {list_of_bjj_positions[:1]}')
   ...: print(f'Last position: {list_of_bjj_positions[-1:]}')
   ...: print(f'First three positions:\
        {list_of_bjj_positions[0:3]}')
   ...:
First position: ['mount']
Last position: ['open-guard']
First three positions: ['mount', 'full-guard', 'half-guard']
```

Functions

Functions are the building blocks for data science programming in Python, but they are also a way of creating logical, testable structures. There has been a strong debate brewing for decades about whether functional programming is superior to object-oriented programming in Python. This section will not answer that question, but it will show the utility of understanding the fundamentals of functions in Python.

Writing Functions

Learning to write a function is the most fundamental skill to learn in Python. With a basic mastery of functions, it is possible to have an almost full command of the language.

Simple Function

The simplest functions just return a value.

```
In [1]: def favorite_martial_art():
   ...:       return "bjj"
In [2]: favorite_martial_art()
Out[2]: "bjj"
```

Documenting Functions

It is a good idea to document functions. In Jupyter Notebook and IPython, docstrings can be viewed by referring to the function with a ? character appended after the object as shown.

```
In [2]: favorite_martial_art_with_docstring?
Signature: favorite_martial_art_with_docstring()
Docstring: This function returns the name of my favorite martial art
File:      ~/src/functional_intro_to_python/
Type:      function
```

Docstrings of functions can be printed out by referring to __doc__

```
In [4]: favorite_martial_art_with_docstring.__doc__
   ...:
Out[4]: 'This function returns the name of my favorite martial art'
```

Function Arguments: Positional, Keyword

A function is most useful when arguments are passed to the function. New values for times are processed inside the function. This function is also a "positional" argument, not a keyword argument. Positional arguments are processed in the order in which they are created.

```
In [5]: def practice(times):
   ...:     print(f"I like to practice {times} times a day")
   ...:


In [6]: practice(2)
I like to practice 2 times a day

In [7]: practice(3)
I like to practice 3 times a day
```

Positional Arguments: Processed in Order

Positional arguments for functions are processed in the order in which they are defined. So, they are both easy to write and easy to be confused about.

```
In [9]: def practice(times, technique, duration):
   ...:     print(f"I like to practice {technique},\
                {times} times a day, for {duration} minutes")
   ...:


In [10]: practice(3, "leg locks", 45)
I like to practice leg locks, 3 times a day, for 45 minutes
```

Keyword Arguments: Processed by Key or Value, and Can Have Default Values

One handy feature of keyword arguments is that you can set defaults and only change the defaults you want to change.

```
In [12]: def practice(times=2, technique="kimura", duration=60):
   ...:     print(f"I like to practice {technique},\
                {times} times a day, for {duration} minutes")
In [13]: practice()
I like to practice kimura, 2 times a day, for 60 minutes
In [14]: practice(duration=90)
I like to practice kimura, 2 times a day, for 90 minutes
```

**kwargs and *args

Both *kwargs and *args syntax allow dynamic argument passing to functions. However, these syntaxes should be used with discretion because they can make code hard to understand. This is also a powerful technique to know how to use when appropriate.

```
In [15]: def attack_techniques(**kwargs):
    ...:     """This accepts any number of keyword arguments"""
    ...:
    ...:     for name, attack in kwargs.items():
    ...:         print(f"This is an attack I would like\
    ...:           to practice: {attack}")
    ...:
```

```
In [16]: attack_techniques(arm_attack="kimura",
    ...:                    leg_attack="straight_ankle_lock", neck_attack="arm_triangle")
    ...:
This is an attack I would like to practice: kimura
This is an attack I would like to practice: straight_ankle_lock
This is an attack I would like to practice: arm_triangle
```

Passing Dictionary of Keywords to Function

**kwargs syntax can also be used to pass in arguments all at once.

```
In [19]: attacks = {"arm_attack":"kimura",
    ...:            "leg_attack":"straight_ankle_lock",
    ...:            "neck_attack":"arm_triangle"}
In [20]: attack_techniques(**attacks)
This is an attack I would like to practice: kimura
This is an attack I would like to practice: straight_ankle_lock
This is an attack I would like to practice: arm_triangle
```

Passing Around Functions

Object-oriented programming is a popular way to program, but it isn't the only style available in Python. For concurrency and for data science, functional programming fits as a complementary style.

In this example, a function can be used inside of another function by being passed into the function itself as an argument.

```
In [21]: def attack_location(technique):
    ...:     """Return the location of an attack"""
    ...:
    ...:     attacks = {"kimura": "arm_attack",
    ...:                "straight_ankle_lock":"leg_attack",
    ...:                "arm_triangle":"neck_attack"}
    ...:     if technique in attacks:
    ...:         return attacks[technique]
    ...:     return "Unknown"
    ...:
```

```
In [22]: attack_location("kimura")
Out[22]: 'arm_attack'
```

```
In [24]: attack_location("bear hug")
    ...:
Out[24]: 'Unknown'

In [25]: def multiple_attacks(attack_location_function):
    ...:         """Takes a function that categorizes attacks
                    and returns location"""
    ...:
    ...:         new_attacks_list = ["rear_naked_choke",
                "americana", "kimura"]
    ...:         for attack in new_attacks_list:
    ...:             attack_location = attack_location_function(attack)
    ...:             print(f"The location of attack {attack} \
                        is {attack_location}")
    ...:

In [26]: multiple_attacks(attack_location)
The location of attack rear_naked_choke is Unknown
The location of attack americana is Unknown
The location of attack kimura is arm_attack
```

Closures and Functional Currying

Closures are functions that contain other functions. In Python, a common way to use them is to keep track of the state. In the example below, the outer function *attack_counter* keeps track of counts of attacks. The inner function *attack_filter* uses the *"nonlocal"* keyword in Python3 to modify the variable in the outer function.

This approach is called *functional currying*. It allows for a specialized function to be created from general functions. As shown, this style of function could be the basis of a simple video game or may be used by the statistics crew of an MMA match.

```
In [1]: def attack_counter():
    ...:     """Counts number of attacks on part of body"""
    ...:     lower_body_counter = 0
    ...:     upper_body_counter = 0
    ...:     def attack_filter(attack):
    ...:         nonlocal lower_body_counter
    ...:         nonlocal upper_body_counter
    ...:         attacks = {"kimura": "upper_body",
    ...:             "straight_ankle_lock":"lower_body",
    ...:             "arm_triangle":"upper_body",
    ...:             "keylock": "upper_body",
    ...:             "knee_bar": "lower_body"}
    ...:         if attack in attacks:
    ...:             if attacks[attack] == "upper_body":
    ...:                 upper_body_counter +=1
    ...:             if attacks[attack] == "lower_body":
    ...:                 lower_body_counter +=1
    ...:         print(f"Upper Body Attacks {upper_body_counter},\
                    Lower Body Attacks {lower_body_counter}")
```

```
...:        return attack_filter
...:

In [2]: fight = attack_counter()

In [3]: fight("kimura")
Upper Body Attacks 1, Lower Body Attacks 0

In [4]: fight("knee_bar")
Upper Body Attacks 1, Lower Body Attacks 1

In [5]: fight("keylock")
Upper Body Attacks 2, Lower Body Attacks 1
```

Functions that Yield (Generators)   A useful style of programming is "lazy evaluation." A generator is one example of this style. Generators yield items at a time.

This example returns an "infinite" random sequence of attacks. The lazy portion comes into play in that while there is an infinite amount of values, they are only returned when the function is called.

```
In [6]: def lazy_return_random_attacks():
...:        """Yield attacks each time"""
...:        import random
...:        attacks = {"kimura": "upper_body",
...:              "straight_ankle_lock":"lower_body",
...:              "arm_triangle":"upper_body",
...:               "keylock": "upper_body",
...:               "knee_bar": "lower_body"}
...:        while True:
...:            random_attack = random.choices(list(attacks.keys()))
...:            yield random_attack
...:

In [7]: attack = lazy_return_random_attacks()

In [8]: next(attack)
Out[8]: ['straight_ankle_lock']

In [9]: attacks = {"kimura": "upper_body",
...:              "straight_ankle_lock":"lower_body",
...:              "arm_triangle":"upper_body",
...:               "keylock": "upper_body",
...:               "knee_bar": "lower_body"}
...:
```

```
In [10]: for _ in range(10):
    ...:         print(next(attack))
    ...:
['keylock']
['arm_triangle']
['arm_triangle']
['arm_triangle']
['knee_bar']
['arm_triangle']
['knee_bar']
['kimura']
['arm_triangle']
['kimura'
```

Decorators: Functions That Wrap Other Functions

Another useful technique in Python is to use the decorator syntax to wrap one function with another function. In the example below, a decorator is written that adds random sleep to each function call. When combined with the previous "infinite" attack generator, it generates random sleeps between each function call.

```
In [12]: def randomized_speed_attack_decorator(function):
    ...:         """Randomizes the speed of attacks"""
    ...:
    ...:         import time
    ...:         import random
    ...:
    ...:         def wrapper_func(*args, **kwargs):
    ...:             sleep_time = random.randint(0,3)
    ...:             print(f"Attacking after {sleep_time} seconds")
    ...:             time.sleep(sleep_time)
    ...:             return function(*args, **kwargs)
    ...:         return wrapper_func

In [13]: @randomized_speed_attack_decorator
    ...: def lazy_return_random_attacks():
    ...:         """Yield attacks each time"""
    ...:         import random
    ...:         attacks = {"kimura": "upper_body",
    ...:                 "straight_ankle_lock":"lower_body",
    ...:                 "arm_triangle":"upper_body",
    ...:                  "keylock": "upper_body",
    ...:                  "knee_bar": "lower_body"}
    ...:         while True:
    ...:             random_attack = random.choices(list(attacks.keys()))
    ...:             yield random_attack
    ...:
```

```
In [14]: for _ in range(10):
   ...:         print(next(lazy_return_random_attacks()))
   ...:
Attacking after 1 seconds
['knee_bar']
Attacking after 0 seconds
['arm_triangle']
Attacking after 2 seconds
['knee_bar']
```

Using Apply in Pandas

The final lesson on functions is to make use of this knowledge on a DataFrame in Pandas. One of the more fundamental concepts in Pandas is to use apply on a column versus iterating through all of the values. In this example, all of the numbers are rounded to a whole digit.

```
In [1]: import pandas as pd
   ...: iris = pd.read_csv('https://raw.githubusercontent.com/mwaskom/seaborn-data/master/iris.csv')
   ...: iris.head()
   ...:
Out[1]:
   sepal_length  sepal_width  petal_length  petal_width species
0           5.1          3.5           1.4          0.2  setosa
1           4.9          3.0           1.4          0.2  setosa
2           4.7          3.2           1.3          0.2  setosa
3           4.6          3.1           1.5          0.2  setosa
4           5.0          3.6           1.4          0.2  setosa

In [2]: iris['rounded_sepal_length'] =\
          iris[['sepal_length']].apply(pd.Series.round)
   ...: iris.head()
   ...:
Out[2]:
   sepal_length  sepal_width  petal_length  petal_width species  \
0           5.1          3.5           1.4          0.2  setosa
1           4.9          3.0           1.4          0.2  setosa
2           4.7          3.2           1.3          0.2  setosa
3           4.6          3.1           1.5          0.2  setosa
4           5.0          3.6           1.4          0.2  setosa

   rounded_sepal_length
0                   5.0
1                   5.0
2                   5.0
3                   5.0
4                   5.0
```

This was done with a built-in function, but a custom function can also be written and applied to a column. In the example below, the values are multiplied by 100. The alternative way to accomplish this would be to create a loop, transform the data, and then write it back. In Pandas, it is straightforward and simple to apply custom functions instead.

```
In [3]: def multiply_by_100(x):
   ...:     """Multiplies by 100"""
   ...:     return x*100
   ...: iris['100x_sepal_length'] =\
 iris[['sepal_length']].apply(multiply_by_100)
   ...: iris.head()
   ...:

   rounded_sepal_length  100x_sepal_length
0                   5.0              510.0
1                   5.0              490.0
2                   5.0              470.0
3                   5.0              460.0
4                   5.0              500.0
```

Using Control Structures in Python

This section describes common control structures in Python. The workhorse of control structures in regular Python is the "for loop." One thing to be aware of, however, is that for loops are not commonly used with Pandas, so what works well for Python doesn't fit with the paradigm in Pandas. Some examples are

- For loops
- While loops
- If/else statements
- Try/Except
- Generator expressions
- List comprehensions
- Pattern matching

All programs eventually need a way to control the flow of execution. This section describes some techniques to do so.

for Loops

The for loop is one of the most fundamental control structures in Python. One common pattern is to use the range function to generate a range of values, then to iterate on them.

```
In [4]: res = range(3)
   ...: print(list(res))
   ...:
[0, 1, 2]
```

```
In [5]: for i in range(3):
   ...:       print(i)
   ...:
0
1
2
```

For Loop over List

Another common pattern is to iterate on a list.

```
In [6]: martial_arts = ["Sambo", "Muay Thai", "BJJ"]
   ...: for martial_art in martial_arts:
   ...:       print(f"{martial_art} has influenced\
               modern mixed martial arts")
   ...:
Sambo has influenced modern mixed martial arts
Muay Thai has influenced modern mixed martial arts
BJJ has influenced modern mixed martial arts
```

While **Loops**

A while loop is often used as a way of looping until a condition is met. A common use of a while loop is to create an infinite loop. In the example, a while loop is used to filter a function that returns 1 of 2 types of attacks.

```
In [7]: def attacks():
   ...:       list_of_attacks = ["lower_body", "lower_body",
                 "upper_body"]
   ...:       print(f"There are a total of {len(list_of_attacks)}\
                 attacks coming!")
   ...:       for attack in list_of_attacks:
   ...:           yield attack
   ...: attack = attacks()
   ...: count = 0
   ...: while next(attack) == "lower_body":
   ...:       count +=1
   ...:       print(f"crossing legs to prevent attack #{count}")
   ...: else:
   ...:       count +=1
   ...:       print(f"This is not a lower body attack, \
         I will cross my arms for #{count}")
   ...:
There are a total of 3 attacks coming!
crossing legs to prevent attack #1
crossing legs to prevent attack #2
This is not a lower body attack, I will cross my arms for #3
```

If/Else

If/Else statements are a common way to branch between decisions. In the example, if/elif are used to match a branch. If there are no matches, the last else statement is run.

```
In [8]: def recommended_attack(position):
   ...:     """Recommends an attack based on the position"""
   ...:     if position == "full_guard":
   ...:         print(f"Try an armbar attack")
   ...:     elif position == "half_guard":
   ...:         print(f"Try a kimura attack")
   ...:     elif position == "full_mount":
   ...:         print(f"Try an arm triangle")
   ...:     else:
   ...:         print(f"You're on your own, \
                  there is no suggestion for an attack")
In [9]: recommended_attack("full_guard")
Try an armbar attack

In [10]: recommended_attack("z_guard")
You're on your own, there is no suggestion for an attack
```

Generator Expression

Generator expressions build further on the concept of yield by allowing for the lazy evaluation of a sequence. The benefit of generator expressions is that nothing is evaluated or brought into memory until it is actually evaluated. This is why the example below can be operating on an infinite sequence of random attacks that are generated.

In the generator pipeline, a lower-case attack such as "arm_triangle" is converted to "ARM_TRIANGLE"; next, the underscore is removed in "ARM TRIANGLE".

```
In [11]: def lazy_return_random_attacks():
    ...:     """Yield attacks each time"""
    ...:     import random
    ...:     attacks = {"kimura": "upper_body",
    ...:         "straight_ankle_lock":"lower_body",
    ...:         "arm_triangle":"upper_body",
    ...:          "keylock": "upper_body",
    ...:          "knee_bar": "lower_body"}
    ...:     while True:
    ...:         random_attack = random.choices(list(attacks.keys()))
    ...:         yield random_attack
    ...:
    ...: #Make all attacks appear as Upper Case
    ...: upper_case_attacks = \
              (attack.pop().upper() for attack in \
              lazy_return_random_attacks())
```

```
In [12]: next(upper_case_attacks)
Out[12]: 'ARM_TRIANGLE'


In [13]: ## Generator Pipeline:  One expression chains into the next
    ...: #Make all attacks appear as Upper Case
    ...: upper_case_attacks =\
             (attack.pop().upper() for attack in\
             lazy_return_random_attacks())
    ...: #Remove the underscore
    ...: remove_underscore =\
             (attack.split("_") for attack in\
             upper_case_attacks)
    ...: #Create a new phrase
    ...: new_attack_phrase =\
             (" ".join(phrase) for phrase in\
             remove_underscore)
    ...:

In [19]: next(new_attack_phrase)
Out[19]: 'STRAIGHT ANKLE LOCK'

In [20]: for number in range(10):
    ...:     print(next(new_attack_phrase))
    ...:
KIMURA
KEYLOCK
STRAIGHT ANKLE LOCK
...
```

List Comprehension

A list comprehension is syntactically similar to a generator expression, but in direct contrast, it is evaluated in memory. Additionally, it is optimized C code that can be a substantial improvement over a traditional for loop.

```
In [21]: martial_arts = ["Sambo", "Muay Thai", "BJJ"]
new_phrases = [f"Mixed Martial Arts is influenced by \
        {martial_art}" for martial_art in martial_arts]
In [22]: print(new_phrases)
['Mixed Martial Arts is influenced by Sambo', \
'Mixed Martial Arts is influenced by Muay Thai', \
'Mixed Martial Arts is influenced by BJJ']
```

Intermediate Topics

With those basics out of the way, it is important to understand not just how to "create code," but how to create code that is "maintainable." One way of doing this is to create a library; another way is to use code that has already been written by installing third-party libraries. In general, the idea is to minimize and break up complexity.

Writing a Library in Python

It doesn't take long into a project before writing a library in Python becomes important. These are the basics: In this repository there is a folder called *funclib*, and inside is a *__init__.py* file. To create a library, a module is needed in this directory with a function in it.

Create a file.

```
touch funclib/funcmod.py
```

Inside this file, a function is created.

```
"""This is a simple module"""


def list_of_belts_in_bjj():
    """Returns a list of the belts in Brazilian jiu-jitsu"""

    belts = ["white", "blue", "purple", "brown", "black"]
    return belts
```

Importing the Library

With Jupyter, if a library is directory above, *sys.path.append* can be added so it will be imported. Next, the module is imported using the namespace of the folder/filename/function name that was created earlier.

```
In [23]: import sys;sys.path.append("..")
    ...: from funclib import funcmod
In [24]: funcmod.list_of_belts_in_bjj()
Out[24]: ['white', 'blue', 'purple', 'brown', 'black']
```

Installing Other Libraries Using pip install

Installing other libraries can be done with the `pip install` command. Note that conda (https://conda.io/docs/user-guide/tasks/manage-pkgs.html) is both an alternative and replacement for pip. If you are using conda, pip will work just fine, since it is a replacement for virtualenv, but it also has the ability to directly install packages.

To install the pandas package:

```
pip install pandas
```

Alternately, packages can be installed using a requirements.txt file.

```
> ca requirements.txt
pylint
pytest
pytest-cov
click
jupyter
nbval

> pip install -r requirements.txt
```

Here is an example of how to use a small library in Jupyter Notebook. This is an important subtlety that is worth calling out. It is easy to create a giant spider web of procedural code in a Jupyter Notebook, and it's a very simple fix is to create some libraries that are then tested and imported.

```
"""This is a simple module"""

import pandas as pd

def list_of_belts_in_bjj():
    """Returns a list of the belts in Brazilian jiu-jitsu"""

    belts = ["white", "blue", "purple", "brown", "black"]
    return belts

def count_belts():
    """Uses Pandas to count number of belts"""

    belts = list_of_belts_in_bjj()
    df = pd.DataFrame(belts)
    res = df.count()
    count = res.values.tolist()[0]
    return count

In [25]: from funclib.funcmod import count_belts
    ...:

In [26]: print(count_belts())
    ...:
5
```

Classes

Using classes and interacting with them can be done iteratively in Jupyter Notebook. The simplest type of class is just a name, as shown here.

```
class Competitor: pass
```

But, that class can be instantiated into multiple objects.

```
In [27]: class Competitor: pass
In [28]:
    ...: conor = Competitor()
    ...: conor.name = "Conor McGregor"
    ...: conor.age = 29
    ...: conor.weight = 155
In [29]: nate = Competitor()
    ...: nate.name = "Nate Diaz"
    ...: nate.age = 30
    ...: nate.weight = 170
```

```
In [30]: def print_competitor_age(object):
    ...:       """Print out age statistics about a competitor"""
    ...:
    ...:       print(f"{object.name} is {object.age} years old")
In [31]: print_competitor_age(nate)
Nate Diaz is 30 years old
In [32]:
    ...: print_competitor_age(conor)
Conor McGregor is 29 years old
```

Differences between Classes and Functions

The key differences between classes and functions are

- Functions are much easier to reason about.

- Functions (typically) have state inside the function only, whereas classes have state that persists outside the function.

- Classes can offer a more advanced level of abstraction at the cost of complexity.

Final Thoughts

This chapter sets the stage for this book. It started with a brief tutorial on "functional" Python and how it can be used for machine learning application development. In later chapters, the nuts and bolts of cloud-based machine learning are covered in detail.

The core components of machine learning can be broken down into a couple of broad categories. Supervised machine learning techniques are used when the correct answer is already known. An example would be to predict housing prices from previous historical data. Unsupervised machine learning techniques are used when the correct answer is not known. The most common examples of unsupervised machine learning are clustering algorithms.

In the case of supervised machine learning, the data has already been labeled, and the objective is to correctly predict an outcome. From a practical point of view with AI, some techniques can make supervised machine learning even more powerful and feasible. One such approach is transfer learning, tweaking a pretrained model with a much smaller data set to fit to a new problem. Another approach is active learning, choosing which data to add to an expensive manual tagging, based on the improvements it can add.

In contrast, unsupervised machine learning has no labels, and the objective is to find hidden structures in the data. There is a third type of machine learning, reinforcement learning, that is less commonly used and will not be covered in detail in this book. Reinforcement learning is often used to do things like learning to play Atari games from raw pixels or playing Go (https://gogameguru.com/i/2016/03/deepmind-mastering-go.pdf). Deep learning is a machine learning technique that is often used with graphics processing unit (GPU) farms via cloud providers. Deep learning is often used to solve classification problems like image recognition, but it is also use for many other problems. There are over a dozen companies currently working on developing deep learning chips, signaling how important deep learning is becoming to machine learning practitioners.

Two subcategories of supervised machine learning are regression and classification. Regression-based supervised learning techniques predict a continuous value. Classification-based supervised learning is focused on predicting labels based on historical data.

Finally, AI will be covered in the context of both automation and the imitation of cognitive functions. Many off-the-shelf AI solutions are now available via APIs from the big technologies companies: Google, Amazon, Microsoft, and IBM. The integration of these APIs into AI projects will be covered in detail.

AI and ML Toolchain

We're talking about practice. We're talking about practice. We ain't talking about the game.

Allen Iverson

There is a growing wave of articles, videos, courses, and degrees in AI and machine learning (ML). What isn't covered as much is the toolchain. What are the fundamental skills needed to be a data scientist creating production machine learning? What are the fundamental processes a company must establish to develop reliable automated systems that can make predictions?

The toolchain needed to be successful in data science has exploded in complexity in some areas and shrunk in others. Jupyter Notebook is one of the innovations that has shrunk the complexity of developing solutions, as have cloud computing and SaaS build systems. The philosophy of DevOps touches on many areas including data security and reliability. The 2017 Equifax hack and the 2018 Facebook/Cambridge Analytica scandal that released the information of a significant portion of Americans highlights that data security is one of most pressing issues of our time. This chapter covers these issues and presents recommendations on how to develop processes that increase the reliability and security of ML systems.

Python Data Science Ecosystem: IPython, Pandas, NumPy, Jupyter Notebook, Sklearn

The Python ecosystem is unique because of the history of how it all came together. I remember first hearing about Python in 2000 when I was working at Caltech. At the time, it was an almost unheard-of language but was gaining some ground in academic circles because there was talk about how great a language it would be for teaching fundamental computer science.

One of the issues with teaching computer science with C or Java is that there is a lot of extra overhead to worry about other than fundamental concepts like a for loop. Almost 20 years later we are finally there, and Python is perhaps becoming the standard to teach computer science concepts the world over.

It is no surprise that it has also made tremendous strides in three areas I am also passionate about: DevOps, cloud architecture, and of course data science. For me it is natural to think about all of topics as interrelated. This accidental evolution has made me smile when I realize I can contribute to just about the entire stack of a company with just one language; what is more, I can do it very, very quickly with tremendous scale characteristics because of services like AWS Lambda.

Jupyter Notebook is also an interesting beast. I coauthored a book around 10 years ago in which we used IPython for the majority of the book examples (much like this book), and I have literally never stopped using IPython. So when Jupyter became a big deal, it fit just like a glove. The accidents have kept evolving in my favor with Python.

As I get more analytical, though, I did spend years working with R and came to appreciate that it has very different style from Python. For one, data frames are embedded into the language as well as plotting and advanced statistical functions and more "pure" functional programming.

In comparison to R, Python has tremendously more real-world applicability considering the cloud integration options and libraries, but for "pure" data science it does have a slightly disjointed feel to it. For example, you would never use a `for` loop in Pandas, but in regular Python it is very common. There are some paradigm clashes as regular Python mixes with Pandas, scikit-learn, and NumPy, but this is a pretty good problem to have if you're a Python user.

R, RStudio, Shiny, and ggplot

Even if the reader is only a Python user, I still think it is useful to have some familiarity with R and the R tools. The R ecosystem has some features that are worth discussing. You can download R from a mirror at https://cran.r-project.org/mirrors.html.

The predominant integrated development environment (IDE) for the R language is RStudio (https://www.rstudio.com/). RStudio has many great features, including the ability to create Shiny (http://shiny.rstudio.com/) applications and R Markdown documents (https://rmarkdown .rstudio.com/). If you are just getting started with R, it is almost mandatory to at least give it a try.

Shiny is a technology that is evolving but is worth exploring for interactive data analysis. It allows for the creation of interactive web applications that can be deployed to production by writing pure R code. There are many examples in the gallery (https://rmarkdown.rstudio.com/gallery .html) to provide inspiration.

Another area in which R is strong is having cutting-edge statistical libraries. Because of the history of R, created in Auckland, New Zealand for statisticians, it has enjoyed a strong history in that community. For that reason alone, it is recommended to have R in your toolbox.

Finally, the graphing library ggplot is so good and so complete that in many cases I find myself exporting code from a Python project as a CSV file, bringing it into RStudio, and creating a beautiful visualization in R and ggplot. An example of this is covered in Chapter 6, "Predicting Social-Media Influence in the NBA."

Spreadsheets: Excel and Google Sheets

Excel has gotten a lot of criticism in recent years. But as tools that are not the entire solution, Excel and Google Sheets have been extremely helpful. In particular, one of the powerful ways to use Excel is as a way of preparing and cleaning data. During the process of rapidly prototyping a data science problem, it can be faster to clean up and format data sets in Excel.

Similarly, Google Sheets is wonderful technology that solves real-world problems. In Chapter 4, "Cloud AI Development with Google Cloud Platform," an example shows how easy it is to programmatically create Google Sheets. Spreadsheets may be legacy technology, but they are still incredibly useful tools to create production solutions.

Cloud AI Development with Amazon Web Services

Amazon Web Services (AWS) is the 800-pound gorilla of the cloud. At Amazon, there are about a baker's dozen leadership principles (https://www.amazon.jobs/principles) outlining the way the employees think as an organization. Near the end of the list is "Deliver results." The cloud platform has been doing just that since it launched in 2006. Prices continuously drop, existing services get better, and new services are added at a rapid pace.

In recent years, there has been huge progress in Big Data, AI, and ML on AWS. There has also been a move in the direction of serverless technologies, like AWS Lambda. With many new technologies, there is an initial version that has a link to the past, and then a next iteration that leaves much of the past behind. The first version of the cloud has definite roots in the data center: virtual machines, relational databases, etc. The next iteration, serverless, is "cloud-native" technology. The operating system and other details are abstracted away, and what is left is code to solve the problem.

This streamlined way to write code is a natural fit for ML and AI applications being developed on the cloud. This chapter covers these new technologies as they relate to building cloud AI applications.

DevOps on AWS

I have heard many data scientists and developers say, "DevOps is not my job." DevOps isn't a job, however; it is a state of mind. The most sophisticated forms of AI are automating difficult human tasks like driving cars. DevOps has common roots with this way of thinking. Why wouldn't an ML engineer want to create a highly efficient feedback loop for deploying software to production?

The cloud—and in particular, the AWS cloud—has enabled automation and efficiency at a scale that has never been seen before. Some of the solutions available that are DevOps heavy are Spot instances, OpsWorks, Elastic Beanstalk, Lambda, CodeStar, CodeCommit, CodeBuild, CodePipeline, and CodeDeploy. This chapter shows examples of all these services along with an overview on how an ML engineer can make use of them.

Continuous Delivery

Software is always ready to be released in a continuous-delivery environment. The conceptual model is a factory assembly line. There is a great online resource, DevOps Essentials on AWS (http://www.devopsessentialsaws.com/), codeveloped by Pearson Education and Stelligent, that covers much of this. It gives a good overview of DevOps on AWS.

Creating a Software Development Environment for AWS

An easy-to-miss detail in working with AWS is getting a basic development environment set up. Because Python is such a large portion of this setup for many ML developers, it makes sense to design around Python. This involves setting up a Makefile, creating a virtual environment, adding a shortcut in bash or zsh to switch into it, automatically sourcing an AWS profile, and more.

A quick note on Makefiles: They first appeared in 1976 from Bell Labs and are used as a dependency-tracking build utility. Makefile systems can get very complex, but for many ML projects they can be invaluable. One good reason is they are available on any Unix or Linux system without installing software. Second, they are a standard that, generally speaking, people on a project will understand.

Virtual environments were something I used quite a bit while working in the film industry. Film could be considered one of the first "Big Data" industries. Even in the late 2000s there were near, or actual, petabyte file servers at film studios where I worked, and the only way to get a grip on the directory trees was to have tools that set environmental variables for projects.

When I was working for Weta Digital doing Python programming for the movie *Avatar,* I remember the file servers got so big they couldn't grow anymore so they had to sync huge copies of the data around to several file servers. In fact, one of my side projects was to help fix the way Python worked on the file servers. Because the Python import system was so greedy in the way it looked for imports, often a script would take 30 seconds to launch because it was searching nearly a hundred thousand files in its path. We discovered this by using strace on Linux, then hacking the Python interpreter to ignore Python paths.

Virtualenv in Python and conda by Anaconda do similar things to what I experienced in the film world. They create isolated environmental variables for a project. This then allows a user to toggle among the projects they work on and not get conflicting versions of libraries.

In Listing 2.1, there is the start of a basic Makefile.

Listing 2.1 **Basic Python AWS Project Makefile**

```
setup:
    python3 -m venv ~/.pragai-aws
install:
    pip install -r requirements.txt
```

A Makefile is best practice because it serves as a common reference point for building a project locally, on a build server, in a docker container, and in production. To use this Makefile in a new git repository type:

```
➜    pragai-aws git:(master) ✗  make setup
python3 -m venv ~/.pragai-aws
```

This make command creates a new Python virtual environment in the ~/.pragai-aws location. As mentioned other places in this book, it is generally a good idea to create an alias that will source the environment and cd into it all at once. For a Z shell or bash user, you would edit the .zshrc or .bashrc and add an alias to this git checkout repository.

```
Alias pawstop="cd ~/src/pragai-aws &&\
        source ~/.pragai-aws/bin/activate"
```

Then sourcing this environment is as easy as typing this alias.

```
➜    pragai-aws git:(master) ✗ pawstop
(.pragai-aws) ➜    pragai-aws git:(master) ✗
```

The magic that makes this happen is the activate script. This same activate script will serve as a useful mechanism to control other environmental variables for the project, namely PYTHONPATH and AWS_PROFILE, which will be covered in detail. The next step to set up a project for AWS is to create an account if you don't have one, and a user in that account if you haven't already. Amazon has excellent instructions on creating Identity and Access Management (IAM) user accounts: http://docs.aws.amazon.com/IAM/latest/UserGuide/id_users_create.html.

Once the account is set up (following the official AWS instructions), the next setup step is to create a named profile. There is good official reference material from AWS on this as well: http://docs.aws.amazon.com/cli/latest/userguide/cli-multiple-profiles.html. The key idea is to create profiles that make it explicit that a project is using a particular profile username or role; refer to AWS materials for more detail: http://docs.aws.amazon.com/cli/latest/userguide/cli-roles.html.

To install the AWS CLI tool and Boto3 (note: Boto3 is the latest version of Boto as of this writing), place both in the requirements.txt file and run make install.

```
(.pragai-aws) ➜    ✗ make install
pip install -r requirements.txt
```

With the aws command installed, it needs to be configured with a new user.

```
(.pragai-aws) ➜    ✗ aws configure --profile pragai
AWS Access Key ID [****************XQDA]:
AWS Secret Access Key [****************nmkH]:
Default region name [us-west-2]:
Default output format [json]:
```

The command-line aws tool can now be used with the –profile option. An easy way to test this out is to attempt to list the contents of one of the ML data sets hosted on AWS, like the Global Database of Events, Language and Tone Project (GDELT; https://aws.amazon.com/public-datasets/gdelt/).

```
(.pragai-aws) ➜ aws s3 cp\
        s3://gdelt-open-data/events/1979.csv .
fatal error: Unable to locate credentials
```

By selecting the –profile option, the download command is able to grab the file from S3. There is certainly no problem with always remembering to type the –profile flag, but this could get tedious for heavy command-line use of AWS.

```
(.pragai-aws) aws --profile pragai s3 cp\
        s3://gdelt-open-data/events/1979.csv .
download: s3://gdelt-open-data/events/1979.csv to ./1979.csv
(.pragai-aws) ➜    du -sh 1979.csv
110M    1979.csv
```

A solution to this is to put the AWS_PROFILE variable in the activate script for virtualenv.

```
(.pragia-aws) ➜  vim ~/.pragai-aws/bin/activate
#Export AWS Profile
AWS_PROFILE="pragai"
export AWS_PROFILE
```

Now when the virtual environment is sourced, the correct AWS profile is automatically used.

```
(.pragia-aws) ➜  echo $AWS_PROFILE
pragai
(.pragia-aws) ➜  aws s3 cp\
        s3://gdelt-open-data/events/1979.csv .
download: s3://gdelt-open-data/events/1979.csv to ./1979.csv
```

Python AWS Project Configuration

With the virtualenv and AWS credentials set up, the next thing to configure is the Python code. Having a valid project structure goes a long way in making development efficient and productive. Here is an example of creating a basic Python/AWS project structure.

```
(.pragia-aws) ➜  mkdir paws
(.pragia-aws) ➜  touch paws/__init__.py
(.pragia-aws) ➜  touch paws/s3.py
(.pragia-aws) ➜  mkdir tests
(.pragia-aws) ➜  touch tests/test_s3.py
```

Next, a simple S3 module can be written that uses this layout. An example is seen in Listing 2.2. The Boto3 library is used to create a function to download a file from S3. The additional import is a logging library.

Listing 2.2 **S3 Module**

```
"""
S3 methods for PAWS library
"""

import boto3
from sensible.loginit import logger

log = logger("Paws")


def boto_s3_resource():
    """Create boto3 S3 Resource"""

    return boto3.resource("s3")

def download(bucket, key, filename, resource=None):
    """Downloads file from s3"""
```

```
if resource is None:
    resource = boto_s3_resource()
log_msg = "Attempting download: {bucket}, {key}, {filename}".\
    format(bucket=bucket, key=key, filename=filename)
log.info(log_msg)
resource.meta.client.download_file(bucket, key, filename)
return filename
```

To use this newly created library from the IPython command line, it is a couple of lines of code, and the namespace of "paws" has been created.

```
In [1]: from paws.s3 import download

In [2]: download(bucket="gdelt-open-data",\
        key="events/1979.csv", filename="1979.csv")
2017-09-02 11:28:57,532 - Paws - INFO - Attempting download:
        gdelt-open-data, events/1979.csv, 1979.csv
```

With a successful library started, it is time to create a PYTHONPATH variable in the activate script that reflects the location of this library.

```
#Export PYTHONPATH
PYTHONPATH="paws"
export PYTHONPATH
```

Next, the virtual environment is sourced again using the alias pawstop set up earlier.

```
(.pragia-aws) ➜  pawstop
(.pragia-aws) ➜  echo $PYTHONPATH
paws
```

Next, a unit test can be created using *pytest* and *moto*, two useful libraries for testing AWS. Moto is used for mocking AWS and pytest is a test framework. This can be seen in Listing 2.3. Pytest fixtures are used to create temporary resources, and then moto is used to create mock objects that simulate Boto actions. The test function test_download then asserts that after the resource is created properly. Note that to actually test the download function, a resource object must be passed in. This is a great example of how writing tests for code helps make code less brittle.

Listing 2.3 **Testing S3 Module**

```
import pytest
import boto3
from moto import mock_s3
from paws.s3 import download

@pytest.yield_fixture(scope="session")
def mock_boto():
    """Setup Mock Objects"""

    mock_s3().start()
```

```
    output_str = 'Something'
    resource = boto3.resource('s3')
    resource.create_bucket(Bucket="gdelt-open-data")
    resource.Bucket("gdelt-open-data").\
        put_object(Key="events/1979.csv",
                        Body=output_str)
    yield resource
    mock_s3().stop()

def test_download(mock_boto):
    """Test s3 download function"""

    resource = mock_boto
    res = download(resource=resource, bucket="gdelt-open-data",
            key="events/1979.csv",filename="1979.csv")
    assert res == "1979.csv"
```

To install the libraries needed to test the project, the contents of the requirements.txt file should look like this.

```
awscli
boto3
moto
pytest
pylint
sensible
jupyter
pytest-cov
pandas
```

To install the packages, a make install command is run. Then to run the tests, the Makefile should be changed to look like this.

```
setup:
    python3 -m venv ~/.pragia-aws

install:
    pip install -r requirements.txt

test:
    PYTHONPATH=. && pytest -vv --cov=paws tests/*.py

lint:
    pylint --disable=R,C paws
```

Then, running the tests and the coverage looks like this.

```
(.pragia-aws) ➜  pragai-aws git:(master) ✗ make test
PYTHONPATH=. && pytest -vv --cov=paws tests/*.py
================================================
test session starts ============================
platform darwin -- Python 3.6.2, pytest-3.2.1,
```

```
/Users/noahgift/.pragia-aws/bin/python3
cachedir: .cache
rootdir: /Users/noahgift/src/pragai-aws, inifile:
plugins: cov-2.5.1
collected 1 item

tests/test_s3.py::test_download PASSED

---------- coverage: platform darwin, python 3.6.2-final-0
Name                    Stmts   Miss  Cover
----------------------------------------
paws/__init__.py            0      0   100%
paws/s3.py                 12      2    83%
----------------------------------------
TOTAL                      12      2    83%
```

There are many ways to set up Pylint, but my preferred method is to only show warnings and errors for a continuous delivery project: `pylint --disable=R,C paws`. Running the lint, then, works like this.

```
(.pragia-aws) ➜  pragai-aws git:(master) ✗ make lint
pylint --disable=R,C paws
No config file found, using default configuration

-------------------------------------------------------------------
Your code has been rated at 10.00/10 (previous run: 10.00/10, +0.00)
```

Finally, it may be useful to create an all statement to install, lint, and test: `all: install lint test`. Then a `make all` command will start all three actions sequentially.

Integrating Jupyter Notebook

Getting Jupyter Notebook to work with the project layout and having notebooks automatically tested are great benefits to add. To do that, a notebook will be created in a notebooks folder and a data folder at the root of the checkout: `mkdir -p notebooks`. Next, `jupyter notebook` is run and a new notebook is created called `paws.ipynb`. Inside this notebook, the previous library can be used to download the CSV file and do a brief exploration in Pandas. First, the path is appended to the root and Pandas is imported.

```
In [1]: #Add root checkout to path
   ...: import sys
   ...: sys.path.append("..")
   ...: import pandas as pd
   ...:
```

The library that was created earlier is loaded, and the CSV file is downloaded.

```
In [2]: from paws.s3 import (boto_s3_resource, download)

In [3]: resource = boto_s3_resource()
```

```
In [4]: csv_file = download(resource=resource,
    ...:                     bucket="gdelt-open-data",
    ...:                     key="events/1979.csv",
    ...:                     filename="1979.csv")
    ...:
2017-09-03 11:57:35,162 - Paws - INFO - Attempting

events/1979.csv, 1979.csv
```

Because the data is irregularly shaped, a trick to fit it into the data frame is used: names=range(5). Also, at 100MB, the file is too big to fit into a Git repo as a test data set. It will be truncated and saved back out.

```
In [7]: #Load the file, truncate it and save.
    ...: df = pd.read_csv(csv_file, names=range(5))
    ...: df = df.head(100)
    ...: df.to_csv(csv_file)
    ...:
```

Next the file is read back in and described.

```
In [8]: df = pd.read_csv("1979.csv", names=range(5))
    ...: df.head()
    ...:
Out[8]:
    Unnamed: 0
0          NaN
1          NaN
2          0.0  0\t19790101\t197901\t1979\t1979.0027\t\t\t\t\t\t...
3          1.0  1\t19790101\t197901\t1979\t1979.0027\t\t\t\t\t\t...
4          2.0  2\t19790101\t197901\t1979\t1979.0027\t\t\t\t\t\t...

      3    4
0     3    4
1     3    4
2   NaN  NaN
3   NaN  NaN
4   NaN  NaN

In [9]: df.describe()
Out[9]:
        Unnamed: 0
count    98.000000
mean     48.500000
std      28.434134
min       0.000000
25%      24.250000
50%      48.500000
75%      72.750000
max      97.000000
```

With this basic notebook set up, it can also be integrated into the Makefile build system by using the pytest plugin nbval and adding it to the requirements.txt file. The lines below should be commented out (so the S3 file won't be downloaded on each run, and then the notebook can be saved and closed).

```
#csv_file = download(resource=resource,
#                    bucket="gdelt-open-data",
#                    key="events/1979.csv",
#                    filename="1979.csv")
#Load the file, truncate it and save.
#df = pd.read_csv(csv_file, names=range(5))
#df = df.head(100)
#df.to_csv(csv_file)
```

In the Makefile, a new line can be added to also test the notebooks.

```
test:
    PYTHONPATH=. && pytest -vv --cov=paws tests/*.py
    PYTHONPATH=. && py.test --nbval-lax notebooks/*.ipynb
```

The output of the notebook test run looks like this now.

```
PYTHONPATH=. && py.test --nbval-lax notebooks/*.ipynb
================================================================
test session starts
================================================================
platform darwin -- Python 3.6.2, pytest-3.2.1, py-1.4.34
rootdir: /Users/noahgift/src/pragai-aws, inifile:
plugins: cov-2.5.1, nbval-0.7
collected 8 items

notebooks/paws.ipynb ........

======================================================
warnings summary ====================================
notebooks/paws.ipynb::Cell 0
  /Users/noahgift/.pragia-aws/lib/python3.6/site-
packages/jupyter_client/connect.py:157: RuntimeWarning:
'/var/folders/vl/sskrtrf17nz4nww5zr1b64980000gn/T':
'/var/folders/vl/sskrtrf17nz4nww5zr1b64980000gn/T'
    RuntimeWarning,

-- Docs: http://doc.pytest.org/en/latest/warnings.html
======================================================
8 passed, 1 warnings in 4.08 seconds
======================================================
```

There is a now a repeatable and testable structure for adding notebooks to the project and sharing the common library that has been created. Additionally, this structure can be used for a continuous-delivery environment, which will be shown later in the chapter. By testing the Jupyter Notebooks as they are built, it also serves a useful double purpose of integration testing an ML project.

Integrating Command-Line Tools

An often-overlooked tool in both traditional software engineering projects and ML projects is the addition of command-line tools. Some interactive exploration is much more conducive to a command-line tool. For cloud architecture, creating a command-line prototype of say, an SQS-based application, is often much quicker than only using a traditional technique like an IDE. To get started with building a command-line tool, the requirements.txt file will be updated with the Click library and `make install` will be run.

```
(.pragia-aws) ➜  tail -n 2 requirements.txt
click
```

Next, a command-line script is created in the root.

```
(.pragia-aws) ➜  pragai-aws git:(master) touch pcli.py
```

The script will perform a set of actions similar to those of the Jupyter Notebook, except that it will be more flexible and allow the user to pass in the arguments to the function from the command line. In Listing 2.4, the click framework is used to create a wrapper around the Python library created previously.

Listing 2.4   **pcli Command-Line Tool**

```python
#!/usr/bin/env python

"""
Command-line Tool for Working with PAWS library
"""

import sys

import click
import paws
from paws import s3

@click.version_option(paws.__version__)
@click.group()
def cli():
    """PAWS Tool"""

@cli.command("download")
@click.option("--bucket", help="Name of S3 Bucket")
@click.option("--key", help="Name of S3 Key")
@click.option("--filename", help="Name of file")
def download(bucket, key, filename):
    """Downloads an S3 file
    ./paws-cli.py --bucket gdelt-open-data --key \
        events/1979.csv --filename 1979.csv
    """
```

```
    if not bucket and not key and not filename:
        click.echo("--bucket and --key and --filename are required")
        sys.exit(1)
    click.echo(
        "Downloading s3 file with: bucket-\
        {bucket},key{key},filename{filename}".\
        format(bucket=bucket, key=key, filename=filename))
    res = s3.download(bucket, key,filename)
    click.echo(res)

if __name__ == "__main__":
    cli()
```

To get this script to be executable, it needs to have a Python shebang line added to the top of the script.

```
#!/usr/bin/env python
```

It also needs to be made executable, as follows.

```
(.pragia-aws) ➜  pragai-aws git:(master) chmod +x pcli.py
```

Finally, a good trick is to create a __version__ variable inside of the __init__.py portion of a library and set it to a version number that is a string. It can then be called in a script or a command-line tool.

To get this script to run help, the following commands are run.

```
(.pragia-aws) ➜  ./pcli.py --help
Usage: paws-cli.py [OPTIONS] COMMAND [ARGS]...

  PAWS Tool

Options:
  --version  Show the version and exit.
  --help     Show this message and exit.

Commands:
  download  Downloads an S3 file ./pcli.py --bucket...
```

To get the script to run the download, the commands and output are

```
(.pragia-aws) ➜  ./pcli.py download –bucket\
        gdelt-open-data --key events/1979.csv \
        --filename 1979.csv


Downloading s3 file with: bucket-gdelt-open-data,
keyevents/1979.csv,filename1979.csv
2017-09-03 14:55:39,627 - Paws - INFO - Attempting download:
 gdelt-open-data, events/1979.csv, 1979.csv
1979.csv
```

This is all it takes to start adding powerful command-line tools to an ML project. One last step is to integrate this into the test infrastructure. Fortunately, Click has great support for testing as well (http://click.pocoo.org/5/testing/). A new file is created with this command: `touch tests/ test_paws_cli.py` In Listing 2.5, the test code is written that verifies the __version__ variable flows through the command-line tool.

Listing 2.5 **Click Command-line Testing of pcli**

```
import pytest
import click
from click.testing import CliRunner

from pcli import cli
from paws import __version__

@pytest.fixture
def runner():
    cli_runner = CliRunner()
    yield cli_runner


def test_cli(runner):
    result = runner.invoke(cli, ['--version'])
    assert __version__ in result.output
```

The Makefile needs to be altered to allow coverage reporting to show for the newly created command-line tool. This is shown below in the output of the make command `make test`. By adding –cov=pli, everything just works, and the code coverage is computed.

```
(.pragia-aws) ➜  make test
PYTHONPATH=. && pytest -vv --cov=paws --cov=pcli tests/*.py
==========================================================
test session starts
==========================================================
platform darwin -- Python 3.6.2, pytest-3.2.1, py-1.4.34,
/Users/noahgift/.pragia-aws/bin/python3
cachedir: .cache
rootdir: /Users/noahgift/src/pragai-aws, inifile:
plugins: cov-2.5.1, nbval-0.7
collected 2 items

tests/test_paws_cli.py::test_cli PASSED
tests/test_s3.py::test_download PASSED

---------- coverage: platform darwin, python 3.6.2-final-0
Name                 Stmts   Miss  Cover
------------------------------------
paws/__init__.py         1      0   100%
```

```
paws/s3.py            12       2      83%
pcli.py               19       7      63%
------------------------------------------
TOTAL                 32       9      72%
```

Integrating AWS CodePipeline

A rich project skeleton for working on AWS projects is working, tested, and building. A next step is to integrate the AWS CodePipeline toolchain. AWS CodePipeline is a very powerful collection of tools on AWS that acts like a Swiss Army Knife of continuous delivery. It has the flexibility to be extended in many different directions. In this example, a basic build server configuration will be set up that triggers on changes to GitHub. First, a new file touch buildspec.yml is created; then, it is populated with the same make commands that are run locally, as seen in Listing 2.6.

To get this building, a new CodePipeline will be created in the AWS Console (https://us-west-2.console.aws.amazon.com/codepipeline/home?region=us-west-2#/create/Name [user must be logged in to access]). Note, in the buildspec.yml, that a "fake" set of credentials is created in the docker container that CodeBuild uses. This is for the Moto library that mocks out Python Boto calls.

Listing 2.6   **Click Command-line Testing of pcli**

```
version: 0.2

phases:
  install:
    commands:
      - echo "Upgrade Pip and install packages"
      - pip install --upgrade pip
      - make install
            # create the aws dir
      - mkdir -p ~/.aws/
      # create fake credential file
      - echo "[default]\naws_access_key_id = \
        FakeKey\naws_secret_access_key = \
        FakeKey\naws_session_token = FakeKey" >\
        ~/.aws/credentials

  build:
    commands:
      - echo "Run lint and test"
      - make lint
      - PYTHONPATH=".";make test
  post_build:
    commands:
      - echo Build completed on `date`
```

In the console for AWS CodePipeline, there are few steps to get the build working. First, in Figure 2.1, the pipeline name "paws" is created.

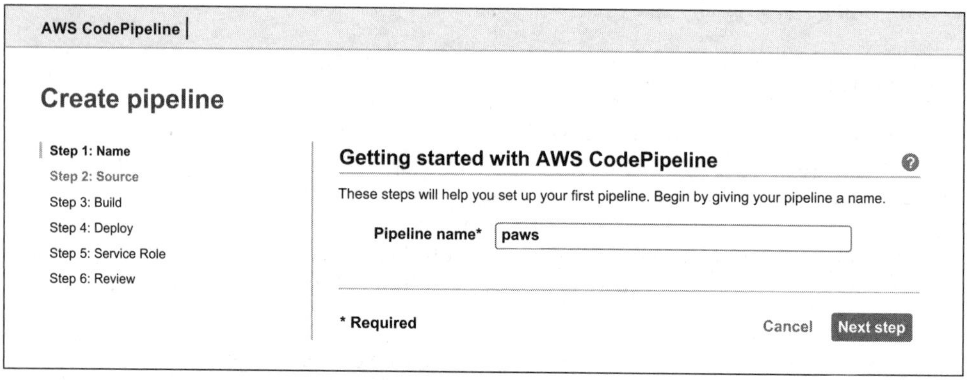

Figure 2.1   Representation of Creating a CodePipeline Name

In Figure 2.2, GitHub is selected as a source from which to pull, and a GitHub repository name and branch is selected. In this case, it triggers a change every time the master branch is updated.

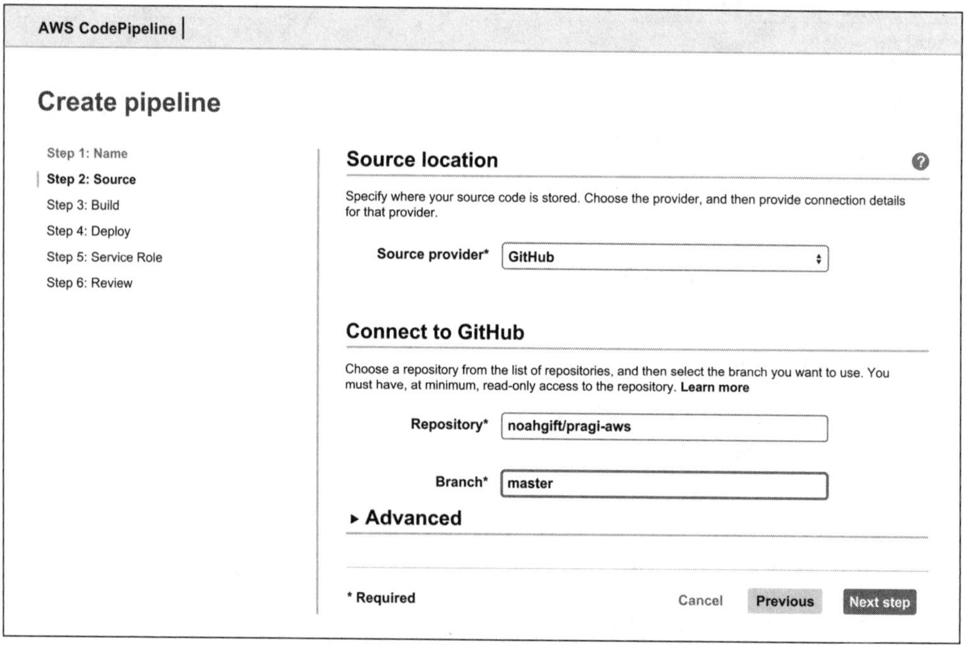

Figure 2.2   Representation of Creating a CodePipeline Source

The next step is the build step, which has more going on than any other step (see Figure 2.3). The most important part to pay attention to is the use of a custom docker image, which shows the power of CodePipeline. Additionally, the build step is told to look for a buildspec.yml file in the root of the GitHub repository. This is the file that was created in Listing 2.5.

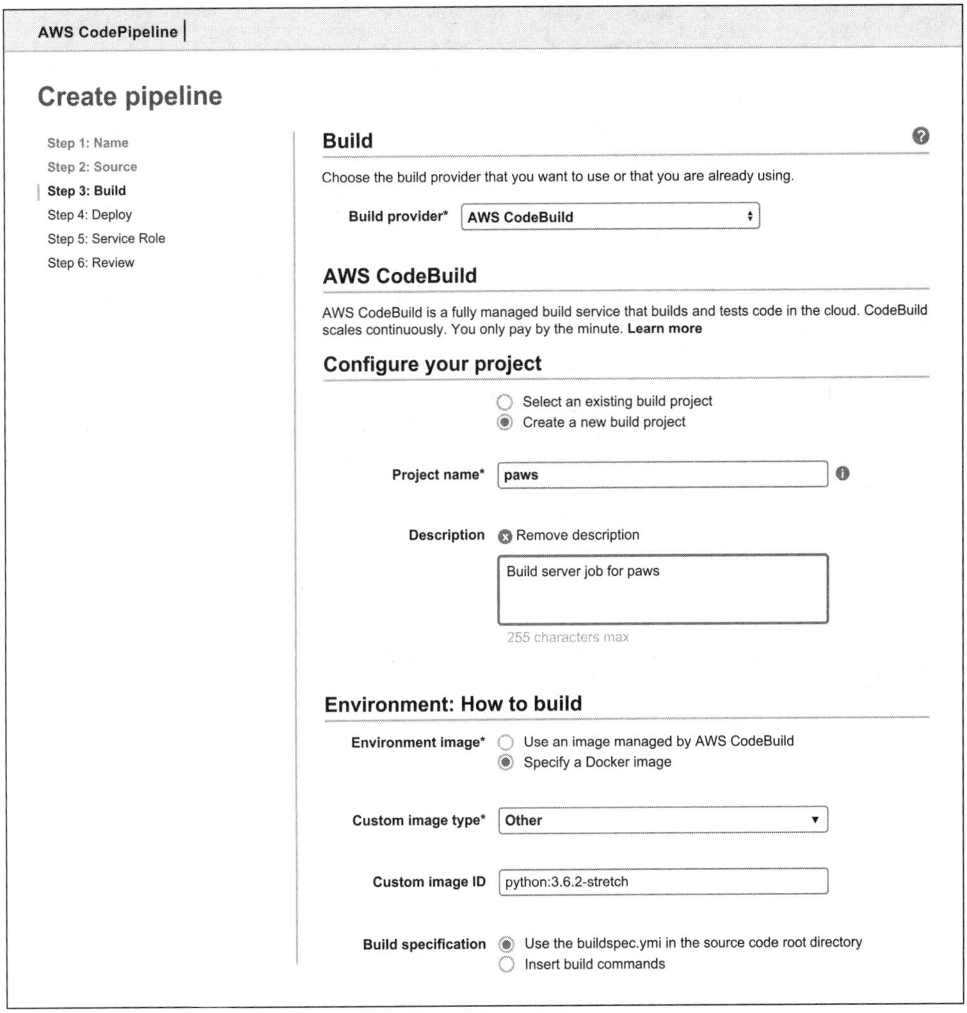

AWS CodePipeline |

Create pipeline

Step 1: Name
Step 2: Source
Step 3: Build
Step 4: Deploy
Step 5: Service Role
Step 6: Review

Build

Choose the build provider that you want to use or that you are already using.

Build provider*   AWS CodeBuild   ⬍

AWS CodeBuild

AWS CodeBuild is a fully managed build service that builds and tests code in the cloud. CodeBuild scales continuously. You only pay by the minute. **Learn more**

Configure your project

○ Select an existing build project
◉ Create a new build project

Project name*   paws   ⓘ

Description   ⊗ Remove description

Build server job for paws

255 characters max

Environment: How to build

Environment image*   ○ Use an image managed by AWS CodeBuild
◉ Specify a Docker image

Custom image type*   Other   ▼

Custom image ID   python:3.6.2-stretch

Build specification   ◉ Use the buildspec.ymi in the source code root directory
○ Insert build commands

Figure 2.3   Representation of Creating a CodePipeline Build

Figure 2.4 is the deploy step, which is not something that will be set up. This step could deploy the project to, say, Elastic Beanstalk.

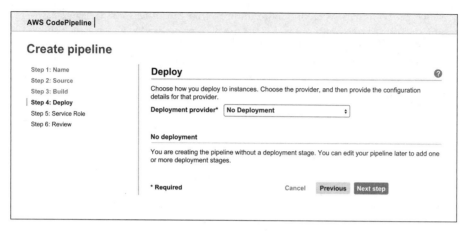

Figure 2.4   Representation of Creating a CodePipeline Deploy

Figure 2.5 shows the final screen of the wizard to create a pipeline, and Figure 2.6 shows a successful build after a trigger from GitHub. This completes a basic setup of CodePipeline for a project, but there is much more that can be done. Lambda functions can be triggered, SNS messages can be sent, and multiple simultaneous builds can be triggered that test, say, multiple versions of your code base on different versions of Python.

AWS CodePipeline |

Create pipeline

Step 1: Name
Step 2: Source
Step 3: Build
Step 4: Deploy
Step 5: Service Role
Step 6: Review ·

Review your pipeline

We will create your pipeline with the following resources.

Source Stage

Source provider   GitHub

Repository   noahgift/pragai-aws

Branch   master

Build Stage

Build provider   AWS CodeBuild

Project name*   paws   ☑ View project details

Staging Stage

Deployment provider   No Deployment

Pipeline settings

Pipeline name   paws

Artifact location   s3://codepipeline-us-west-2-862037486407/
AWS CodePipeline will use this existing S3 bucket to store artifacts for this pipeline. Depending on the size of your artifacts, you might be charged for storage costs. For more information, see **Amazon S3 storage pricing.**

Role name   AWS-CodePipeline-Service

To save this configuration with these resources, choose Create pipeline.
Would you like to create this pipeline?

Cancel   **Previous**   Create pipeline

Figure 2.5   Representation of a CodePipeline Review

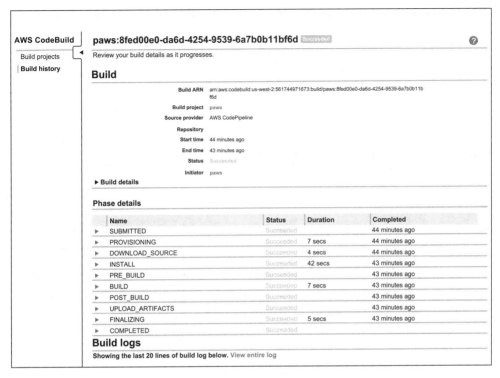

Figure 2.6   Representation of a Successful CodePipeline Build

Basic Docker Setup for Data Science

In dealing with students new to data science, there is a constant stream of questions about the same topic: their environment doesn't work anymore. This is a huge problem that is slowly getting much better due to tools like Docker. At least for Mac users, there are similarities in the Mac Unix environment and a production Linux environment, but Windows is a completely foreign world. This is why Docker on Windows is such a powerful tool for data scientists who use that platform.

To install Docker on OS X, Linux, or Windows, you can refer to the instructions on https://www. docker.com/. A good place to experiment with a default data science stack is to use the jupyter/ datascience-notebook (https://hub.docker.com/r/jupyter/datascience-notebook/). One you have Docker installed and you do a "docker pull," to launch the notebook it is a one-line command.

```
docker run -it --rm -p 8888:8888 jupyter/datascience-notebook
```

To run batch jobs with AWS Batch, a production team could develop against a dockerfile on the team's laptop, check it into source code, then register it against the AWS private Docker registry. Then when batch jobs are run, there would be a guarantee they are executed in exactly the same way as they were on the team's laptop. This is absolutely the future, and pragmatic-minded teams would be advised to get up to speed with Docker. Not only does it save a ton of time in local development, but for many real-world problems with running jobs, Docker isn't just optional, it is required.

Other Build Servers: Jenkins, CircleCI, and Travis

Although CodePipeline was covered in this chapter, it is an AWS-specific product. Other services that are very good as well include Jenkins (https://jenkins.io/), CircleCI (https://circleci.com/), Codeship (https://codeship.com/), and Travis (https://travis-ci.org/). They all have strengths and weaknesses, but in general they are also Docker-based build systems. This is yet another reason to get a strong foundation around Docker.

For further inspiration, you can look at a sample project I created that builds on CircleCI: https://github.com/noahgift/myrepo. There is also a video you can watch from a workshop I taught where I go over the details step by step.

Summary

This chapter covered the fundamentals of DevOps as it relates to ML. A sample continuous-delivery pipeline and project structure was created that could be used as the building blocks of an ML pipeline. It's easy to get months down the road on a project and realize that a lack of fundamental infrastructure is going to eventually cause an existential threat to the project's long-term viability.

Finally, Docker was covered in detail because, frankly, it is the future. All data teams need to know about it. And for truly large problems, like building a large-scale production AI system, it will absolutely part of the deployed solution.

Spartan AI Lifecycle

I'm going to go out there and be ridiculous and see what happens. I've got nothing to lose.

Wayde Van Niekerk

In building software, many things may seem unimportant but later turn out to be critical. Alternately, many things seem important that could be a false path. One heuristic that I have found useful is to think of things in terms of a feedback loop. At a task, is the thing you are doing speeding up the feedback loop(s) or blocking it?

The Spartan AI lifecycle is the spirit of this heuristic. Either you are speeding things up and making them more efficient, or you are not. If one inner ring of feedback loop needs to be optimized, say getting better unit tests or more reliable extract, transform, and load (ETL) services, then it should be done in a way that it doesn't block other feedback loops.

In this chapter, approaches to thinking in this manner are discussed in real-world problems, like building your own ML model versus calling an API, or being "vendor locked in" versus building it yourself. Thinking like a Spartan AI warrior means not working on things that don't improve the efficiency of the entire system and each subsystem. Having a heuristic to live by is refreshing and empowering. Ultimately, some things matter more than others, which is another way of saying no to nonsense.

Pragmatic Production Feedback Loop

In Figure 3.1, the technology feedback loop describes the thought process behind creating technology. Technology, whether it is creating ML models or web applications, has a feedback loop that needs to be accounted for. If the feedback loop is slow, broken, or not interconnected, there will be hell to pay. A few examples of broken feedback loops at places I have worked are presented in this chapter.

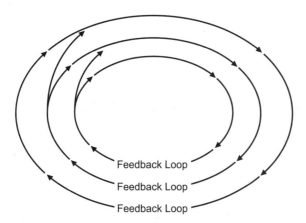

Figure 3.1 Technology Feedback Loop

Developers committing code infrequently is a common problem for startups and other companies. A ratio I have created in an open source project devml called Active Ratio looks at the percentage of time a developer checks in code on average. For example, are developers checking in code on average 4 out of 5 days per week, or are they checking in code about once a week, or in extreme situations, once every three months?

A common misconception is for developers and managers to smugly talk about how source code metrics are misleading, as in, the number of lines of code per day doesn't mean anything. Just because it is hard to reason about source code metrics doesn't mean the information isn't valuable. Active Ratio looks at the behavioral aspects of source code, which are much more interesting than vanity metrics. A good example of this would be to look in the physical world. If a painter is subcontracted to paint a house and only spend 25 percent of his time painting, what is going on? There are a few options that come to mind, and the obvious ones are that the painter may be doing a bad job or is taking advantage of the client. Less obvious, but possible, is that the project may be horribly managed. What if the main contractor keeps blocking the main road to the house with cement trucks and the painter cannot get to the worksite several days in a row? This is a broken feedback loop.

It is true that software developers can be abused into working horrible conditions by asking developers to work 12-hour days, 7 days a week, but there are ways to look at behavioral signals in a company in a way that sanely optimizes performance and helps teams deliver more efficiently. In an ideal situation, a painter paints Monday through Friday, and a software team writes code Monday through Friday. With software, there is an "invention" aspect to it that makes it different from physical labor, and this also needs to be accounted for; this means that burning the candle at both ends can lead to poor "inventions," i.e., software. This is why I am not encouraging people to look at the Active Ratio and encourage developers to work 7 days a week and commit every day, nor to encourage developers to go on epic 400-day commit streak binges where they commit code to GitHub every day.

Instead, what behavioral metrics around the feedback loops do is encourage sophisticated teams to look at what is really going on. Maybe there is a lack of effective project management in the software team that is committing code only a couple of days per week. I have absolutely seen companies that let a "scrum master" or the "founder" suck developers into all-day or frequent-day meetings that just waste everyone's time. In fact, the company most certainly will fail if this doesn't get fixed. The road to the worksite is quite definitely dropped. These are the types of situations that can be spotted by diving into the metrics around feedback loops.

Another feedback loop is the data science feedback loop. How does a company really solve data-related problems, and what is the feedback loop? Ironically, many data science teams are not really adding value to organizations because the feedback loop is broken. How is it broken? Mainly because there is no feedback loop. Here are a few questions to ask.

- Can the team run experiments at will on the production system?
- Is the team running experiments in Jupyter Notebook and Pandas on small, unrealistic data sets only?
- How often does the data science team ship trained models to production?
- Is the company unwilling to use or unaware of pretrained ML models like the Google Cloud Vision API or Amazon Rekognition?

One of the open secrets about ML is that often the tools that are taught—Pandas, scikit-learn, R DataFrames, etc.—don't work well in production workflows by themselves. Instead, a balanced approach of using Big Data tools such as PySpark and propriety tools like AWS SageMaker, Google TPUs (TensorFlow Processing Units), and others are a necessary part of creating pragmatic solutions.

A great example of a broken feedback loop is a production SQL database that wasn't designed to account for an ML architecture. The developers are happily coding away, while the data engineering tasks are at the mercy of transforming the tables in the SQL database to something useful using home-grown Python scripts that convert files into CSV files, which are analyzed with Pandas in an ad-hoc manner with scikit-learn. What is the feedback loop here?

It is a dead end, because even though the data eventually gets turned into something marginally useful, it is analyzed with tools that cannot be used in production, and the ML model doesn't get deployed to production. As a manager, I have seen many data scientists who are not all that concerned about getting the ML model shipped into production, but they should be, because it completes the feedback loop. There is a pragmatism that is missing in the industry, and one of the solutions is a focus on making sure there is an ML feedback loop that gets code into production.

Through 2017 and 2018 there has been incredible progress made in tools that complete this feedback loop. A few of these tools mentioned in this chapter—such as AWS SageMaker, which focuses on rapid iteration on training ML models and deploying them to API endpoints—are aiming to solve this. Another AWS tool, AWS Glue, manages ETL processes by connecting data sources, like an SQL database, performing ETL on them and writing them back to another data source like S3 or another SQL database.

Google also toolchains like this, including BigQuery, which is one of the crown jewels of production ML in that it handles just about any performance workload that can be thrown at it. Other parts of the Google ecosystem also allow an efficient ML/AI feedback loop, such as TPUs (https://cloud.google.com/tpu/), Datalab (https://cloud.google.com/datalab/), and AI APIs.

There is an expression that data is the new oil; to stick with that analogy, you cannot put oil in an internal combustion engine. A petroleum-based feedback loop is necessary for that. It starts with finding and extracting oil with industrial-strength machines (i.e., what cloud providers are starting to expose), and then the oil has to be transported and refined before it is delivered to gas stations. Imagine a situation in which a bunch of engineers are drilling holes into a pit, and with an ad hoc laboratory, trying to refine oil, then putting batches of gas into cars that somehow found their way to the drilling site. This is what data science is currently in many companies and why it is going to rapidly change.

Recognizing this challenge and opportunity and doing something about it is going to be a fork in the road for many organizations. The status quo of tinkering with data just isn't going to cut it, and the laboratory will need to be converted into a refinery capable of delivering high-quality, high-volume quantities back into production. Creating bespoke batches of high-octane fuel by a dig site is just as practical as doing data science in a vacuum.

AWS SageMaker

SageMaker is an exciting piece of technology coming out of Amazon that tackles a big problem—in fact, the problem discussed earlier in this chapter. It closes one of the loops for ML in the real world. Figure 3.2 highlights the process: First an EDA and/or model training is performed via a notebook instance. Next, a job is kicked off on a machine, a model is trained, and then an endpoint is deployed...potentially to production.

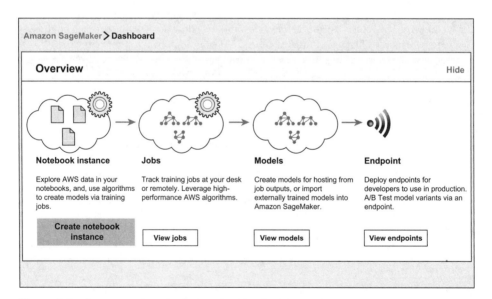

Figure 3.2   Representation of a Sagemaker Feedback Loop

Finally, what makes this incredibly powerful is by using Boto; this can be easily put into an API using chalice or raw AWS Lambda, or even the endpoint itself, as seen in Figure 3.3.

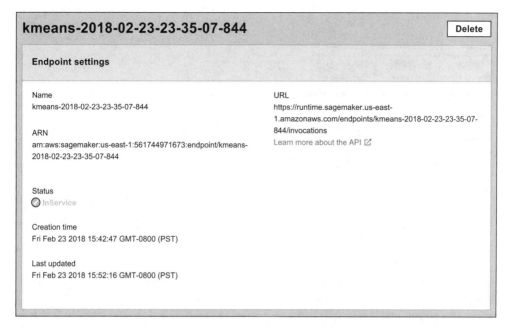

kmeans-2018-02-23-23-35-07-844   Delete

Endpoint settings

Name
kmeans-2018-02-23-23-35-07-844

URL
https://runtime.sagemaker.us-east-
1.amazonaws.com/endpoints/kmeans-2018-02-23-23-35-07-
844/invocations
Learn more about the API ☑

ARN
arn:aws:sagemaker:us-east-1:561744971673:endpoint/kmeans-
2018-02-23-23-35-07-844

Status
◉ InService

Creation time
Fri Feb 23 2018 15:42:47 GMT-0800 (PST)

Last updated
Fri Feb 23 2018 15:52:16 GMT-0800 (PST)

Figure 3.3   Representation of Sagemaker

How does this look in practice from Boto? It's pretty simple.

```
import boto3
sm_client = boto3.client('runtime.sagemaker')
response = sm_client.invoke_endpoint(EndpointName=endpoint_name,
                                     ContentType='text/x-libsvm',
                                     Body=payload)
result = response['Body'].read()
result = result.decode("utf-8")
print(result)
```

SageMaker also has built-in ML models that it maintains such as k-means, Neural Topic Model, principal component analysis, and more. The SageMaker algorithms are packaged as Docker images, and it is possible to use almost any algorithm. What is powerful about this approach is that by using SageMaker k-means implementation, there are going to be reasonable guarantees about performance and compatibility in generating repeatable production workflows. At the same time, though, highly optimized custom algorithms can be generated as repeatable Docker builds.

AWS Glue Feedback Loop

AWS Glue is a great example of a feedback loop inside of the main feedback loop. There is a crisis of legacy SQL and NoSQL databases being internally "crawled" by bad scripts. AWS Glue goes a long way in solving this problem. It is a fully managed ETL service that mitigates much of the typical nastiness of ETL.

How does it work? Figure 3.4 shows what it does.

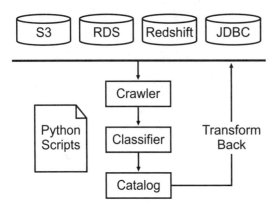

Figure 3.4   AWS Glue ETL Pipeline

One example of how AWS Glue works is as follows. You have a legacy PostgreSQL database that stores the customer database for your startup. You connect AWS Glue to this database and it "infers" that schema for you. You can see what this looks like in Figure 3.5.

Schema			
	Column name	**Data type**	**Key**
1	updated_at	timestamp	
2	name	string	
3	created_at	timestamp	
4	id	int	
5	locale	string	

Figure 3.5   Representation of AWS Glue

Next, a job is created that can be a Python or Scala script that will translate the schema into another format and destination. These scripts look something like this (abbreviated for space). You can accept these default scripts, which are stored in S3, or tweak them.

```
import sys
from awsglue.transforms import *
from awsglue.utils import getResolvedOptions
from pyspark.context import SparkContext
from awsglue.context import GlueContext
from awsglue.job import Job
## @params: [JOB_NAME]
args = getResolvedOptions(sys.argv, ['JOB_NAME'])
####abbreviated
```

```
sc = SparkContext()
glueContext = GlueContext(sc)
spark = glueContext.spark_session
job = Job(glueContext)
job.init(args['JOB_NAME'], args)
####abbreviated
## @inputs: [frame = applymapping1]
datasink2 = glueContext.write_dynamic_frame.\
        from_options(frame = applymapping1,
        connection_type = "s3",
        connection_options =\
        {"path": "s3://dev-spot-etl-pg/tables/scrummaster"},
        format = "csv", transformation_ctx = "datasink2")
job.commit()
```

After that, these jobs can be scheduled via triggers: events or cron jobs. Of course, this can also be scripted via Python using Boto. The best part of this service? There is business continuity. If a developer quits or is fired, the service is easily maintained by the next developer. This is a reliable feedback loop that doesn't hinge on the individual strength of a specific key hire.

AWS Glue is also a good fit as part of a larger pipeline of data processing. Beyond just connecting to a relational database, AWS Glue can do ETL on data stored in S3. One potential source of this data is the Amazon Kinesis service, which could be dumping a stream of data into an S3 bucket. Here is an example of what that pipeline could look like with some async firehose events getting sent to S3. First, a connection to the Boto3 Firehose client is created and an `asyncio` event is made.

```
import asyncio
import time
import datetime
import uuid
import boto3
import json


LOG = get_logger(__name__)

def firehose_client(region_name="us-east-1"):
    """Kinesis Firehose client"""

    firehose_conn = boto3.client("firehose", region_name=region_name)
    extra_msg = {"region_name": region_name,\
        "aws_service": "firehose"}
    LOG.info("firehose connection initiated", extra=extra_msg)
    return firehose_conn

async def put_record(data,
            client,
            delivery_stream_name="test-firehose-nomad-no-lambda"):
    """
```

```
    See this:
        http://boto3.readthedocs.io/en/latest/reference/services/
        firehose.html#Firehose.Client.put_record
    """
    extra_msg = {"aws_service": "firehose"}
    LOG.info(f"Pushing record to firehose: {data}", extra=extra_msg)
    response = client.put_record(
        DeliveryStreamName=delivery_stream_name,
        Record={
            'Data': data
        }
    )
    return response
```

Next, a unique user ID (UUID) is created, which will be used for the events that get sent in the async stream.

```
def gen_uuid_events():
    """Creates a time stamped UUID based event"""

    current_time = 'test-{date:%Y-%m-%d %H:%M:%S}'.\
    format(date=datetime.datetime.now())
    event_id = str(uuid.uuid4())
    event = {event_id:current_time}
    return json.dumps(event)
```

Finally, an async event loop fires these messages into Kinesis, which again, will eventually put them into S3 for AWS Glue to transform. Completing the loop then requires hooking up the Glue S3 Crawler, as shown in Figure 3.6, which will "inspect" the schema and create tables that can then be turned into an ETL job that later runs.

```
def send_async_firehose_events(count=100):
    """Async sends events to firehose"""

    start = time.time()
    client = firehose_client()
    extra_msg = {"aws_service": "firehose"}
    loop = asyncio.get_event_loop()
    tasks = []
    LOG.info(f"sending aysnc events TOTAL {count}",extra=extra_msg)
    num = 0
    for _ in range(count):
        tasks.append(asyncio.ensure_future(
                put_record(gen_uuid_events(), client)))
        LOG.info(f"sending aysnc events: COUNT {num}/{count}")
        num +=1
    loop.run_until_complete(asyncio.wait(tasks))
    loop.close()
    end = time.time()
    LOG.info("Total time: {}".format(end - start))
```

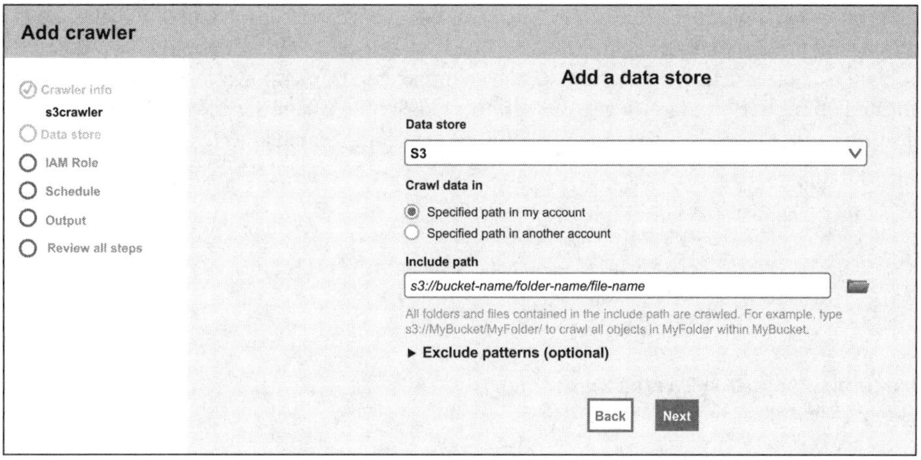

Figure 3.6   Representation of AWS Glue S3 Crawler

AWS Batch

AWS Batch is another service that frees companies and data science teams from writing meaning-less code. It is very common to need to run batch jobs that do things like k-means clustering or preprocessing parts of a data pipeline. Again, often this is a broken feedback loop teetering on the verge of collapse when a couple of key employees quit.

In Figure 3.7, an example AWS Batch pipeline shows how piecing prebuilt services can create a very reliable service that uses "off-the-shelf image classification" with AWS Recognition and "off-the-shelf" batch and event processing tools from AWS.

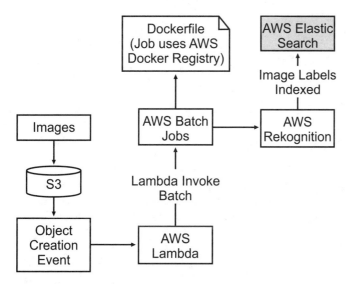

Figure 3.7   AWS Batch Image Classification ML Pipeline

Similar to other parts of the pipeline, AWS Batch can be invoked via Python and Boto; with AWS Lambda, it could mean something like the AWS chalice framework. AWS Batch solves a pretty big problem that used to involve either extremely complicated home-grown messes or a less complicated orchestration of low-level AWS services like Simple Queue Service (SQS) and Simple Notification Service (SNS), which while powerful, can get complicated as well.

```python
def batch_client():
    """Create AWS Batch Client
    {"message": "Create AWS Batch Connection"}
    {"message": "Found credentials in shared credentials file:
        ~/.aws/credentials"}
    """

    log.info(f"Create AWS Batch Connection")
    client = boto3.client("batch")
    return client


def submit_job(job_name="1", job_queue="first-run-job-queue",
               job_definition="Rekognition",
               command="uname -a"):
    """Submit AWS Batch Job"""

    client = batch_client()
    extra_data = {"jobName":job_name,
                  "jobQueue":job_queue,
                  "jobDefinition":job_definition,
                  "command":command}
    log.info("Submitting AWS Batch Job", extra=extra_data)
    submit_job_response = client.submit_job(
        jobName=job_name,
        jobQueue=job_queue,
        jobDefinition=job_definition,
        containerOverrides={'command': command}
    )
    log.info(f"Job Response: {submit_job_response}",
        extra=extra_data)
    return submit_job_response
```

Docker-based Feedback Loops

Many techniques listed in this book, at the core, have Docker files included. This is an extremely powerful "micro" feedback loop. With both AWS and Google Cloud Platform (GCP), there is also the ability to package your own Docker containers and serve them out of their registry services. Up until recently, Docker was fairly fragile, but today there is very little reason to doubt that it is game-changing technology.

There are many reasons to use Docker for ML. Starting at the most micro level, dealing with packaging hell on a laptop is just a waste of time when you can have a file that can be invoked in a clean sandbox that gives you a clean environment.

Why get lost in pip install and conda package management tools conflicting and fighting with themselves all over your organization, when you can declare a Dockerfile with exactly the environment that is guaranteed to work in both production and on OS X, Linux, and Windows machines?

Additionally, look at this example Dockerfile for testing a Lambda-based application. It is both short (because it builds off the Amazon Linux Dockerfile) and descriptive.

```
FROM amazonlinux:2017.09

RUN yum -y install python36 python36-devel gcc \
    procps libcurl-devel mod_nss crypto-utils \
    unzip

RUN python3 --version

# Create app directory and add app
ENV APP_HOME /app
ENV APP_SRC $APP_HOME/src
RUN mkdir "$APP_HOME"
RUN mkdir -p /artifacts/lambda
RUN python3 -m venv --without-pip ~/.env && \
 curl https://bootstrap.pypa.io/get-pip.py | \
    ~/.env/bin/python3

#copy all requirements files
COPY requirements-testing.txt requirements.txt ./

#Install both using pip
RUN source ~/.env/bin/activate && \
    pip install --install-option="--with-nss" pycurl && \
    pip install -r requirements-testing.txt && \
        source ~/.env/bin/activate && \
            pip install -r requirements.txt
COPY . $APP_HOME
```

To integrate this with the AWS container registry, you would need to log in.

```
AWS_PROFILE=metamachine
AWS_DEFAULT_REGION=us-east-1
export AWS_PROFILE
export AWS_DEFAULT_REGION

aws ecr get-login --no-include-email --region us-east
```

Then build this image locally.

```
docker build -t metamachine/lambda-tester .
```

Next, it gets tagged.

```
docker tag metamachine/lambda-tester:latest\
  907136348507.dkr.ecr.us-east-1.amazonaws.com\
/metamachine/myorg/name:latest
```

Then it gets pushed to the AWS registry.

```
docker push 907136348507.dkr.ecr.us-east-1.amazonaws.com\
/metamachine/lambda-tester:latest
```

At this point, other members of the organization can run this image by pulling it down locally.

```
docker pull 907136348507.dkr.ecr.us-east-1.amazonaws.com\
/metamachine/lambda-tester:latest
```

Next, running the image is pretty straightforward. So here is an example of you running the image and mounting your local filesystem as well.

```
docker run -i -t -v `pwd`:/project 907136348507.\
dkr.ecr.us-east-1.amazonaws.com/ \
metamachine/lambda-tester /bin/bash
```

This is just one example of how to use Docker, but essentially service in this book can somehow interact with Docker—from running batch jobs to running customized Jupyter Notebook data science workflows.

Summary

Feedback loops are essential to moving past the laboratory mentality of data science in organizations. In a way, data science as a term may be the wrong way to classify solving ML problems in an organization. Pragmatically solving AI problems involves looking at the results more than the technique. Ultimately, spending months on selecting the best ML algorithm for something that never makes it to production is just an exercise in futility and a waste of money.

One way to ship more ML to production is to quit working so hard. Using off-the-shelf solutions from cloud providers is a powerful technique to accomplish this. Moving past "hero-driven development" and moving into an organizational behavior that encourages business continuity and shipping solutions is good for everyone: good for individual contributors, good for the business, and good for the dawn of AI.

II

AI in the Cloud

4

Cloud AI Development with Google Cloud Platform

There are no shortcuts to building a team each season. You build the foundation brick by brick.

Bill Belichick

For both developers and data scientists, there is a lot to like about the GCP. Many of their services are targeted toward making the development experience fun and powerful. In some ways, Google has been a leader in several aspects of the cloud that AWS has only recently started to address in a serious way. App Engine was way ahead of its time, released in 2008 as a Python-based Platform as a Service (PAAS) with access to Google Cloud Datastore, a fully managed NoSQL database service.

In other ways, Amazon has created considerable moats in directly addressing the needs of the customer as their top priority. Amazon has customer obsession as one of its core values, as well as frugality. This combination has led to an onslaught of low-cost cloud services and features that Google at first seemed unwilling or unable to compete with. For years it was impossible to even find a phone number for any Google service, and even early innovations like Google App Engine were left to almost die on the vine through neglect. The real driver of revenue at Google has always been advertising, where at Amazon it has been products. The result has been for AWS to create a crushing lead of around 30 to 35 percent market share of the cloud worldwide.

The explosion of interest in AI and "applied" Big Data has created opportunities for the Google Cloud, and it has pounced on them. Google has arguably been an ML and Big Data company from Day 1, which creates considerable weapons to attack the cloud market leader, AWS. While Google has been behind the curve on some of its cloud offerings, it has also been ahead on some its ML and AI offerings. A new battleground in cloud ML and AI services has emerged, and GCP is poised to be one of the strongest competitors in this arena.

GCP Overview

Google cleared about approximately 74 billion dollars in net digital ad sales, but only about 4 billion dollars from cloud services in 2017. The upside to this disparity is that there is plenty of money to subsidize research and development on new innovations in cloud services. A good example of this is TPUs, which are 15 to 30 times faster (https://cloud.google.com/blog/big-data/2017/05/an-in-depth-look-at-googles-first-tensor-processing-unit-tpu) than contemporary GPUs and CPUs.

Beyond building dedicated chips for AI, Google has also been busy creating useful AI services with out-of-the-box pretrained models like the Cloud Vision API, Cloud Speech API, and the Cloud Translation API. One theme in this book is the concept of pragmatism. There is no shortage of companies in the San Francisco Bay Area stacked full of engineers and data scientists working on things that don't matter. They busily toil away at Jupyter Notebooks that may never add real value to an organization.

This is as real a problem as the front-end developer who keeps rewriting the web site from backbone to Angular to Vue.js on a predictable 6-month cadence. For the developer, yes, there is some value in doing this because it means they can update their resume with that framework. They are also hurting themselves because they are failing to learn how to create useful production solutions from what they have.

Here is where pretrained models and high-level tools from GCP come into play. Many companies would benefit from calling these APIs versus doing the data science equivalent of porting their front-end to the Javascript framework of the month. This could also serve to add some buffer to teams in allowing them to deliver results quickly and simultaneously work on harder problems.

Other high-level services that GCP provides can add a lot of value to a data science team. One of these services is Datalab, which has a similar "free" product associated with it called Colaboratory (https://colab.research.google.com/). These services create incredible value right out of the gate by eliminating package management hell. Additionally, because they have easy integration with the GCP platform, it becomes much easier to test out services and prototype solutions. Moreover, with the purchase of Kaggle (http://kaggle.com/), there is a much deeper integration with the Google Suite of tools, which may make it easier to hire data scientists who understand how to use BigQuery, for example. This was a smart move on the part of Google.

One direction the GCP platform has taken that also distinguishes it from AWS is the exposure of high-level PaaS services, like Firebase (https://firebase.google.com/).

Colaboratory

Colaboratory is a research project out of Google that requires no setup and runs in the cloud (https://colab.research.google.com/). It is based on Jupyter Notebook, is free to use, and has a lot of packages preinstalled like Pandas, matplotlib, and TensorFlow. There are some extremely useful features right out of the box that make it interesting for many use cases.

The features that I found the most interesting are as follows.

- Easy integration with Google Sheets, Google Cloud Storage, and your local filesystem with the ability to convert them to Pandas DataFrames

- Support for both Python 2 and 3

- Ability to upload notebooks

- Notebooks are stored in Google Drive and can piggyback on the same sharing features that make Google Drive documents easy to work with

- Ability for two users to edit the notebook at the same time

One of the more fascinating parts of Colaboratory is the ability to create a shared training lab for Jupyter Notebook–based projects. Several incredibly tricky problems are solved right away like sharing, dealing with data sets, and having libraries installed. An additional use case would be to programmatically create Colaboratory notebooks that have hooks into the AI pipeline of your organization. A directory of notebooks could be prepopulated with access to a BigQuery query or an ML model that is a template for a future project.

Here is a hello-world workflow. You can refer to this notebook in GitHub: https://github.com/noahgift/pragmaticai-gcp/blob/master/notebooks/dataflow_sheets_to_pandas.ipynb. In Figure 4.1, a new notebook is created.

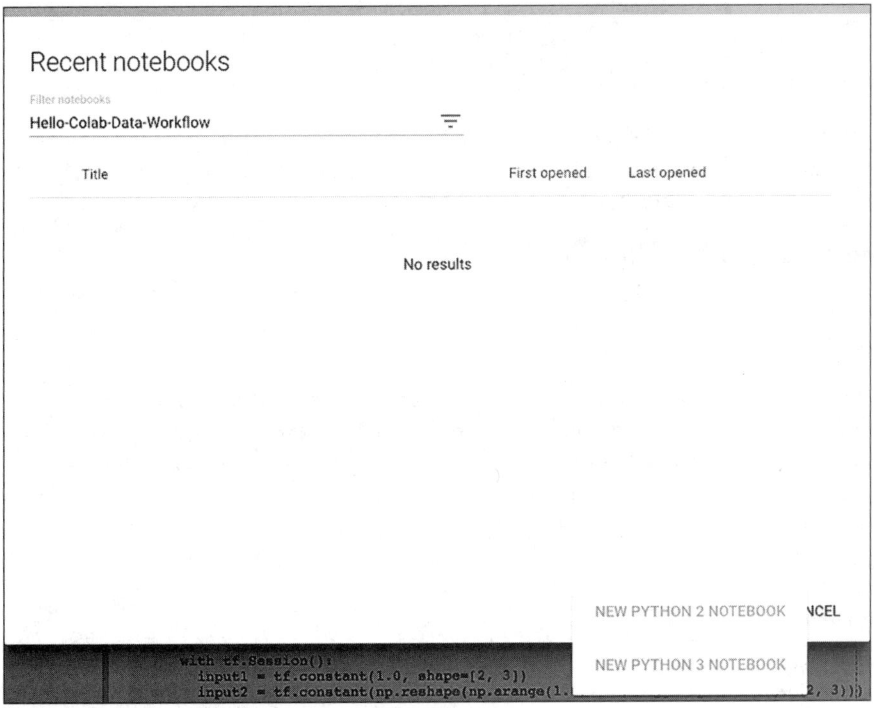

Figure 4.1   Colaboratory Notebook Creation

Next, the gspread library is installed.

```
!pip install --upgrade -q gspread
```

Authentication is necessary to write to a spreadsheet as shown, and a "gc" object is created as a result.

```
from google.colab import auth
auth.authenticate_user()

import gspread
from oauth2client.client import GoogleCredentials

gc = gspread.authorize(GoogleCredentials.get_application_default())
```

The gc object is now used to create a spreadsheet that has one column populated with values from 1 to 10.

```
sh = gc.create('pramaticai-test')
worksheet = gc.open('pramaticai-test').sheet1
cell_list = worksheet.range('A1:A10')

import random
count = 0
for cell in cell_list:
  count +=1
  cell.value = count
worksheet.update_cells(cell_list)
```

Finally, the spreadsheet is converted to a Pandas DataFrame:

```
worksheet = gc.open('pramaticai-test').sheet1
rows = worksheet.get_all_values()
import pandas as pd
df = pd.DataFrame.from_records(rows)
```

Datalab

The next stop on the tour of GCP is Datalab (https://cloud.google.com/datalab/docs/quickstart). The entire gcloud ecosystem requires the software development kit (SDK) be installed from https://cloud.google.com/sdk/downloads. Another option to install is to use the terminal as follows.

```
curl https://sdk.cloud.google.com | bash
exec -l $SHELL
gcloud init
gcloud components install datalab
```

Once the gcloud environment is initialized, a Datalab instance can be launched. There are a few interesting things to note. Docker is an incredible technology for running isolated versions of Linux that will run the same on your laptop as it will in a data center, or some other laptop of a future collaborator.

Extending Datalab with Docker and Google Container Registry

You can run Datalab locally in Docker by referring to the getting-started guide here: https://github.com/googledatalab/datalab/wiki/Getting-Started. Just having a local, friendly version of Datalab you can run free of charge is useful, but what is even more powerful is the ability to extend this Datalab base image, store it in your own Google Container Registry, then launch it with a more powerful instance than your workstation or laptop, like an n1-highmem-32, for example, which has 16 cores and 104GB of memory.

All of a sudden, problems that were just not addressable from your local laptop become pretty straightforward. The workflow to extend the Datalab Docker core image is covered in the guide mentioned in this section. The main takeaway is that after cloning the repository, a change will need to be made to Dockerfile.in.

Launching Powerful Machines with Datalab

To launch one of these mega instances of Jupyter Notebook, it looks like this, as seen in Figure 4.2.

```
➜  pragmaticai-gcp git:(master) datalab create\
 --machine-type n1-highmem-16 pragai-big-instance
Creating the instance pragai-big-instance
Created [https://www.googleapis.com/compute/v1
/projects/cloudai-194723/zones/us-central1-f/
instances/pragai-big-instance].
Connecting to pragai-big-instance.
This will create an SSH tunnel and may prompt you
to create an rsa key pair. To manage these keys, see
https://cloud.google.com/compute/docs/instances/\
adding-removing-ssh-keys
Waiting for Datalab to be reachable at http://localhost:8081/
Updating project ssh metadata...-
```

Name ^	Zone	Creation time	Machine type	Recommendation	Internal IP	External IP	Connect
pragai-big-instance	us-central1-f	Feb 27, 2018, 3:11:12 PM	16 vCPUs, 104 GB		10.128.0.2	35.224.142.212	SSH ▾
tpu-demo-vm	us-central1-f	Feb 12, 2018, 1:03:07 PM	4 vCPUs, 15 GB		10.128.0.2	None	SSH ▾

Figure 4.2   Datalab Instance Running in GCP Console

To make the instance do something useful, Major League Baseball game logs from 1871 to 2016 that were found at data.world (https://data.world/dataquest/mlb-game-logs) are synced to a bucket in GCP. Figure 4.3 shows that 171,000 rows were loaded into Pandas DataFrame via the describe command.

```
gsutil cp game_logs.csv gs://pragai-datalab-test
Copying file://game_logs.csv [Content-Type=text/csv]...
- [1 files][129.8 MiB/129.8 MiB]
  628.9 KiB/s
Operation completed over 1 objects/129.8 MiB.
```

```
In [19]:  df.describe()
```

Out[19]:

	date	number_of_game	v_game_number	h_game_number	v_score	h_score	length_outs	attendanc
count	171907.000	171907.000	171907.000	171907.000	171907.000	171907.000	140841.000	118877.00C
mean	19534616.307	0.261	76.930	76.954	4.421	4.701	53.620	20184.247
std	414932.618	0.606	45.178	45.163	3.278	3.356	5.572	14257.382
min	18710504.000	0.000	1.000	1.000	0.000	0.000	0.000	0.000
25%	19180516.000	0.000	38.000	38.000	2.000	2.000	51.000	7962.000
50%	19530530.000	0.000	76.000	76.000	4.000	4.000	54.000	18639.00C
75%	19890512.000	0.000	115.000	115.000	6.000	6.000	54.000	31242.00C
max	20161002.000	3.000	165.000	165.000	49.000	38.000	156.000	99027.00C

8 rows × 83 columns

Figure 4.3   171,000 Rows in DataFrame from GCP Bucket

The entire notebook can be found in GitHub (https://github.com/noahgift/pragmaticai-gcp/blob/master/notebooks/pragai-big-instance.ipynb), and the commands are as follows. First, some imports.

```
Import pandas as pd
pd.set_option('display.float_format', lambda x: '%.3f' % x)
import seaborn as sns
from io import BytesIO
```

Next, a special Datalab command assigns the output to a variable called game_logs.

```
%gcs read --object gs://pragai-datalab-test/game_logs.csv\
        --variable game_logs
```

A new DataFrame is now created.

```
df = pd.read_csv(BytesIO(game_logs))
```

Finally, the DataFrame is plotted as shown in Figure 4.4.

```
%timeit
ax = sns.regplot(x="v_score", y="h_score", data=df)
```

The takeaway from this exercise is that using Datalab to spin up ridiculously powerful machines to do exploratory data analysis (EDA) is a good idea. Billing is by the second, and it can save hours to do heavy crunching and EDA. Another takeaway is that GCP is leading this section of cloud services versus AWS because the developer experience does a quite nice job in moving large sets of data into a notebook and using familiar "small data" tools like Seaborn and Pandas.

Another takeaway is that Datalab is a great foundation for building production ML pipelines. GCP buckets can be explored, BigQuery has straightforward integration, and other parts of the GCP ecosystem can be integrated like ML Engine, TPUs, and the container registry.

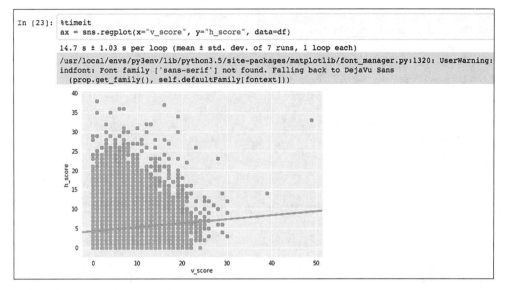

```
In [23]:  %timeit
          ax = sns.regplot(x="v_score", y="h_score", data=df)

          14.7 s ± 1.03 s per loop (mean ± std. dev. of 7 runs, 1 loop each)
          /usr/local/envs/py3env/lib/python3.5/site-packages/matplotlib/font_manager.py:1320: UserWarning:
          indfont: Font family ['sans-serif'] not found. Falling back to DejaVu Sans
            (prop.get_family(), self.defaultFamily[fontext]))
```

Figure 4.4 Timed Seaborn Plot Takes 17 seconds to Plot 171,000 Rows on 32 Core Machine with 100GB of Memory

BigQuery

BigQuery is one of crown jewels of the GCP ecosystem and an excellent service around which to build pragmatic production ML and AI pipelines. In many ways, this too has some developer usability advantages over AWS. While AWS is stronger on complete end-to-end solutions, GCP seems to cater to the tools and paradigms developers are already used to. It is trivial to move data in and out in a variety of different ways, from the command line on a local machine to GCP buckets to API calls.

Moving Data into BigQuery from the Command Line

Speaking of moving data into BigQuery, a straightforward way to do this is to use the bq command-line tool. Here is the recommended approach.

First, check whether the default project has any existing data sets.

```
➜  pragmaticai-gcp git:(master) bq ls
```

In this case, there isn't an existing data set in the default project, so a new data set will be created.

```
➜  pragmaticai-gcp git:(master) bq mk gamelogs
Dataset 'cloudai:gamelogs' successfully created.
```

Next, bq ls is used to verify the data set was created.

```
➜  pragmaticai-gcp git:(master) bq ls
  datasetId
 -----------

  gamelogs
```

Next, a local CSV file that is 134MB and has 171,000 records is uploaded with the flag `-autodetect`. This flag enables a lazier way to upload data sets with many columns since you don't have to define the schema up front.

```
→  pragmaticai-gcp git:(master) ✗ bq load\
 --autodetect gamelogs.records game_logs.csv
Upload complete.
Waiting on bqjob_r3f28bca3b4c7599e_00000161daddc035_1
        ... (86s) Current status: DONE
→  pragmaticai-gcp git:(master) ✗ du -sh game_logs.csv
134M    game_logs.csv
```

Now that the data has been loaded, it can be queried easily from Datalab as shown in Figure 4.5.

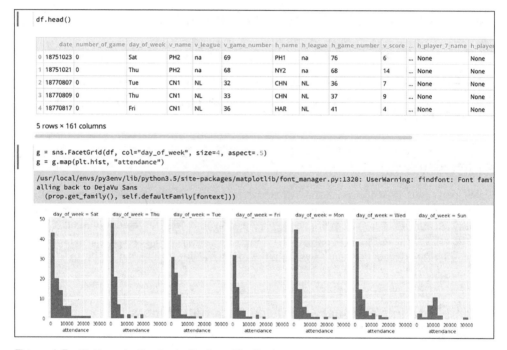

Figure 4.5 BigQuery to Pandas to Seaborn Pipeline

First, imports are created. Note the google.datalab.bigquery import, which allows for easy access to BigQuery.

```
import pandas as pd
import google.datalab.bigquery as bq
pd.set_option('display.float_format', lambda x: '%.3f' % x)
import seaborn as sns
from io import BytesIO
```

Next, a query is turned into a DataFrame. There are 171,000 rows, but for this query, it is limited to 10 rows.

```
some_games = bq.Query('SELECT * FROM `gamelogs.records` LIMIT 10000')
df = some_games.execute(output_options=\
        bq.QueryOutput.dataframe()).result()
```

Finally, that DataFrame is converted into a Seaborn visualization that facets the plots by day of the week.

```
g = sns.FacetGrid(df, col="day_of_week", size=4, aspect=.5)
g = g.map(plt.hist, "attendance")
```

The takeaway from this pipeline example is that BigQuery and Datalab are very impressive and facilitate the creation of easy ML pipelines. Within minutes, it is possible to upload gigantic data sets to BigQuery, fire up a "God" Jupyter workstation to do EDA, and then convert it into actionable notebooks.

This toolchain could next plug right into the ML services of Google or plug into training custom classification models using TPUs. As mentioned before, one of the more powerful differences from the AWS platform is the workflow that encourages the use of the common open-source libraries like Seaborn and Pandas. On one hand, it is true that these tools will eventually fall over under large enough data sets; however, it does add a layer of convenience to be able to reach for familiar tools.

Google Cloud AI Services

As mentioned in the title of this book, pragmatism in AI is heavily encouraged. Why not use off-the-shelf tools when they are available? Fortunately, GCP includes quite a few services, ranging from wild experiments to legitimate "build your company around them" services. Here is brief list of some of the highlights.

- Cloud AutoML (https://cloud.google.com/automl/)
- Cloud TPU (https://cloud.google.com/tpu/)
- Cloud Machine Learning Engine (https://cloud.google.com/ml-engine/)
- Cloud Job Discovery (https://cloud.google.com/job-discovery/)
- Cloud Dialogflow Enterprise Edition (https://cloud.google.com/dialogflow-enterprise/)
- Cloud Natural Language (https://cloud.google.com/natural-language/)
- Cloud Speech-to API (https://cloud.google.com/speech/)
- Cloud Translation API (https://cloud.google.com/translate/)
- Cloud Vision API (https://cloud.google.com/vision/)
- Cloud Video Intelligence (https://cloud.google.com/video-intelligence/)

Another use case for the AI services is to supplement your existing data center or cloud. Why not try the Cloud Natural Language service on your AWS data sets and compare how both work instead of, God forbid, training your own natural language model? Pragmatic AI teams are wise to pick these off-the-shelf solutions, put them into production, and focus on doing bespoke ML training for areas where it really matters to be different.

To use these services, the recommended workflow would be much like other examples in this chapter: fire up a Datalab instance, upload some data, and play around with the API. Another way to explore the API, though, is by just uploading data in the API explorer for each of these services. In many situations, this is the ideal way to start.

Classifying my Crossbreed Dog with the Google Vision API

To use the Computer Vision API via the API explorer, https://cloud.google.com/vision/docs/quickstart contains a quickstart example. To test it out, I uploaded a picture of my dog into a bucket `pragai-cloud-vision` and called it `titan_small.jpg`.

Next, in Figure 4.6 an API call is formulated to that bucket/file. In Figure 4.7, it's Titan the family dog.

```
Request body

{
  "requests": [
    {
      "features": [
        {
          "type": "LABEL_DETECTION"
        }
      ],
      "image": {
        "source": {
          "imageUri": "gs://pragai-cloud-vision/titan_small.jpg"
        }
      }
    }
  ]
}

Press ctrl+space or click one of the hint bubbles for suggestions.
```

Figure 4.6   Google Vision API Request in Browser

Figure 4.7   Titan's Cute Stare Didn't Fool Google's AI

So, what did the image classification system discover about the family dog? It turns out our dog has a greater then 50% chance of being a Dalmatian. It also looks like our dog is a crossbreed.

```
{
  "responses": [
    {
      "labelAnnotations": [
        {
          "mid": "/m/0bt9lr",
          "description": "dog",
          "score": 0.94724846,
          "topicality": 0.94724846
        },
        {
          "mid": "/m/0kpmf",
          "description": "dog breed",
          "score": 0.91325045,
          "topicality": 0.91325045
        },
```

```
    {
      "mid": "/m/05mqq3",
      "description": "snout",
      "score": 0.75345945,
      "topicality": 0.75345945
    },
    {
      "mid": "/m/01z5f",
      "description": "dog like mammal",
      "score": 0.7018985,
      "topicality": 0.7018985
    },
    {
      "mid": "/m/02rjc05",
      "description": "dalmatian",
      "score": 0.6340561,
      "topicality": 0.6340561
    },
    {
      "mid": "/m/02x147d",
      "description": "dog breed group",
      "score": 0.6023531,
      "topicality": 0.6023531
    },
    {
      "mid": "/m/03f5jh",
      "description": "dog crossbreeds",
      "score": 0.51500386,
      "topicality": 0.51500386
    }
  ]
  }
 ]
}
```

Cloud TPU and TensorFlow

An emerging trend in 2018 is the appearance of custom ML accelerators. In February 2018, Google put TPUs into beta release, but they have been in use internally at Google on products such as Google Image Search, Google Photos, and Google Cloud Vision API. A more technical read of TPUs can be found by reading In-Datacenter Performance of a Tensor Processing Unit (https://drive.google.com/file/d/0Bx4hafXDDq2EMzRNcy1vSUxtcEk/view). This mentions the "Cornucopia Corollary" to Amdah's Law: *Low utilization of a huge cheap resource can still deliver high, cost-effective performance.*

TPUs, like some of the other AI services coming out of Google, have the ability to be game-changing technological moats. TPU, in particular, is an interesting bet. If Google can make it easy to train deep learning models with the TensorFlow SDK and enable significant efficiencies by utilizing dedicated hardware AI accelerators, it could have a massive advantage over other clouds.

Ironically though, although Google has made incredible strides at making parts of its cloud ecosystem ridiculously developer friendly, the TensorFlow SDK continues to be problematic. It is very low level, complex, and seemingly designed for Math PhDs who prefer to write in Assembly and C++. There are some solutions that help mitigate this though, like PyTorch. As much as I am personally excited about TPUs, I do think there needs to be a "come to Jesus" moment on the complexity of TensorFlow. It probably will happen, but it is worth noting, HBD... "Here Be Dragons."

Running MNIST on Cloud TPUs

This tutorial is going to piggyback off an existing tutorial for the TPUs that are in beta at the time of this book's publishing. That tutorial can be found at https://cloud.google.com/tpu/docs/tutorials/mnist. To get started, not only is it necessary to have the gcloud SDK installed, but the beta components are needed as well.

```
gcloud components install beta
```

Next, a virtual machine (VM) is needed that will be the job controller. The gcloud cli is used to create a 4-core VM in the central region.

```
(.tpu) ➜  google-cloud-sdk/bin/gcloud compute instances\
    create tpu-demo-vm \
  --machine-type=n1-standard-4 \
  --image-project=ml-images \
  --image-family=tf-1-6 \
  --scopes=cloud-platform
Created [https://www.googleapis.com/compute/v1/\
        projects/cloudai-194723/zones/us-central1-f/\
        instances/tpu-demo-vm].
NAME         ZONE          MACHINE_TYPE
STATUS
tpu-demo-vm  us-central1-f n1-standard-4  _
RUNNING
```

After the VM is created, a TPU instance needs to be provisioned.

```
google-cloud-sdk/bin/gcloud beta compute tpus create demo-tpu \
  --range=10.240.1.0/29 --version=1.6
Waiting for [projects/cloudai-194723/locations/us-central1-f/\
operations/operation-1518469664565-5650a44f569ac-9495efa7-903
9887d] to finish...done.
Created [demo-tpu].

google-cloud-sdk/bin/gcloud compute ssh tpu-demo-vm -- -L \
        6006:localhost:6006
```

Next, some data for the project is downloaded and then uploaded to Cloud Storage. Note that my bucket is called `tpu-research`, but your bucket will be different.

```
python /usr/share/tensorflow/tensorflow/examples/how_tos/\
       reading_data/convert_to_records.py --directory=./data
gunzip ./data/*.gz
export GCS_BUCKET=gs://tpu-research
gsutil cp -r ./data ${STORAGE_BUCKET}
```

Finally, the `TPU_NAME` variable needs to match the name of the TPU instance created earlier.

```
export TPU_NAME='demo-tpu'
```

The last step is to train the model. In this example, the iterations are pretty low, and since the TPUs are powerful, it may make sense to experiment with adding a few zeros to the iterations.

```
python /usr/share/models/official/mnist/mnist_tpu.py \
  --tpu_name=$TPU_NAME \
  --data_dir=${STORAGE_BUCKET}/data \
  --model_dir=${STORAGE_BUCKET}/output \
  --use_tpu=True \
  --iterations=500 \
  --train_steps=1000
```

The model will then print out the loss value, and it is also possible to look at the tensorboard, which has many interesting graphical features. However, a final bit of cleanup will need to be done. Cleaning up the TPUs is necessary to eliminate further charges, as shown.

```
noahgift@tpu-demo-vm:~$ gcloud beta compute tpus delete demo-tpu
Your TPU [demo-tpu] will be deleted.
Do you want to continue (Y/n)?  y
Waiting for [projects/cloudai-194723/locations/us-central1-f/\
operations/operation-1519805921265-566416410875e-018b840b
-1fd71d53] to finish...done.
Deleted [demo-tpu].
```

Summary

GCP is a legitimate contender for building pragmatic AI solutions. It has some advantages and unique offerings over AWS, mainly around the hyper-focus on the developer experience and the off-the-shelf, high-level AI services.

Recommended next steps for the curious AI practitioner would be to go through some of the AI APIs and see how they can be wired together to create solutions that "just work." One of the opportunities and challenges that Google has created is the TPU and TensorFlow ecosystem. On one hand, it is extremely complex to get started with; on the other hand, the power is seductive. Being an expert at TPUs, at the very least, seems like a wise course of action for any company trying to be a leader in the AI space.

Cloud AI Development with Amazon Web Services

Your love makes me strong. Your hate makes me unstoppable.

Ronaldo

FANG stocks (i.e., Facebook, Amazon, Netflix, and Google) have been growing at an unchecked pace in the last several years. Amazon alone in the last three years, from March 2015 to March 2018, has risen 300 percent. Netflix runs its operations on top of AWS as well. From a career perspective, there is a lot of momentum and money going into the AWS cloud. Understanding the platform and what it provides is crucial to the success of many AI applications in the coming years.

A takeaway from this large shift in capital is that the cloud is not only here to stay but is changing fundamental paradigms for the development of software. In particular, AWS has made a bet on serverless technology. The crown jewel of this stack is the Lambda technology, which allows functions in multiple languages—Go, Python, Java, C#, and Node—to be executed as events inside of a larger ecosystem. One way to think about this is that the cloud itself is a new operating system.

Python is famous for having some severe limitations for scalability because of the nature of the language. Despite the inspired, wrong, and *almost convincing*, arguments that the global interpreter lock (GIL) doesn't matter and performance of Python doesn't matter, it does in the real world at scale. What makes Python easy to use has historically also cursed it in terms of performance. In particular, the GIL effectively puts the brakes on efficient parallelization compared to other languages like Java at scale. Sure, there are workarounds on a Linux target host, but this often results in a lot of wasted engineering time rewriting the Erlang language concurrency ideas within Python poorly, or it results in idle cores.

With AWS Lambda, that weakness becomes irrelevant because the operating system is AWS itself. Instead of using threads or processes to parallelize code, a cloud developer can use SNS, SQS, Lambda, and other building-block technologies. These primitives then take the place of threads, processes, and other traditional operating system paradigms. Further proof of the problems with scaling traditional Python on Linux center around deep investigation about supposed high scaling Python projects.

If you dig deep, you will find that what actually is doing the hard work is something like RabbitMQ and/or Celery (written in Erlang), or Nginx, written in highly optimized C. But before you get too excited about Erlang (I ran a company that extensively used it), it is almost impossible to hire anyone who can write in it. The Go language does start to address some of these same scale problems, and you can actually hire Go developers. On the other hand, maybe the best of both worlds is to kick the concurrency can into the back yard of the cloud OS and let them deal with it for you. Then when your expensive Go or Erlang developer quits, it doesn't destroy your entire company.

Fortunately, though, with serverless technology, the weakness of Python on the Linux operating system suddenly becomes accidently irrelevant. A good example of this comes from my days running engineering at the Big Data company Loggly. We attempted to write a highly performant async-based Python log ingestion system in Python, and yes, running on one core it was pretty impressive, getting 6,000 to 8,000 requests per second. The problem, though, was that other cores sat idle, and the solution to start scaling that "async" Python collector to multiple cores ultimately wasn't worth the engineering ROI. With the creation of serverless components from AWS, however, writing the entire system in Python is an excellent idea because the scalability is inherent to their platform.

There is more to consider than just this with these new cloud operating systems. Many technologies like web frameworks are abstractions built on abstractions from decades previous. The relational database was invented in the 1970s, and yes, it is a solid technology—but in the early 2000s, web framework developers took this technology, which evolved in a PC and data center era, and slapped a bunch of web frameworks on top of it using object-relational mappers and code-generation tools. Almost by design, building web applications is an investment into legacy thought processes. They can absolutely solve problems, and they are powerful, but are they the future, especially within the context of large-scale AI projects? I would say no.

Serverless technology is a completely different way of thinking. Databases can be self-scalable, and the schemas can be both flexible and efficient to manage. Instead of running web front ends like Apache or Nginx, which proxy down to code, there are stateless application servers that only run in response to events.

Complexity isn't free. With the complexity increasing with ML and AI applications, something has to give, and one way of decreasing complexity in an application is to no longer have servers that need to be maintained. This may also mean doing an `rm  -rf` to traditional web frameworks. This won't happen overnight though, so this chapter covers both a traditional web application, Flask, but with a cloud operating system twist to it. Other chapters have many examples of pure serverless architectures, specifically with AWS Chalice.

Building Augmented Reality and Virtual Reality Solutions on AWS

Working in the film industry and at Caltech gave me an appreciation for high-performance Linux file servers that were mounted across all workstations in the organization. It is very powerful to have thousands of machines and thousands of users all use a central mount point to configure the operating system, distribute data, and share disk I/O.

A little known fact is that many film companies are ranked in the Top 500 list of supercomputers, and have been for years (https://www.top500.org/news/new-zealand-to-join-petaflop-club/). This is because render farms, which point to high-performance centralized file servers, use tremendous computing and disk I/O resources. When I was at Weta Digital in New Zealand working on Avatar back in 2009 (https://www.geek.com/chips/the-computing-power-that-created-avatar-1031232/), they had 40,000 processors with 104TB of memory. They were processing up to 1.4 million tasks per day, so many film veterans laugh a little at current Spark and Hadoop-based workloads.

The point in bringing up this story—outside of saying, "Get off my lawn!" to newcomers to Big Data—is that a centralized file server is a thing of beauty in large-scale computing. Historically, though, these "Ferrari" file servers took a whole crew of specialized "mechanics" to keep them running. With the cloud era, all of a sudden, you just point and click to get a Ferrari-based file server.

Computer Vision: AR/VR Pipelines with EFS and Flask

AWS has a service Elastic File System (EFS), which is exactly that—a point-and-click "Ferrari" file server. One of the ways I have used it in the past was to create centralized file server for a virtual reality(VR)–based computer vision pipeline on AWS. The assets, code, and produced artifacts were all stored on EFS. In Figure 5.1, this is what a VR pipeline on AWS could look like using EFS. The camera stations could involve 48 or 72 or more cameras all generating large frames that will later be ingested into a VR scene-stitching algorithm.

One subtle but powerful point is that EFS also makes deployment of Python application code a breeze because an EFS mount point can be created for each environment, say DEV, STAGE, and PRODUCTION. Then a "deployment" is an rsync of code, which can be done subsecond from the build server to the EFS mount point depending on the branch; say the DEV EFS mount point is the master branch, and the STAGE EFS mount point is the staging branch, etc. Then Flask will always have the latest version of code on disk, making deployment a trivial issue. An example of what that could look like in is Figure 5.2.

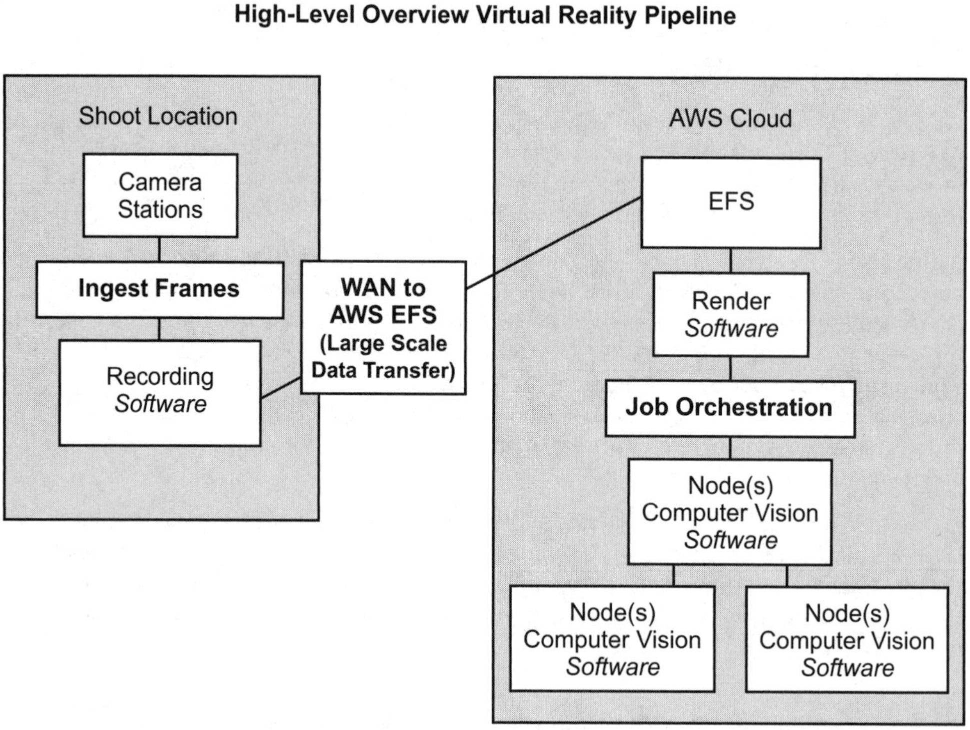

High-Level Overview Virtual Reality Pipeline

Figure 5.1   AWS VR Pipeline with EFS

The ability to use serverless technology when it helps make things easier, plus EFS and Flask together is a powerful tool for building AI products of all kinds. In the examples shown, this was for a computer vision/VR/AR pipeline, but another place EFS comes in handy is for data engineering for traditional ML as well.

Finally, one reason I know this architecture worked is that I wrote it from scratch for a VR/AR company, and it was so popular we quickly burned through 100,000 in credits from AWS in just a few months, spinning up giant multi-hundred-node jobs. Sometimes success does burn a hole in your pocket.

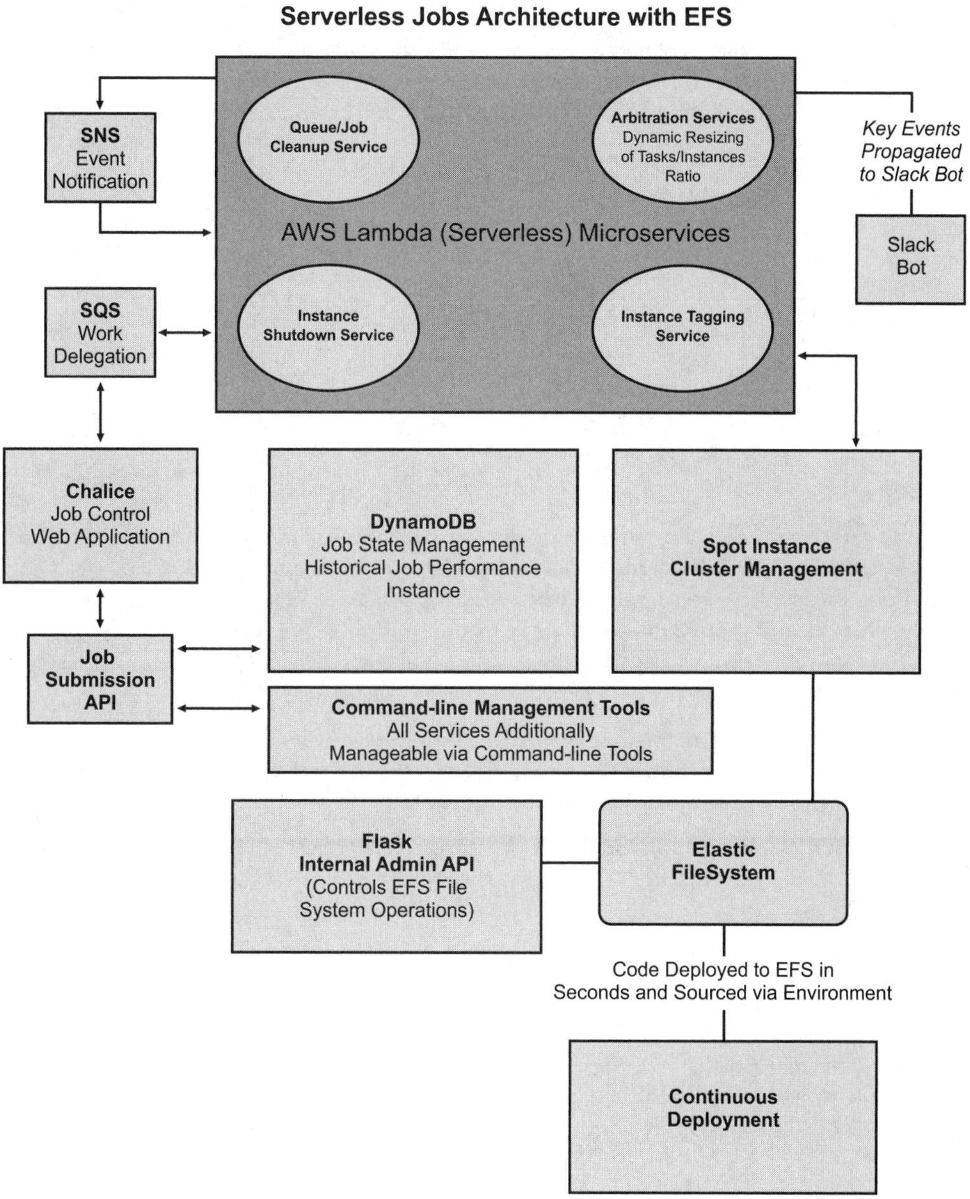

Serverless Jobs Architecture with EFS

Figure 5.2   Detailed Serverless and Flask Architecture

Data Engineering Pipeline with EFS, Flask, and Pandas

In building a production AI pipeline, data engineering can often be the biggest challenge. The following section will describe in detail how the start of a production API could be created in a company, like say, Netflix, AWS, or a unicorn startup. Data teams often need to build libraries and services to make it easier to work with data on the platform at their organization.

In this example, there is a need to create a proof of concept aggregation of CSV data. A REST API that will accept a CSV file, a column to group on, and a column to aggregate returns the result. A further note on this example is that it is very real world in the sense that little details like API documentation, testing, continuous integration, plugins, and benchmarking are all included.

The input to the problem should look like this.

```
first_name,last_name,count
chuck,norris,10
kristen,norris,17
john,lee,3
sam,mcgregor,15
john,mcgregor,19
```

When run against the API, it would then be

```
norris,27
lee,3
mcgregor,34
```

The code for this entire project can be found here: https://github.com/noahgift/pai-aws. Because using Makefiles and virtualenv are covered extensively in other chapters, this chapter will get right into the code. This project will contain five major pieces: the Flask app, a library "nlib," notebooks, tests, and a command-line tool.

Flask App

The Flask app is composed of three components: static directory, which has a favicon.ico in it; a templates directory, which contains an index.html; and the core web application, which is about 150 lines of code. Here is a walkthrough of the core Flask app.

This initial section imports Flask and flasgger (a swagger API doc generator; https://github.com/rochacbruno/flasgger), and defines logging and the Flask app.

```
import os
import base64
import sys
from io import BytesIO

from flask import Flask
from flask import send_from_directory
from flask import request
from flask_api import status
from flasgger import Swagger
from flask import redirect
from flask import jsonify

from sensible.loginit import logger
from nlib import csvops
from nlib import utils

log = logger(__name__)
```

```
app = Flask(__name__)
Swagger(app)
```

A helper function is created to do Base64 decoding of payloads.

```
def _b64decode_helper(request_object):
    """Returns base64 decoded data and size of encoded data"""

    size=sys.getsizeof(request_object.data)
    decode_msg = "Decoding data of size: {size}".format(size=size)
    log.info(decode_msg)
    decoded_data = BytesIO(base64.b64decode(request.data))
    return decoded_data, size
```

Next, a couple of routes are created that are really boilerplate routes that serve out the favicon and redirect to the main docs.

```
@app.route("/")
def home():
    """/ Route will redirect to API Docs: /apidocs"""

    return redirect("/apidocs")


@app.route("/favicon.ico")
def favicon():
    """The Favicon"""

    return send_from_directory(os.path.join(app.root_path, 'static'),
                    'favicon.ico',
                    mimetype='image/vnd.microsoft.icon')
```

Things start to get more interesting with the /api/funcs route. This lists dynamically installable plugins. These could be custom algorithms. This will be described in more detail in the library section.

```
@app.route('/api/funcs', methods = ['GET'])
def list_apply_funcs():
    """Return a list of appliable functions


        GET /api/funcs
        ---
        responses:
            200:
                description: Returns list of appliable functions.


    """

    appliable_list = utils.appliable_functions()
    return jsonify({"funcs":appliable_list})
```

This section creates a groupby route and it contains detailed docstring documentation, so that swagger API docs can be dynamically created.

```
@app.route('/api/<groupbyop>', methods = ['PUT'])
def csv_aggregate_columns(groupbyop):
    """Aggregate column in an uploaded csv

    ---

        consumes: application/json
        parameters:
            - in: path
              name: Appliable Function (i.e. npsum, npmedian)
              type: string
              required: true
              description: appliable function,
               which must be registered (check /api/funcs)
            - in: query
              name: column
              type: string
              description: The column to process in an aggregation
              required: True
            - in: query
              name: group_by
              type: string
              description:\
                  The column to group_by in an aggregation
              required: True
            - in: header
              name: Content-Type
              type: string
              description: \
                  Requires "Content-Type:application/json" to be set
              required: True
            - in: body
              name: payload
              type: string
              description: base64 encoded csv file
              required: True

    responses:
        200:
            description: Returns an aggregated CSV.

    """
```

Finally, the meat of the API call is created below. Note that many "messy" real-world problems are addressed here, like ensuring the correct content type, looking for a specific HTTP method, logging dynamically loading plugins, and returning a correct JSON response with a 200 Status Code if things are correct, but returning other HTTP status codes if they are incorrect.

```
content_type = request.headers.get('Content-Type')
content_type_log_msg =\
```

```
                "Content-Type is set to: {content_type}".\
            format(content_type=content_type)
    log.info(content_type_log_msg)
    if not content_type == "application/json":
        wrong_method_log_msg =\
                "Wrong Content-Type in request:\
          {content_type} sent, but requires application/json".\
              format(content_type=content_type)
        log.info(wrong_method_log_msg)
        return jsonify({"content_type": content_type,
                "error_msg": wrong_method_log_msg}),
status.HTTP_415_UNSUPPORTED_MEDIA_TYPE


    #Parse Query Parameters and Retrieve Values
    query_string = request.query_string
    query_string_msg = "Request Query String:
{query_string}".format(query_string=query_string)
    log.info(query_string_msg)
    column = request.args.get("column")
    group_by = request.args.get("group_by")

    #Query Parameter logging and handling
    query_parameters_log_msg =\
        "column: [{column}] and group_by:\
        [{group_by}] Query Parameter values".\
        format(column=column, group_by=group_by)
    log.info(query_parameters_log_msg)
    if not column or not group_by:
        error_msg = "Query Parameter column or group_by not set"
        log.info(error_msg)
        return jsonify({"column": column, "group_by": group_by,
                "error_msg": error_msg}), status.HTTP_400_BAD_REQUEST

    #Load Plugins and grab correct one
    plugins = utils.plugins_map()
    appliable_func = plugins[groupbyop]

    #Unpack data and operate on it
    data,_ = _b64decode_helper(request)
    #Returns Pandas Series
    res = csvops.group_by_operations(data,
        groupby_column_name=group_by, \
        apply_column_name=column, func=appliable_func)
    log.info(res)
    return res.to_json(), status.HTTP_200_OK
```

This code block sets flags like debug and includes boilerplate code to run a Flask app as a script.

```
if __name__ == "__main__": # pragma: no cover
    log.info("START Flask")
```

```
app.debug = True
app.run(host='0.0.0.0', port=5001)
log.info("SHUTDOWN Flask")
```

Next to run the app, I created a Makefile command as shown.

```
(.pia-aws) ➜  pai-aws git:(master) make start-api
#sets PYTHONPATH to directory above,
#would do differently in production
cd flask_app && PYTHONPATH=".." python web.py
2018-03-17 19:14:59,807 - __main__ - INFO - START Flask
 * Running on http://0.0.0.0:5001/ (Press CTRL+C to quit)
 * Restarting with stat
2018-03-17 19:15:00,475 - __main__ - INFO - START Flask
 * Debugger is active!
 * Debugger PIN: 171-594-84
```

In Figure 5.3, the swagger documentation conveniently lets a user list the available funcs, that is, plugins from nlib. The output shows that there is a npmedian, npsum, numpy, and tanimoto function loaded. In Figure 5.4, there is a useful web form that allows a developer to fully complete the API call without using curl or a programming language. The really powerful thing about this system is that the core web app was only 150 lines of code, yet is real world and about ready for production!

Figure 5.3   Listing of Plugins Available

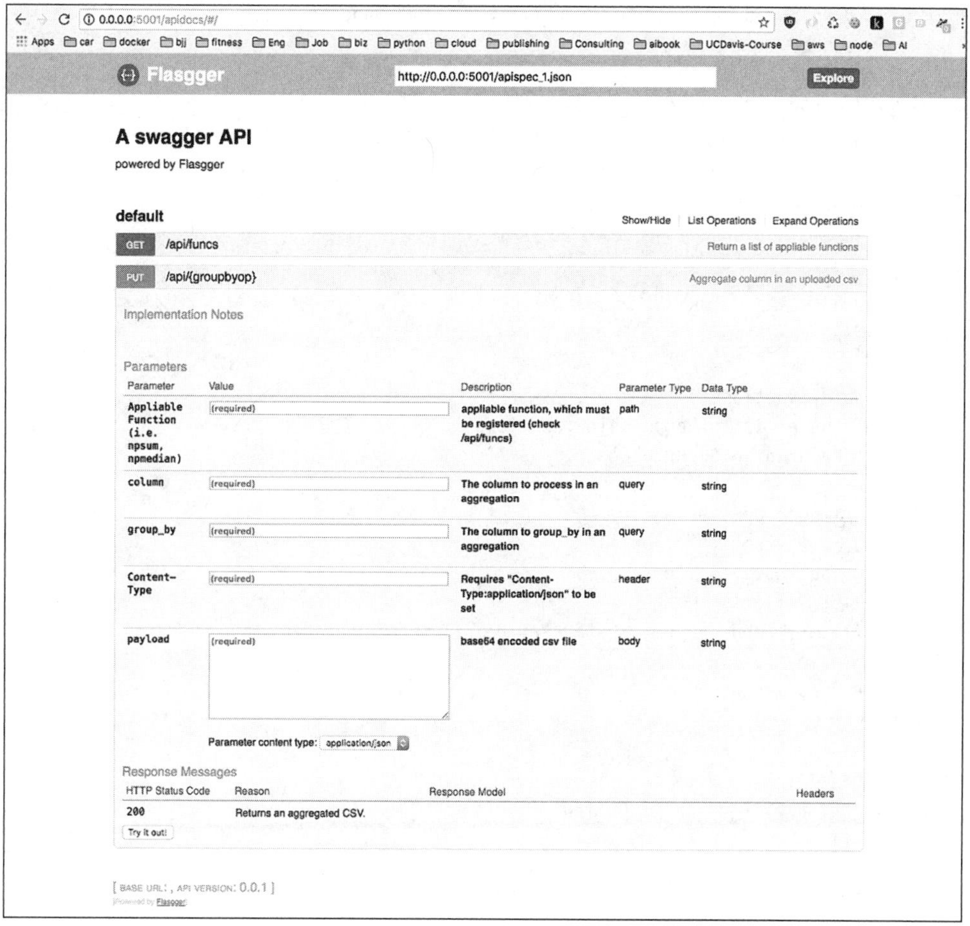

Figure 5.4   Using the API

Library and Plugins

Inside of the nlib directory there are four files: __init__.py, applicable.py, csvops.py, and utils.py. Here is a breakdown of each file.

The __init__.py is very simple, it contains a version variable.

```
__version__ = 0.1
```

Next is the utils.py file, which is a plugin loader and it finds "appliable" functions from appliable.py file.

```
"""Utilities
```

```
Main use it to serve as a 'plugins' utility so that functions can be:
    * registered
    * discovered
    * documented


"""

import importlib

from sensible.loginit import logger

log = logger(__name__)

def appliable_functions():
    """Returns a list of appliable functions
        to be used in GroupBy Operations"""

    from . import appliable
    module_items = dir(appliable)
    #Filter out special items __
    func_list = list(
        filter(lambda x: not x.startswith("__"),
        module_items))
    return func_list



def plugins_map():
    """Create a dictionary of callable functions

    In [2]: plugins = utils.plugins_map()
Loading appliable functions/plugins: npmedian
Loading appliable functions/plugins: npsum
Loading appliable functions/plugins: numpy
Loading appliable functions/plugins: tanimoto

    In [3]: plugins
    Out[3]:
    {'npmedian': <function nlib.appliable.npmedian>,
     'npsum': <function nlib.appliable.npsum>,
     'numpy': <module 'numpy' from site-packages...>,
     'tanimoto': <function nlib.appliable.tanimoto>}

    In [4]: plugins['npmedian']([1,3])
    Out[4]: 2.0
    """

    plugins = {}
    funcs = appliable_functions()
```

```
    for func in funcs:
        plugin_load_msg =\
          "Loading appliable functions/plugins:\
          {func}".format(func=func)
        log.info(plugin_load_msg)
        plugins[func] = getattr(
        importlib.import_module("nlib.appliable"), func
        )
    return plugins
```

The appliable.py file is where custom functions can be created. These functions are "applied" to column in a Pandas DataFrame and could be completely customized to do anything that can be done to a column.

```
"""Appliable Functions to a Pandas GroupBy Operation (I.E Plugins)"""

import numpy


def tanimoto(list1, list2):
    """tanimoto coefficient

    In [2]: list2=['39229', '31995', '32015']
    In [3]: list1=['31936', '35989', '27489',
        '39229', '15468', '31993', '26478']
    In [4]: tanimoto(list1,list2)
    Out[4]: 0.1111111111111111

    Uses intersection of two sets to determine numerical score

    """

    intersection = set(list1).intersection(set(list2))
    return float(len(intersection))\
        /(len(list1) + len(list2) - len(intersection))

def npsum(x):
    """Numpy Library Sum"""

    return numpy.sum(x)

def npmedian(x):
    """Numpy Library Median"""

    return numpy.median(x)
```

Finally, the cvops module deals with csv ingest and operations as shown.

```
"""
```

```
CSV Operations Module:
See this for notes on I/O Performance in Pandas:
    http://pandas.pydata.org/pandas-docs/stable/io.html#io-perf
"""

from sensible.loginit import logger
import pandas as pd

log = logger(__name__)
log.debug("imported csvops module")


def ingest_csv(data):
    """Ingests a CSV using Pandas CSV I/O"""

    df = pd.read_csv(data)
    return df

def list_csv_column_names(data):
    """Returns a list of column names from csv"""

    df = ingest_csv(data)
    colnames = list(df.columns.values)
    colnames_msg = "Column Names: {colnames}".\
        format(colnames=colnames)
    log.info(colnames_msg)
    return colnames

def aggregate_column_name(data,
        groupby_column_name, apply_column_name):
    """Returns aggregated results of csv by column name as json"""


    df = ingest_csv(data)
    res = df.groupby(groupby_column_name)[apply_column_name].sum()
    return res

def group_by_operations(data,
        groupby_column_name, apply_column_name, func):
    """

    Allows a groupby operation to take arbitrary functions

    In [14]: res_sum = group_by_operations(data=data,
        groupby_column_name="last_name", columns="count",
        func=npsum)
    In [15]: res_sum
    Out[15]:
```

```
last_name
eagle    34
lee       3
smith    27
Name: count, dtype: int64
"""


df = ingest_csv(data)
grouped = df.groupby(groupby_column_name)[apply_column_name]
#GroupBy with filter to specific column(s)
applied_data = grouped.apply(func)
return applied_data
```

Command-line Tool

In yet another "get off my lawn" moment, I am going to create a command-line tool because I believe they are useful in just about any project. Despite how powerful Jupyter Notebooks are, there things that command-line tools just do better.

Here is what cvscli.py looks like. At the start, boilerplate documentation and imports are created.

```
#!/usr/bin/env python
"""

Commandline Tool For Doing CSV operations:

    * Aggregation
    * TBD

"""


import sys

import click
from sensible.loginit import logger

import nlib
from nlib import csvops
from nlib import utils

log = logger(__name__)
```

Next, the meat of the command-line tool does the same thing as the HTTP API. There is documentation enclosed and a sample file in ext/input.csv that allows the tool be tested. The output is included in the docstring to be helpful to a user of the tool.

```
@click.version_option(nlib.__version__)
@click.group()
def cli():
    """CSV Operations Tool

    """
```

```
@cli.command("cvsops")
@click.option('--file', help='Name of csv file')
@click.option('--groupby', help='GroupBy Column Name')
@click.option('--applyname', help='Apply Column Name')
@click.option('--func', help='Appliable Function')
def agg(file,groupby, applyname, func):
    """Operates on a groupby column in a csv file
 and applies a function

    Example Usage:
    ./csvcli.py cvsops --file ext/input.csv –groupby\
 last_name --applyname count --func npmedian
    Processing csvfile: ext/input.csv and groupby name:\
 last_name and applyname: count
    2017-06-22 14:07:52,532 - nlib.utils - INFO - \
Loading appliable functions/plugins: npmedian
    2017-06-22 14:07:52,533 - nlib.utils - INFO - \
Loading appliable functions/plugins: npsum
    2017-06-22 14:07:52,533 - nlib.utils - INFO - \
Loading appliable functions/plugins: numpy
    2017-06-22 14:07:52,533 - nlib.utils - INFO - \
Loading appliable functions/plugins: tanimoto
    last_name
    eagle    17.0
    lee       3.0
    smith    13.5
    Name: count, dtype: float64

    """

    if not file and not groupby and not applyname and not func:
        click.echo("--file and --column and –applyname\
 --func are required")
        sys.exit(1)

    click.echo("Processing csvfile: {file} and groupby name:\
 {groupby} and applyname: {applyname}".\
            format(file=file, groupby=groupby, applyname=applyname))
    #Load Plugins and grab correct one
    plugins = utils.plugins_map()
    appliable_func = plugins[func]
    res = csvops.group_by_operations(data=file,
            groupby_column_name=groupby, apply_column_name=applyname,
            func=appliable_func)
    click.echo(res)
```

Finally, just the web api, the command-line tool allows a user to list the plugins that are available.

```
@cli.command("listfuncs")
def listfuncs():
    """Lists functions that can be applied to a GroupBy Operation
```

Example Usage:

```
./csvcli.py listfuncs
Appliable Functions: ['npmedian', 'npsum', 'numpy', 'tanimoto']
"""

funcs = utils.appliable_functions()
click.echo("Appliable Functions: {funcs}".format(funcs=funcs))


if __name__ == "__main__":
    cli()
```

Benchmarking and Testing the API

When creating production APIs in the real world, it would be shameful to not do some benchmarking before putting them into production. Here is what that looks like via a Makefile command.

```
➜  pai-aws git:(master) make benchmark-web-sum
#very simple benchmark of api on sum operations
ab -n 1000 -c 100 -T 'application/json' -u ext/input_base64.txt\
http://0.0.0.0:5001/api/npsum\?column=count\&group_by=last_name
This is ApacheBench, Version 2.3 <$Revision: 1757674 $>
......
Benchmarking 0.0.0.0 (be patient)
Completed 100 requests
Finished 1000 requests


Server Software:        Werkzeug/0.14.1
Server Hostname:        0.0.0.0
Server Port:            5001

Document Path:          /api/npsum?column=count&group_by=last_name
Document Length:        31 bytes

Concurrency Level:      100
Time taken for tests:   4.105 seconds
Complete requests:      1000
Failed requests:        0
Total transferred:      185000 bytes
Total body sent:        304000
HTML transferred:       31000 bytes
Requests per second:    243.60 [#/sec] (mean)
Time per request:       410.510 [ms] (mean)
```

In this case, the application has a reasonable performance for what it does, and it will scale reasonably well behind an Elastic Load Balancer (ELB) with multiple Nginx nodes. However, it should be pointed out that yes, this is one of those examples of how powerful and fun Python is to code with, but also how languages like C++, Java, C#, and Go blow it away in terms of performance. It isn't uncommon for an Erlang or Go application to be doing something similar and getting thousands of requests per second.

In this case, though, the speed of what was developed and the specific data science use case make it a reasonable tradeoff, for now. Version two ideas include switching this over to AWS Chalice and using something like Spark and/or Redis to cache requests and store results in memory. Note that AWS Chalice also has the ability to do API request caching by default, so adding several layers of caching would be fairly trivial.

Ideas for Deploying into EFS

The final thing to do to deploy this into production is have a build server that mounts several EFS mount points: one for the development environment, one for production, etc. When code is pushed out to a branch, a build job rsyncs it to the correct mount point. One way to add some smarts into code to ensure it knows where the correct environments are is to use the EFS name as a way to route to an environment. Here is what that could look like with a file called env.py.

By hacking the df command on Linux, the code can always be sure it is running in the right spot. A further improvement could be to store the ENV data in the AWS Systems Manager Parameter Store (https://docs.aws.amazon.com/systems-manager/latest/userguide/systems-manager-paramstore.html).

```
"""
Environmental Switching Code:

    Assumptions here are that EFS is essentially a key to map off of
"""

from subprocess import Popen, PIPE

ENV = {
    "local": {"file_system_id": "fs-999BOGUS",\
        "tools_path": ".."}, #used for testing
    "dev": {"file_system_id": "fs-203cc189"},
    "prod": {"file_system_id": "fs-75bc4edc"}
}

def df():
    """Gets df output"""

    p = Popen('df', stdin=PIPE, stdout=PIPE, stderr=PIPE)
    output, err = p.communicate()
    rc = p.returncode
    if rc == 0:
        return output
    return rc,err

def get_amazon_path(dfout):
    """Grab the amazon path out of a disk mount"""
```

```
    for line in dfout.split():
        if "amazonaws" in line:
            return line
    return False

def get_env_efsid(local=False):
    """Parses df to get env and efs id"""

    if local:
        return ("local", ENV["local"]["file_system_id"])
    dfout = df()
    path = get_amazon_path(dfout)
    for key, value in ENV.items():
        env = key
        efsid = value["file_system_id"]
        if path:
            if efsid in path:
                return (env, efsid)
    return False

def main():
    env, efsid = get_env_efsid()
    print "ENVIRONMENT: %s | EFS_ID: %s" % (env,efsid)

if __name__ == '__main__':
    main()%
```

Summary

AWS is a very reasonable choice around which to base the technology decisions for a company. Just from looking at the market cap alone of Amazon, it will be innovating and lowering costs for quite some time. If you look at what they have done with serverless technology, it becomes very exciting.

It is easy to get caught up in being deeply worried about vendor lock-in, but using Erlang on DigitalOcean or your data center doesn't mean you aren't locked into a vendor. You are locked into your small, exotic development team, or your systems admins.

This chapter showed real-world APIs and solutions based on problems I have solved in consulting on AWS. Many of the other ideas in chapters in this book could be hooked into ideas from this chapter, and the marriage could be a production solution.

III

Creating Practical AI Applications from Scratch

Predicting Social-Media Influence in the NBA

Talent wins games, but teamwork and intelligence wins championships.

Michael Jordan

Sports is a fascinating topic for data scientists because there is always a story behind every number. Just because an NBA player scores more points than another player, it doesn't necessarily mean he adds more value to the team. As a result, there has been a recent explosion in individual statistics that try to measure a player's impact. ESPN created the Real Plus-Minus, FiveThirtyEight came up with the CARMELO NBA Player Projections, and the NBA has the Player Impact Estimate. Social media is no different; there is more to the story than just a high follower count.

This chapter will explore the numbers behind the numbers using ML and then creating an API to serve out the ML model. All of this will be done in the spirit of solving real-world problems in a real-world way. This means covering details like setting up your environment, deployment, and monitoring, in addition to creating models on clean data.

Phrasing the Problem

Coming from a cold start in looking at social media and the NBA, there many interesting questions to ask. Here are some examples.

- Does individual player performance impact a team's wins?
- Does on-the-court performance correlate with social-media influence?
- Does engagement on social media correlate with popularity on Wikipedia?
- Is follower count or social-media engagement a better predictor of popularity on Twitter?
- Does salary correlate with on-the-field performance?
- Does winning bring more fans to games?
- What drives the valuation of teams more: attendance or the local real estate market?

To get the answers to these questions and others, data will need to be collected. As previously discussed, the 80/20 rule applies here. Eighty percent of this problem is collecting the data and then transforming the data. The other 20 percent is ML- and data science–related tasks like finding the right model, doing EDA, and feature engineering.

Gathering the Data

In Figure 6.1, there is a list of data sources to extract and transform.

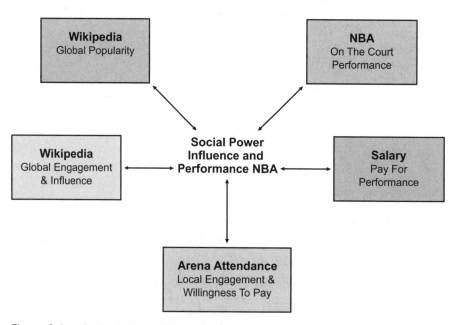

Figure 6.1   NBA Social Power Data Sources

Gathering this data represents a nontrivial software engineering problem. There are many obstacles to overcome, such as finding a good data source, writing code to extract it, abiding by the limitations of the API, and finally getting the data into the correct shape. The first step to collecting all of the data is to figure out which data source to collect first, and where to get it.

Knowing that the ultimate goal is to compare the social-media influence and power of NBA players, a great place to start is with the roster of the NBA players in the 2016–2017 season. In theory, this would be an easy task, but there are a few traps to collecting NBA data. The intuitive place to start would be to go to the official web site at nba.com. For some reason, however, many sports leagues make it difficult to download raw data from their sites. The NBA is no exception, and grabbing stats from their official web site is doable but challenging.

This brings up an interesting point about how to collect data. Often it is easy to collect data manually, that is, downloading from a web site and cleaning it up manually in Excel, Jupyter Notebook, or RStudio. This can be a very reasonable way to get started with a data science problem. If collecting one data source and cleaning it starts to take a few hours, however, it is probably best to look at writing code to solve the problem. There is no hard and fast rule, but experienced people figure out how to continuously make progress on a problem without getting blocked.

Collecting the First Data Sources

Instead of starting with a thorny data source such as the official NBA web site, which actively prevents you from downloading its data, we are going to start with something relatively easy. To collect a first data source from basketball, you can download it directly from this book's GitHub project (https://github.com/noahgift/pragmaticai) or from Basketball Reference (https://www.basketball-reference.com/leagues/NBA_2017_per_game.html).

Doing ML in the real world is beyond just finding the right model for clean data; it means understanding how to set up your local environment as well.

To start running the code, a few steps are needed.

1. Create a virtual environment (based on Python 3.6).

2. Install a few packages that we will use for this chapter: i.e., Pandas, Jupyter.

3. Run this all through a Makefile.

Listing 6.1 shows a setup command that creates a virtual environment for Python 3.6 and installs the packages listed in the requirements.txt file in Listing 6.2. This can be executed all at once with this one liner.

```
make setup && install
```

Listing 6.1   **Makefile Contents**

```
setup:
        python3 -m venv ~/.pragai6
install:
        pip install -r requirements.txt
```

Listing 6.2   **requirements.txt Contents**

```
pytest
nbval
ipython
requests
python-twitter
pandas
pylint
sensible
jupyter
matplotlib
seaborn
statsmodels
sklearn
wikipedia
spacy
ggplot
```

> **Note**
>
> Another handy trick in dealing with Python virtual environments is to create an alias in your .bashrc or .zshrc file that automatically activates the environment and changes into the directory all in one operation. The way I typically do this is by adding this snippet.
>
> ```
> alias pragai6top="cd ~/src/pragai/chapter6\
> && source ~/. Pragai6 /bin/activate"
> ```
>
> To work on this chapter's project, type pragai6top into the shell, and you will cd into the correct project checkout and start your virtual environment. This is the power of using shell aliases in action. There are other tools that automatically do this for you, like pipenv; it may be worth exploring them as well.

To inspect the data, start a Jupyter Notebook using the command: jupyter notebook. Running this will launch a web browser that will allow you to explore existing notebooks or create new ones. If you have checked out the source code for this book's GitHub project, you will see a file named basketball_reference.ipynb.

This is a simple, hello world–type notebook with the data loaded into it. Loading a data set into Jupyter Notebook, or in the case of R, RStudio, is often the most convenient way to do initial validation and exploration of a data set. Listing 6.3 shows how you can also explore the data from a regular IPython shell in addition to or instead of Jupyter.

Listing 6.3 Jupyter Notebook Basketball Reference Exploration

```
import pandas as pd
nba = pd.read_csv("data/nba_2017_br.csv")
nba.describe()
```

> **Note**
>
> Another useful technique is to get in the habit of ensuring Jupyter Notebooks are runnable using the nbval plugin for pytest. You can add a Makefile command test that will run all of your notebooks by issuing
>
> ```
> make test
> ```
>
> You can see what that would look like in a Makefile in the snippet below.
>
> ```
> test:
>         py.test --nbval notebooks/*.ipynb
> ```

Loading a CSV file into Pandas is easy if the CSV file has names for the columns and if the rows of each column are of equal length. If you are dealing with prepared data sets, then it is often if not always the case that the data will be in a suitable shape to load. In the real world, things are never this easy, and it is a battle to get the data into the correct shape as we will see later in this chapter.

Figure 6.2 shows the output in Jupyter Notebook of the describe command. The describe function on a Pandas DataFrame provides descriptive statistics, including the number of columns, in this case 27, and median (this is the 50 percent row), for each column. At this point, it might be a good idea to play around with the Jupyter Notebook that was created and see what other insights you can observe. One of the things this data set doesn't have, however, is a single metric to rank both offensive and defensive performance in a single statistic. To get this, we will need to combine this data set with other sources from ESPN and the NBA. This will raise the difficulty of the project significantly from simply using data to finding it, and then transforming it. One approach that is reasonable is to use a scraping tool like Scrapy, but in our situation, we can use a more ad hoc method. By going to the ESPN and NBA web sites, it is possible to cut and paste the data and put it into Excel. Then the data can be manually cleaned up and saved as a CSV file. For a small data set, this is often much quicker than trying to write a script to perform the same tasks.

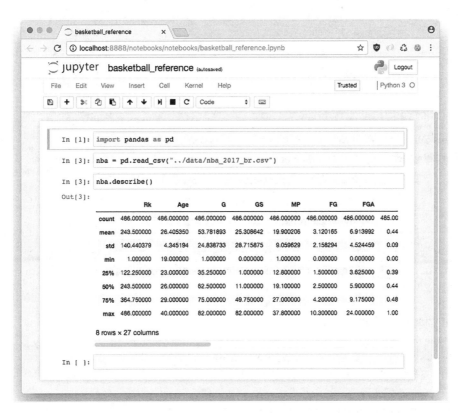

Figure 6.2   Basketball Reference DataFrame Describe Output Jupyter

Later, if this data needs to turn into a bigger project, this approach becomes a poor idea—but for prototyping, it is one of the strongest options. A key takeaway for messy data science problems is to continue to make forward progress without getting bogged down in too much detail. It is very easy to spend a lot of time automating a messy data source only to realize later that the signals are not helpful.

Grabbing the data from ESPN is a similar process as FiveThirtyEight, so I won't describe how to collect it again. A couple of other data sources to collect are salary and endorsements. ESPN has the salary information, and Forbes has a small subset of the endorsement data for eight players. Table 6.1 describes the shape of the data sources, summarizes their content, and defines their source. Mostly accomplished through manual work, there is a fairly impressive list of data sources.

Table 6.1   **NBA Data Sources**

Data Source	Filename	Rows	Summary
Basketball Reference	nba_2017_attendance.csv	30	Stadium attendance
Forbes	nba_2017_endorsements.csv	8	Top players
Forbes	nba_2017_team_valuations.csv	30	All teams
ESPN	nba_2017_salary.csv	450	Most players
NBA	nba_2017_pie.csv	468	All players
ESPN	nba_2017_real_plus_minus.csv	468	All players
Basketball Reference	nba_2017_br.csv	468	All players
FiveThirtyEight	nba_2017_elo.csv	30	Team rank
Basketball Reference	nba_2017_attendance.csv	30	Stadium attendance
Forbes	nba_2017_endorsements.csv	8	Top players
Forbes	nba_2017_team_valuations.csv	30	All teams
ESPN	nba_2017_salary.csv	450	Most players

There is still a lot of work left to get the rest of the data, mainly from Twitter and Wikipedia, and transform it into a unified data set. A couple of initially interesting possibilities are exploring the top eight player's endorsements and exploring the valuation of the teams themselves.

Exploring First Data Sources: Teams

The first thing to do is to use a new Jupyter Notebook. In the GitHub repository, this has already been done for you, and it is called exploring_team_valuation_nba. Next, import a common set of libraries that are typically used in exploring data in a Jupyter Notebook. This is shown in Listing 6.4.

Listing 6.4   **Jupyter Notebook Common Initial Imports**

```
import pandas as pd
import statsmodels.api as sm
import statsmodels.formula.api as smf
import matplotlib.pyplot as plt
import seaborn as sns
color = sns.color_palette()
%matplotlib inline
```

Next, create a Pandas DataFrame for each source, as shown in Listing 6.5.

Listing 6.5   **Create DataFrame for Sources**

```
attendance_df = pd.read_csv("../data/nba_2017_attendance.csv")
endorsement_df = pd.read_csv("../data/nba_2017_endorsements.csv")
valuations_df = pd.read_csv("../data/nba_2017_team_valuations.csv")
salary_df = pd.read_csv("../data/nba_2017_salary.csv")
pie_df = pd.read_csv("../data/nba_2017_pie.csv")
plus_minus_df = pd.read_csv("../data/nba_2017_real_plus_minus.csv")
br_stats_df = pd.read_csv("../data/nba_2017_br.csv")
elo_df = pd.read_csv("../data/nba_2017_elo.csv")
```

In Figure 6.3, a chain of DataFrames are created—a common practice when collecting data in the wild.

Figure 6.3   Multiple DataFrames Output in Jupyter

Here is a merge of attendance data with valuation data and a look at the first few rows.

```
In [14]: attendance_valuation_df =\
 attendance_df.merge(valuations_df, how="inner", on="TEAM")


In [15]: attendance_valuation_df.head()
Out[15]:
                 TEAM  GMS  PCT  TOTAL_MILLIONS  AVG_MILLIONS
0       Chicago Bulls   41  104        0.888882      0.021680
1    Dallas Mavericks   41  103        0.811366      0.019789
2    Sacramento Kings   41  101        0.721928      0.017608
3          Miami Heat   41  100        0.805400      0.019643
4      Toronto Raptors   41  100        0.813050      0.019830
```

Perform a pairplot using Seaborn, which is shown in Figure 6.4.

```
In [15]: from IPython.core.display import display, HTML
    ...: display(HTML("<style>.\
container{ width:100% !important; }</style>"));\
sns.pairplot(attendance_valuation_
    ...: df, hue="TEAM")
```

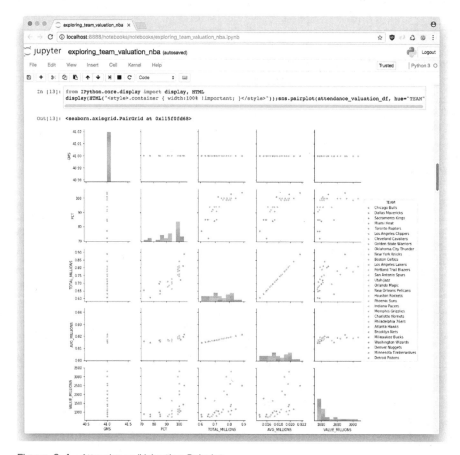

Figure 6.4   Attendance/Valuation Pairplot

In looking at the plots there appears to be a relationship between attendance, either average or total, and the valuation of the team. Another way to dig deeper into this relationship is to create a correlation heatmap, shown in Figure 6.5.

```
In [16]: corr = attendance_valuation_df.corr()
    ...: sns.heatmap(corr,
    ...:             xticklabels=corr.columns.values,
    ...:             yticklabels=corr.columns.values)
    ...:
Out[16]: <matplotlib.axes._subplots.AxesSubplot at 0x111007ac8>
```

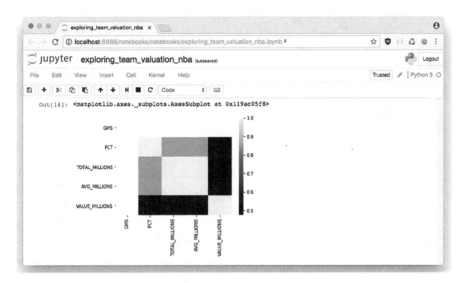

Figure 6.5   Attendance/Valuation Correlation Heatmap

The relationship visible in the pairplot is now more quantifiable. The heatmap shows a medium correlation between valuation and attendance, hovering around 50 percent. Another heatmap shows average attendance numbers versus valuation for every team in the NBA. To generate this type of heatmap in Seaborn, it is necessary to convert the data into a pivot table first. The plot can then be seen in Figure 6.5.

```
In [18]: valuations = attendance_valuation_df.\
pivot("TEAM", "TOTAL_MILLIONS", "VALUE_MILLIONS")
In [19]: plt.subplots(figsize=(20,15))
    ...: ax = plt.axes()
    ...: ax.set_title("NBA Team AVG Attendance vs\
 Valuation in Millions:  2016-2017 Season")
    ...: sns.heatmap(valuations,linewidths=.5, annot=True, fmt='g')
    ...:
Out[19]: <matplotlib.axes._subplots.AxesSubplot at 0x114d3d080>
```

In Figure 6.6, a heatmap shows that there may be some interesting patterns to graph further, perhaps in a 3D plot. There are outliers in New York and Los Angles.

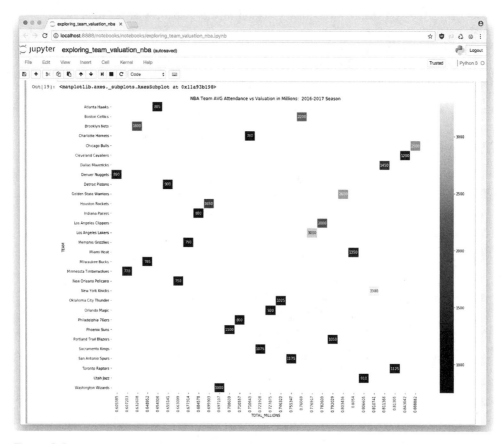

Figure 6.6   NBA Teams Attendance versus Valuation Heatmap

Exploring First Data Sources with Regression

Figure 6.5 shows some fascinating outliers, for example, the Brooklyn Nets are valued at 1.8 billion dollars, yet they have one of the lowest attendance rates in the NBA. Something is going on here that is worth looking at. One way to further investigate is to use linear regression to try to explain the relationship. There are a few different ways to do this if you include both Python and R. In Python, two of the more common approaches are the StatsModels package and scikit-learn. Let's explore both approaches.

With StatsModels, there is a great diagnostic output about performing a linear regression, and it has the feel of classic linear regression software like Minitab and R.

```
In [24]: results = smf.ols(
         'VALUE_MILLIONS ~TOTAL_MILLIONS',
         data=attendance_valuation_df).fit()
```

```
In [25]: print(results.summary())
                        OLS Regression Results
==================================================================
Dep. Variable:          VALUE_MILLIONS   R-squared:           0.282
Model:                             OLS   Adj. R-squared:      0.256
Method:                  Least Squares   F-statistic:         10.98
Date:               Thu, 10 Aug 2017    Prob (F-statistic):0.00255
Time:                       14:21:16    Log-Likelihood:     -234.04
No. Observations:                 30    AIC:                  472.1
Df Residuals:                     28    BIC:                  474.9
Df Model:                          1
Covariance Type:             nonrobust
==================================================================
                    coef    std err        t   P>|t|[0.025 0.975]
------------------------------------------------------------------
.....

Warnings:
[1] Standard Errors assume that the covariance matrix of the errors
is correctly specified.
```

In looking at the results of the regression, it does appear that the variable TOTAL_MILLIONS, which is total attendance in millions is statistically significant (measured in a *P* value of less than .05) in predicting changes in attendance. The R-squared value of .282 (or 28 percent) shows a "goodness of fit"; that is, how well the regression line perfectly fits the data.

Doing a bit more plotting and diagnostics will show how well this model is able to predict. Seaborn has a built in and very useful residplot that plots the residuals. This is shown in Figure 6.7. Having randomly distributed residuals is the ideal scenario; if there are patterns in the plot, it could indicate issues with the model. In this case, there doesn't seem to be a uniformly random pattern.

```
In [88]: sns.residplot(y="VALUE_MILLIONS", x="TOTAL_MILLIONS",
    ...: data=attendance_valuation_df)
    ...:
Out[88]: <matplotlib.axes._subplots.AxesSubplot at 0x114d3d080>
```

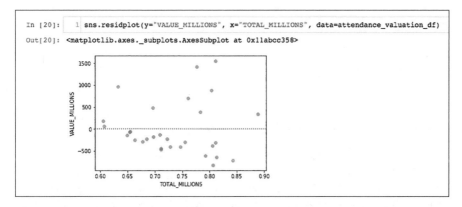

Figure 6.7   NBA Teams Attendance versus Valuation Residual Plot

A common way to measure the accuracy of an ML or statistics prediction is to look at the root mean squared error (RMSE). Here is how to do it with the StatsModels.

```
In [92]: import statsmodels
    ...: rmse = statsmodels.tools.eval_measures.rmse(
         attendance_valuation_predictions_df["predicted"],
         attendance_valuation_predict
    ...: ions_df["VALUE_MILLIONS"])
    ...: rmse
    ...:
Out[92]: 591.33219017442696
```

The lower the RMSE, the better the prediction. To get a better prediction accuracy, we need to figure out a way to lower this RMSE. In addition, having a larger set of data such that the model could be split into test versus training data would ensure better accuracy and reduce the chance of overfitting. A further diagnostic step is to plot the predicted values of the linear regression versus the actual values. In Figure 6.8, an lmplot of the predicted and actual is shown, and it is obvious that this isn't that great a prediction model. It is a good start though, and often this is how ML models are created— by finding correlations and/or statistically significant relationships, then deciding it is worth the effort to collect more data.

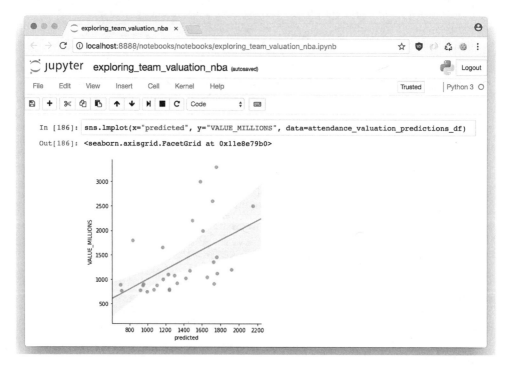

Figure 6.8   Predicted versus Actual Plot of Team Valuation

An initial conclusion is that while there is a relationship between attendance and valuation of an NBA team, there are missing or *latent variables*. An initial hunch is that population of the region, median real estate prices, and how good the team is (ELO ranking and winning percentage) all could play a role here.

```
In [89]: attendance_valuation_predictions_df =\
         attendance_valuation_df.copy()

In [90]: attendance_valuation_predictions_df["predicted"] =\
         results.predict()

In [91]: sns.lmplot(x="predicted", y="VALUE_MILLIONS",\
         data=attendance_valuation_predictions_df)
Out[91]: <seaborn.axisgrid.FacetGrid at 0x1178d2198>
```

Unsupervised Machine Learning: Clustering First Data Sources

A next step in learning more about NBA teams is to use unsupervised ML to cluster the data to find more insights. I was able to manually find median home price data for a county on https://www.zillow.com/research/ and the population for each county from the census on https://www.census.gov/data/tables/2016/demo/popest/counties-total.html.

All this new data can be loaded with a new DataFrame.

```
In [99]: val_housing_win_df =
pd.read_csv("../data/nba_2017_att_val_elo_win_housing.csv")
In [100]: val_housing_win_df.columns
Out[100]:
Index(['TEAM', 'GMS', 'PCT_ATTENDANCE', 'WINNING_SEASON',
       'TOTAL_ATTENDANCE_MILLIONS', 'VALUE_MILLIONS',
       'ELO', 'CONF', 'COUNTY',
       'MEDIAN_HOME_PRICE_COUNTY_MILLONS',
       'COUNTY_POPULATION_MILLIONS'],
     dtype='object')
```

k-nearest neighbors (kNN) clustering works by determining the Euclidean distance between points. Attributes being clustered needed to be scaled so one attribute doesn't have a different scale than another, which would distort the clustering. In addition, clustering is more art than science, and picking the correct number of clusters can be a trial-and-error process. Here is how scaling works in practice.

```
In [102]: numerical_df = val_housing_win_df.loc[:,\
["TOTAL_ATTENDANCE_MILLIONS", "ELO", "VALUE_MILLIONS",
 "MEDIAN_HOME_PRICE_COUNT
     ...: Y_MILLONS"]]
In [103]: from sklearn.preprocessing import MinMaxScaler
     ...: scaler = MinMaxScaler()
     ...: print(scaler.fit(numerical_df))
     ...: print(scaler.transform(numerical_df))
MinMaxScaler(copy=True, feature_range=(0, 1))
[[ 1.         0.41898148  0.68627451  0.08776879]
 [ 0.72637903  0.18981481  0.2745098   0.11603661]
 [ 0.41067502  0.12731481  0.12745098  0.13419221]…
```

In this example, MinMaxScaler is being used from scikit-learn. It converts all numerical values to a value between 0 and 1. Next, sklearn.cluster is performed against the scaled data, and then the cluster results are attached to a new column.

```
In [104]: from sklearn.cluster import KMeans
     ...: k_means = KMeans(n_clusters=3)
     ...: kmeans = k_means.fit(scaler.transform(numerical_df))
     ...: val_housing_win_df['cluster'] = kmeans.labels_
     ...: val_housing_win_df.head()
     ...:
Out[104]:
              TEAM  GMS  PCT_ATTENDANCE  WINNING_SEASON  \
0    Chicago Bulls   41             104               1
1  Dallas Mavericks  41             103               0
2  Sacramento Kings  41             101               0
3       Miami Heat   41             100               1
4   Toronto Raptors  41             100               1
   TOTAL_ATTENDANCE_MILLIONS  VALUE_MILLIONS  ELO  CONF
0                   0.888882            2500  1519  East
1                   0.811366            1450  1420  West
2                   0.721928            1075  1393  West
3                   0.805400            1350  1569  East
4                   0.813050            1125  1600  East
   MEDIAN_HOME_PRICE_COUNTY_MILLONS  cluster
0                         269900.0        1
1                         314990.0        1
2                         343950.0        0
3                         389000.0        1
4                         390000.0        1
```

At this point, there is enough of a solution to provide instant value to a company, and the beginning of a data pipeline is forming. Next let's use R and ggplot to plot the clusters. In order to bring this data set into R, we can write this out to a CSV file.

```
In [105]: val_housing_win_df.to_csv(
"../data/nba_2017_att_val_elo_win_housing_cluster.csv"
)
```

Plotting kNN Clustering in 3D with R

A highlight of the R language is the ability to create advanced plots with meaningful text. Being capable of coding solutions in R and Python opens up a wider variety of solutions in ML. In this particular situation, we are going to use the R 3D scatter plot library along with RStudio to make a sophisticated plot of the relationships we have learned about using kNN cluster. In the GitHub project for this chapter, there is R markdown notebook that has the code and plot; you can also follow along by using the preview function in RStudio for notebooks.

To get started in the console in RStudio (or an R shell), import the scatterplot3d library and load the data using the following commands.

```
> library("scatterplot3d",
        lib.loc="/Library/Frameworks/R.framework/\
        Versions/3.4/Resources/library")
```

```
> team_cluster <- read_csv("~/src/aibook/src/chapter7/data/\
nba_2017_att_val_elo_win_housing_cluster.csv",
+                          col_types = cols(X1 = col_skip()))
```

Next, a function is created to convert the data types into a format that the scatterplot3d library is expecting.

```
> cluster_to_numeric <- function(column){
+      converted_column <- as.numeric(unlist(column))
+      return(converted_column)
+ }
```

A new column is created to hold color data about each cluster.

```
> team_cluster$pcolor[team_cluster$cluster == 0] <- "red"
> team_cluster$pcolor[team_cluster$cluster == 1] <- "blue"
> team_cluster$pcolor[team_cluster$cluster == 2] <- "darkgreen"
```

A skeleton 3D plot is created.

```
> s3d <- scatterplot3d(
+      cluster_to_numeric(team_cluster["VALUE_MILLIONS"]),
+      cluster_to_numeric(
        team_cluster["MEDIAN_HOME_PRICE_COUNTY_MILLIONS"]),
+      cluster_to_numeric(team_cluster["ELO"]),
+      color = team_cluster$pcolor,
+      pch=19,
+      type="h",
+      lty.hplot=2,
+      main="3-D Scatterplot NBA Teams 2016-2017:
  Value, Performance, Home Prices with kNN Clustering",
+      zlab="Team Performance (ELO)",
+      xlab="Value of Team in Millions",
+      ylab="Median Home Price County Millions"
+ )
>
```

To plot the text in the correct location on the 3D space requires a little bit of work.

```
s3d.coords <- s3d$xyz.convert(
cluster_to_numeric(team_cluster["VALUE_MILLIONS"]),
                         cluster_to_numeric(
team_cluster["MEDIAN_HOME_PRICE_COUNTY_MILLIONS"]),
                cluster_to_numeric(team_cluster["ELO"]))

#plot text
text(s3d.coords$x, s3d.coords$y,      # x and y coordinates
     labels=team_cluster$TEAM,        # text to plot
     pos=4, cex=.6)                   # shrink text)
```

The plot shown in Figure 6.9 shows some unusual patterns. The New York Knicks and the Los Angeles Lakers are two of the worst teams in basketball, yet are the most valuable. In addition, you can see that they are in cities that have some of the highest median home prices, which is playing a role in their high valuation. As a result of all of this, they are in their own cluster.

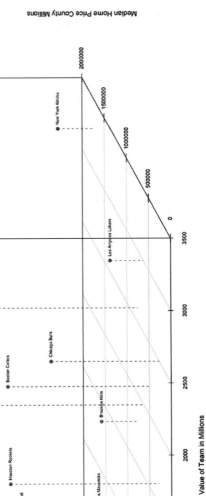

Figure 6.9 3D Scatter Plot of NBA Teams: 2016-2017 with kNN

The blue cluster is mostly a collection of the best teams in the NBA. They also tend to be in cities with higher median home prices but a wide variation of actual value. This makes me suspect that real estate plays a bigger role in team valuation than actual performance (which lines up with previous linear regressions).

The red cluster shows teams that are generally below average in performance, have below-average valuation, and have below-average real estate prices. The exception is the Brooklyn Nets, which is on its way to being a Los Angeles Lakers– and New York Knicks–type team: low performing, yet highly valued.

R has yet one more way to visualize these relationships in multiple dimensions. Next, we are going to create a plot using ggplot in R.

The first thing to do in plotting the relationship in the new graph is to make a logical name for the clusters. The 3D plot gave us some great ideas about how to name clusters. Cluster 0 appears to be a low valuation/low performance cluster, Cluster 1 is a medium valuation/high performance cluster, and Cluster 2 is a high valuation/low performance cluster. One note to add is that cluster number selection is a complex subject. (See Appendix B for more information on the topic.)

```
> team_cluster <- read_csv("nba_cluster.csv",
+                          col_types = cols(X1 = col_skip()))
> library("ggplot2")
>
> #Name Clusters
> team_cluster$cluster_name[team_cluster$cluster == 0] <- "Low"
Unknown or uninitialised column: 'cluster_name'.
> team_cluster$cluster_name[team_cluster$
      cluster == 1] <- "Medium Valuation/High Performance"
> team_cluster$cluster_name[team_cluster$
      cluster == 2] <- "High Valuation/Low Performance"
```

Next, we can use these cluster names to facet (create multiple plots in each plot). In addition, ggplot has the ability to create many other dimensions, and we are going to use them all: color to show winning team percentages and losing team percentages, size to show the differences in median home prices in the county, and the shape to represent the Eastern or Western Conference of the NBA.

```
> p <- ggplot(data = team_cluster) +
+     geom_point(mapping = aes(x = ELO,
+                              y = VALUE_MILLIONS,
+                              color =
factor(WINNING_SEASON, labels=
c("LOSING","WINNING")),
+size = MEDIAN_HOME_PRICE_COUNTY_MILLIONS,
+                              shape = CONF)) +
+     facet_wrap(~ cluster_name) +
+     ggtitle("NBA Teams 2016-2017 Faceted Plot") +
```

```
+     ylab("Value NBA Team in Millions") +
+     xlab("Relative Team Performance (ELO)") +
+     geom_text(aes(x = ELO, y = VALUE_MILLIONS,
+ label=ifelse(VALUE_MILLIONS>1200,
+ as.character(TEAM),'')),hjust=.35,vjust=1)
```

Notice that geom_text only prints the name of the team if the valuation is over 1200. This allows the plot to be more readable and not overwhelmed with overlapping text. In the final snippet, the legend titles are changed. Note also the color is changed to be a factor with one of two values, versus the default of 0, .25, .50, 1. The output of the plot appears in Figure 6.10. The faceting feature of ggplot really shows how clustering has added value to the exploration of data. Using R to do advanced plotting is a great idea even if you are an expert at another ML language like Python or Scala. The results speak for themselves.

```
#Change legends
p +
    guides(color = guide_legend(title = "Winning Season")) +
    guides(size = guide_legend(
+ title = "Median Home Price County in Millions" )) +
    guides(shape = guide_legend(title = "NBA Conference"))
```

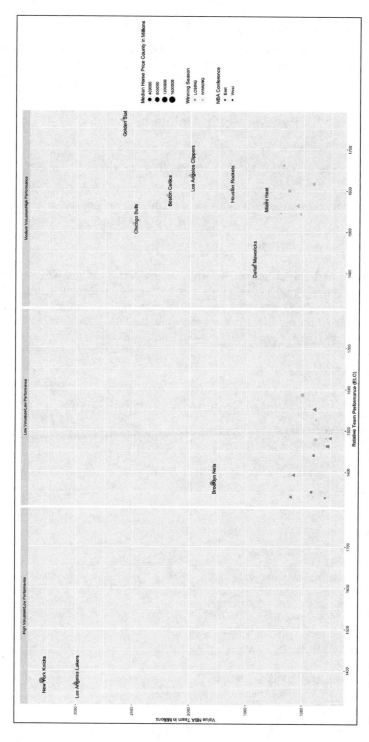

Figure 6.10   ggplot Faceted Plot of NBA Teams: 2016-2017 with kNN

Collecting Challenging Data Sources

With a good set of data around teams already collected, it is time to get into more challenging data sources. This is where things start to get more real. There are some huge issues with collecting random data sources: API limits, undocumented APIs, dirty data, and more.

Collecting Wikipedia Pageviews for Athletes

Here are a few of the problems to solve.

1. How to reverse engineer the Wikipedia system to get pageviews (or find hidden API documentation)

2. How to find a way to generate Wikipedia handles (they may not be the same name as their NBA name)

3. How to join the DataFrame with the rest of the data

Here is how to accomplish this in Python. The entire source for this example is in the GitHub repo for the book, but it will be analyzed in these sections. Below is the example URL for Wikipedia pageviews and the four modules needed. The requests library will make the HTTP calls, Pandas will convert the results into a DataFrame, and the Wikipedia library will be used for a heuristic around detecting the proper Wikipedia URL for an athlete.

```
"""
Example Route To Construct:

https://wikimedia.org/api/rest_v1/ +
metrics/pageviews/per-article/ +
en.wikipedia/all-access/user/ +
LeBron_James/daily/2015070100/2017070500 +

"""
import requests
import pandas as pd
import time
import wikipedia

BASE_URL =\
 "https://wikimedia.org/api/rest_v1/\
metrics/pageviews/per-article/en.wikipedia/all-access/user"
```

Next, the following code constructs a URL that has the data range and username.

```
def construct_url(handle, period, start, end):
    """Constructs a URL based on arguments

    Should construct the following URL:
    /LeBron_James/daily/2015070100/2017070500
    """
```

```
    urls  = [BASE_URL, handle, period, start, end]
    constructed = str.join('/', urls)
    return constructed

def query_wikipedia_pageviews(url):

    res = requests.get(url)
    return res.json()

def wikipedia_pageviews(handle, period, start, end):
    """Returns JSON"""

    constructed_url = construct_url(handle, period, start,end)
    pageviews = query_wikipedia_pageviews(url=constructed_url)
    return pageviews
```

The following function automatically populates a query for 2016. This could later be made more abstract, but for now, this is "hacker" code where hard coding things for speed may be worth the technical debt. Notice as well that a sleep is set to 0 but may need to be enabled if we hit API limits. This is a common pattern when first hitting APIs; they could behave in unexpected ways, so sleeping at some interval can often work around this issue, again, as a temporary hack.

```
def wikipedia_2016(handle,sleep=0):
    """Retrieve pageviews for 2016"""

    print("SLEEP: {sleep}".format(sleep=sleep))
    time.sleep(sleep)
    pageviews = wikipedia_pageviews(handle=handle,
            period="daily", start="2016010100", end="2016123100")
    if not 'items' in pageviews:
        print("NO PAGEVIEWS: {handle}".format(handle=handle))
        return None
    return pageviews
```

Next, the results are converted into a Pandas DataFrame.

```
def create_wikipedia_df(handles):
    """Creates a Dataframe of Pageviews"""

    pageviews = []
    timestamps = []
    names = []
    wikipedia_handles = []
    for name, handle in handles.items():
        pageviews_record = wikipedia_2016(handle)
        if pageviews_record is None:
            continue
        for record in pageviews_record['items']:
            pageviews.append(record['views'])
            timestamps.append(record['timestamp'])
```

```
            names.append(name)
            wikipedia_handles.append(handle)
    data = {
        "names": names,
        "wikipedia_handles": wikipedia_handles,
        "pageviews": pageviews,
        "timestamps": timestamps
    }
    df = pd.DataFrame(data)
    return df
```

A trickier section of the code begins here because some heuristics are needed to guess the right handle. For a first pass, a guess is made that most handles are simply first_last. A second pass appends "(basketball)" to the name, which is a common Wikipedia strategy for disambiguation.

```
def create_wikipedia_handle(raw_handle):
    """Takes a raw handle and converts it to a wikipedia handle"""

    wikipedia_handle = raw_handle.replace(" ", "_")
    return wikipedia_handle

def create_wikipedia_nba_handle(name):
    """Appends basketball to link"""

    url = " ".join([name, "(basketball)"])
    return url

def wikipedia_current_nba_roster():
    """Gets all links on wikipedia current roster page"""

    links = {}
    nba = wikipedia.page("List_of_current_NBA_team_rosters")
    for link in nba.links:
        links[link] = create_wikipedia_handle(link)
    return links
```

This code runs both heuristics and returns verified handles and guesses.

```
def guess_wikipedia_nba_handle(data="data/nba_2017_br.csv"):
    """Attempt to get the correct wikipedia handle"""

    links = wikipedia_current_nba_roster()
    nba = pd.read_csv(data)
    count = 0
    verified = {}
    guesses = {}
    for player in nba["Player"].values:
        if player in links:
            print("Player: {player}, Link: {link} ".\
        format(player=player,
                link=links[player]))
```

```
            print(count)
            count += 1
            verified[player] = links[player] #add wikipedia link
        else:
            print("NO MATCH: {player}".format(player=player))
            guesses[player] = create_wikipedia_handle(player)
    return verified, guesses
```

Next, the Wikipedia Python library is used to convert failed initial guesses of first and last name and looks for "NBA" in the page summary. This is another decent hack to get a few more matches.

```
def validate_wikipedia_guesses(guesses):
    """Validate guessed wikipedia accounts"""

    verified = {}
    wrong = {}
    for name, link in guesses.items():
        try:
            page = wikipedia.page(link)
        except (wikipedia.DisambiguationError,
        wikipedia.PageError) as error:
            #try basketball suffix
            nba_handle = create_wikipedia_nba_handle(name)
            try:
                page = wikipedia.page(nba_handle)
                print("Initial wikipedia URL Failed:\
                 {error}".format(error=error))
            except (wikipedia.DisambiguationError,
                wikipedia.PageError) as error:
                print("Second Match Failure: {error}".\
            format(error=error))
                wrong[name] = link
                continue
        if "NBA" in page.summary:
            verified[name] = link
        else:
            print("NO GUESS MATCH: {name}".format(name=name))
            wrong[name] = link
    return verified, wrong
```

At the end of the script, everything is run and the output is used to create a new CSV file.

```
def clean_wikipedia_handles(data="data/nba_2017_br.csv"):
    """Clean Handles"""

    verified, guesses = guess_wikipedia_nba_handle(data=data)
    verified_cleaned, wrong = validate_wikipedia_guesses(guesses)
    print("WRONG Matches: {wrong}".format(wrong=wrong))
    handles = {**verified, **verified_cleaned}
    return handles
```

```
def nba_wikipedia_dataframe(data="data/nba_2017_br.csv"):
    handles = clean_wikipedia_handles(data=data)
    df = create_wikipedia_df(handles)
    return df

def create_wikipedia_csv(data="data/nba_2017_br.csv"):
    df = nba_wikipedia_dataframe(data=data)
    df.to_csv("data/wikipedia_nba.csv")

if __name__ == "__main__":
    create_wikipedia_csv()
```

All together, something like this can take anywhere from a few hours to a few days and represents the realism of slogging through random data sources to solve a problem.

Collecting Twitter Engagement for Athletes

Collection of data from Twitter has elements that are a bit easier. For one thing, there is a great library in Python, aptly named twitter. There are still some challenges as well, however. Here they are laid out.

1. Summarizing engagement using descriptive statistics

2. Finding the right Twitter handles (handle names on Twitter are even harder to find than on Wikipedia)

3. Joining the DataFrame with the rest of the data

First, create a config file config.py and put credentials for the Twitter API inside of it. Then the `.import config` will create a namespace to use these credentials. Also, Twitter error handling is imported as well as Pandas and NumPy.

```
import time

import twitter
from . import config
import pandas as pd
import numpy as np
from twitter.error import TwitterError
```

The following code talks to Twitter and grabs 200 tweets and converts them into a Pandas DataFrame. Note how this pattern is used frequently in talking with APIs; the columns are put into a list, then the list of columns is used to create a DataFrame.

```
def api_handler():
    """Creates connection to Twitter API"""

    api = twitter.Api(consumer_key=config.CONSUMER_KEY,
    consumer_secret=config.CONSUMER_SECRET,
    access_token_key=config.ACCESS_TOKEN_KEY,
    access_token_secret=config.ACCESS_TOKEN_SECRET)
    return api
```

```
def tweets_by_user(api, user, count=200):
    """Grabs the "n" number of tweets. Defaults to 200"""

    tweets = api.GetUserTimeline(screen_name=user, count=count)
    return tweets

def stats_to_df(tweets):
    """Takes twitter stats and converts them to a dataframe"""

    records = []
    for tweet in tweets:
        records.append({"created_at":tweet.created_at,
            "screen_name":tweet.user.screen_name,
            "retweet_count":tweet.retweet_count,
            "favorite_count":tweet.favorite_count})
    df = pd.DataFrame(data=records)
    return df

def stats_df(user):
    """Returns a dataframe of stats"""

    api = api_handler()
    tweets = tweets_by_user(api, user)
    df = stats_to_df(tweets)
    return df
```

The last function stats_df, can now be used to interactively explore the results of a Twitter API call. Here is an example of LeBron James' descriptive statistics.

```
df = stats_df(user="KingJames")
In [34]: df.describe()
Out[34]:
          favorite_count   retweet_count
count        200.000000      200.000000
mean       11680.670000     4970.585000
std        20694.982228     9230.301069
min            0.000000       39.000000
25%         1589.500000      419.750000
50%         4659.500000     1157.500000
75%        13217.750000     4881.000000
max       128614.000000    70601.000000


In [35]: df.corr()
Out[35]:
                   favorite_count   retweet_count
favorite_count          1.000000        0.904623
retweet_count           0.904623        1.000000
```

In the following code, the Twitter API is called with a slight sleep to avoid running into API throttling. Notice that the Twitter handles are being pulled from a CSV file. Basketball Reference also keeps a large selection of Twitter accounts. Another option would have been to find them manually.

```python
def twitter_handles(sleep=.5,data="data/twitter_nba_combined.csv"):
    """yield handles"""

    nba = pd.read_csv(data)
    for handle in nba["twitter_handle"]:
        time.sleep(sleep) #Avoid throttling in twitter api
        try:
            df = stats_df(handle)
        except TwitterError as error:
            print("Error {handle} and error msg {error}".format(
                handle=handle,error=error))
            df = None
        yield df


def median_engagement(data="data/twitter_nba_combined.csv"):
    """Median engagement on twitter"""

    favorite_count = []
    retweet_count = []
    nba = pd.read_csv(data)
    for record in twitter_handles(data=data):
        print(record)
        #None records stored as Nan value
        if record is None:
            print("NO RECORD: {record}".format(record=record))
            favorite_count.append(np.nan)
            retweet_count.append(np.nan)
            continue
        try:
            favorite_count.append(record['favorite_count'].median())
            retweet_count.append(record["retweet_count"].median())
        except KeyError as error:
            print("No values found to append {error}".\
        format(error=error))
            favorite_count.append(np.nan)
            retweet_count.append(np.nan)

    print("Creating DF")
    nba['twitter_favorite_count'] = favorite_count
    nba['twitter_retweet_count'] = retweet_count
    return nba
```

At the end of all of this, a new CSV file is created.

```python
def create_twitter_csv(data="data/nba_2016_2017_wikipedia.csv"):
    nba = median_engagement(data)
    nba.to_csv("data/nba_2016_2017_wikipedia_twitter.csv")
```

Exploring NBA Athlete Data

To explore the athlete data, a new Jupyter Notebook will be created. This notebook is called nba_player_power_influence_performance. To begin, import a few libraries that are commonly used.

```
In [106]: import pandas as pd
     ...: import numpy as np
     ...: import statsmodels.api as sm
     ...: import statsmodels.formula.api as smf
     ...: import matplotlib.pyplot as plt
     ...: import seaborn as sns
     ...: from sklearn.cluster import KMeans
     ...: color = sns.color_palette()
     ...: from IPython.core.display import display, HTML
     ...: display(HTML("<style>.container\
 { width:100% !important; }</style>"))
     ...: %matplotlib inline
     ...:
<IPython.core.display.HTML object>
```

Next, load the data files in the project and rename the columns.

```
In [108]: attendance_valuation_elo_df =\
 pd.read_csv("../data/nba_2017_att_val_elo.csv")
In [109]: salary_df = pd.read_csv("../data/nba_2017_salary.csv")
In [110]: pie_df = pd.read_csv("../data/nba_2017_pie.csv")
In [111]: plus_minus_df =\
 pd.read_csv("../data/nba_2017_real_plus_minus.csv")
In [112]: br_stats_df = pd.read_csv("../data/nba_2017_br.csv")
In [113]: plus_minus_df.rename(
        columns={"NAME":"PLAYER", "WINS": "WINS_RPM"}, inplace=True)
     ...: players = []
     ...: for player in plus_minus_df["PLAYER"]:
     ...:     plyr, _ = player.split(",")
     ...:     players.append(plyr)
     ...: plus_minus_df.drop(["PLAYER"], inplace=True, axis=1)
     ...: plus_minus_df["PLAYER"] = players
     ...:
```

There are some duplicate sources, so these can also be dropped.

```
In [114]: nba_players_df = br_stats_df.copy()
     ...: nba_players_df.rename(
        columns={'Player': 'PLAYER','Pos':'POSITION',
        'Tm': "TEAM", 'Age': 'AGE', "PS/G": "POINTS"}, i
     ...: nplace=True)
     ...: nba_players_df.drop(["G", "GS", "TEAM"],
        inplace=True, axis=1)
     ...: nba_players_df =\
 nba_players_df.merge(plus_minus_df, how="inner", on="PLAYER")
     ...:
```

```
In [115]: pie_df_subset = pie_df[["PLAYER", "PIE",
          "PACE", "W"]].copy()
     ...: nba_players_df = nba_players_df.merge(
       pie_df_subset, how="inner", on="PLAYER")
     ...:

In [116]: salary_df.rename(columns={'NAME': 'PLAYER'}, inplace=True)
     ...: salary_df["SALARY_MILLIONS"] =\
          round(salary_df["SALARY"]/1000000, 2)
     ...: salary_df.drop(["POSITION","TEAM", "SALARY"],
          inplace=True, axis=1)
     ...:

In [117]: salary_df.head()
Out[117]:
            PLAYER  SALARY_MILLIONS
0      LeBron James            30.96
1       Mike Conley            26.54
2        Al Horford            26.54
3     Dirk Nowitzki            25.00
4   Carmelo Anthony            24.56
```

The salary information is missing for 111 NBA players, so these will be players we will drop as well when we do an analysis.

```
In [118]: diff = list(set(
          nba_players_df["PLAYER"].values.tolist()) -
set(salary_df["PLAYER"].values.tolist()))

In [119]: len(diff)
Out[119]: 111

In [120]: nba_players_with_salary_df =\
 nba_players_df.merge(salary_df);
```

What's left is a Pandas DataFrame with 38 columns.

```
In [121]: nba_players_with_salary_df.columns
Out[121]:
Index(['Rk', 'PLAYER', 'POSITION', 'AGE', 'MP',
       'FG', 'FGA', 'FG%', '3P',
       '3PA', '3P%', '2P', '2PA', '2P%', 'eFG%',
       'FT', 'FTA', 'FT%', 'ORB',
       'DRB', 'TRB', 'AST', 'STL', 'BLK', 'TOV',
       'PF', 'POINTS', 'TEAM', 'GP',
       'MPG', 'ORPM', 'DRPM', 'RPM', 'WINS_RPM',
       'PIE', 'PACE', 'W',
       'SALARY_MILLIONS'],
      dtype='object')
```

```
In [122]: len(nba_players_with_salary_df.columns)
Out[122]: 38
```

Next, the DataFrame can be merged with Wikipedia data. The data is collapsed into a median field so it can be represented as one row in a column.

```
In [123]: wiki_df = pd.read_csv(
        "../data/nba_2017_player_wikipedia.csv")
In [124]: wiki_df.rename(columns=\
        {'names': 'PLAYER', "pageviews": "PAGEVIEWS"}, inplace=True)
In [125]: median_wiki_df = wiki_df.groupby("PLAYER").median()
In [126]: median_wiki_df_small = median_wiki_df[["PAGEVIEWS"]]
In [127]: median_wiki_df_small.reset_index(
        level=0, inplace=True);median_wiki_df_sm.head()
Out[127]:
          PLAYER  PAGEVIEWS
0    A.J. Hammons       1.0
1    Aaron Brooks      10.0
2    Aaron Gordon     666.0
3    Aaron Harrison   487.0
4    Adreian Payne    166.0
In [128]: nba_players_with_salary_wiki_df =\
 nba_players_with_salary_df.merge(median_wiki_df_small)
```

The final columns to add are values from the Twitter data.

```
In [129]: twitter_df = pd.read_csv(
        "../data/nba_2017_twitter_players.csv")


In [130]: nba_players_with_salary_wiki_twitter_df=\
        nba_players_with_salary_wiki_df.merge(twitter_df)
```

There are total of 41 attributes to work with now.

```
In [132]: len(nba_players_with_salary_wiki_twitter_df.columns)
Out[132]: 41
```

A logical next step in exploring the data is to create a correlation heatmap.

```
In [133]: plt.subplots(figsize=(20,15))
    ...: ax = plt.axes()
    ...: ax.set_title("NBA Player Correlation Heatmap")
    ...: corr = nba_players_with_salary_wiki_twitter_df.corr()
    ...: sns.heatmap(corr,
    ...:            xticklabels=corr.columns.values,
    ...:            yticklabels=corr.columns.values)
    ...:
Out[133]: <matplotlib.axes._subplots.AxesSubplot at 0x111e665c0>
<matplotlib.figure.Figure at 0x111e66780>
```

Figure 6.11 shows some fascinating correlations. Twitter engagement and Wikipedia pageviews are highly correlated. Wins attributed to player, or WINS_RPM, is also correlated with Twitter and Wikipedia. Salary and points are highly correlated as well.

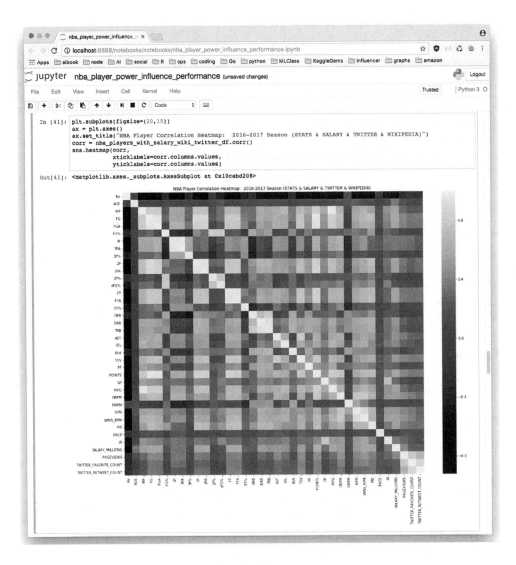

Figure 6.11   NBA Players Correlation Heatmap: 2016–2017

Unsupervised Machine Learning on NBA Players

With a diverse data set and many useful attributes, performing unsupervised ML on NBA players could prove to be very informative. A first step is scale the data and select the attributes against which to cluster (dropping rows with any missing values).

```
In [135]: numerical_df =\
 nba_players_with_salary_wiki_twitter_df.loc[:,\
["AGE", "TRB", "AST", "STL", "TOV", "BLK", "PF", "POINTS",\
 "MPG", "WINS_RPM", "W", "SALARY_MILLIONS", "PAGEVIEWS", \
"TWITTER_FAVORITE_COUNT"]].dropna()
In [142]: from sklearn.preprocessing import MinMaxScaler
     ...: scaler = MinMaxScaler()
     ...: print(scaler.fit(numerical_df))
     ...: print(scaler.transform(numerical_df))
     ...:
MinMaxScaler(copy=True, feature_range=(0, 1))
[[  4.28571429e-01   8.35937500e-01   9.27927928e-01 ...,
     2.43447079e-01   1.73521746e-01]
 [   3.80952381e-01   6.32812500e-01   1.00000000e+00 ...,
     1.86527023e-01   7.89216485e-02]
 [   1.90476190e-01   9.21875000e-01   1.80180180e-01 ...,
     4.58206449e-03   2.99723082e-02]
 ...,
 [   9.52380952e-02   8.59375000e-02   2.70270270e-02 ...,
     1.52830350e-02   8.95911386e-04]
 [   2.85714286e-01   8.59375000e-02   3.60360360e-02 ...,
     1.19532117e-03   1.38459032e-03]
 [   1.42857143e-01   1.09375000e-01   1.80180180e-02 ...,
     7.25730711e-03   0.00000000e+00]]
```

Next, let's cluster again and write out a CSV file to do faceted plotting in R.

```
In [149]: from sklearn.cluster import KMeans
     ...: k_means = KMeans(n_clusters=5)
     ...: kmeans = k_means.fit(scaler.transform(numerical_df))
     ...: nba_players_with_salary_wiki_twitter_df['cluster'] = kmeans.labels_
     ...:
In [150]: nba_players_with_salary_wiki_twitter_df.to_csv(
        "../data/nba_2017_players_social_with_clusters.csv")
```

Faceting Cluster Plotting in R on NBA Players

First, import the CSV file and use the ggplot2 library.

```
> player_cluster <- read_csv(
+ "nba_2017_players_social_with_clusters.csv",
+                        col_types = cols(X1 = col_skip()))

> library("ggplot2")
```

Next, give all four clusters meaningful names.

```
> #Name Clusters
> player_cluster$cluster_name[player_cluster$
```

```
+ cluster == 0] <- "Low Pay/Low"
> player_cluster$cluster_name[player_cluster$
+ cluster == 1] <- "High Pay/Above Average Performance"
> player_cluster$cluster_name[player_cluster$
+ cluster == 2] <- "Low Pay/Average Performance"
> player_cluster$cluster_name[player_cluster$
+ cluster == 3] <- "High Pay/High Performance"
> player_cluster$cluster_name[player_cluster$

+ cluster == 4] <- "Medium Pay/Above Average Performance"
```

Create facets with the cluster names.

```
> #Create faceted plot
> p <- ggplot(data = player_cluster) +
+     geom_point(mapping = aes(x = WINS_RPM,
+                              y = POINTS,
+                              color = SALARY_MILLIONS,
+                              size = PAGEVIEWS))+
+     facet_wrap(~ cluster_name) +
+     ggtitle("NBA Players Faceted") +
+     ylab("POINTS PER GAME") +
+     xlab("WINS ATTRIBUTABLE TO PLAYER (WINS_RPM)") +
+     geom_text(aes(x = WINS_RPM, y = POINTS,
```

There is a bit of work to figure plot text in each facet, and this is accomplished by R and/or statements below. There is also the use of three colors in the salary, which allows for a much clearer view of the differences.

```
label=ifelse(
+ PAGEVIEWS>10000|TOV>5|AGE>37|WINS_RPM>15|cluster
+ == 2 & WINS_RPM > 3,
+
as.character(PLAYER),'')),hjust=.8, check_overlap = FALSE)
>
> #Change legends
> p +
+     guides(color = guide_legend(title = "Salary Millions")) +
+     guides(size = guide_legend(
+ title = "Wikipedia Daily Pageviews" ))+
+     scale_color_gradientn(colours = rainbow(3))
>     geom_text(aes(x = ELO, y = VALUE_MILLIONS, label=ifelse(
VALUE_MILLIONS>1200,as.character(TEAM),'')),hjust=.35,vjust=1)
```

The final result is a nifty, faceted plot as shown in Figure 6.12. The main labels that have been discovered are the differences between popularity, salary, and performance. The cluster with LeBron James and Russell Westbrook has the "best of the best," but they also command the highest salaries.

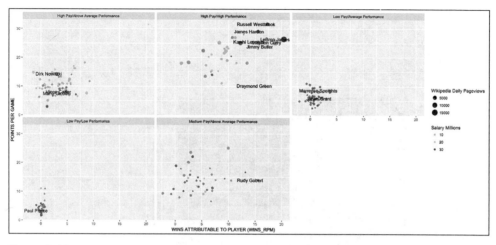

Figure 6.12   ggplot Faceted Plot NBA Players: 2016–2017 with kNN

Putting it All Together: Teams, Players, Power, and Endorsements

With all the data collected, there are some interesting new plots to test out. By combining the endorsement, team, and player data, it is possible to make a couple of fascinating plots. First, the endorsement data can be shown in a correlation heatmap in Figure 6.13. You can see the "copper" color adds an interesting twist to this plot.

```
In [150]: nba_players_with_salary_wiki_twitter_df.to_csv(
"../data/nba_2017_players_social_with_clusters.csv")

In [151]: endorsements = pd.read_csv(
"../data/nba_2017_endorsement_full_stats.csv")

In [152]: plt.subplots(figsize=(20,15))
    ...: ax = plt.axes()
    ...: ax.set_title("NBA Player Endorsement, \
Social Power, On-Court Performance, \
Team Valuation Correlation Heatmap:  2016-2017
    ...: Season")
    ...: corr = endorsements.corr()
    ...: sns.heatmap(corr,
    ...:             xticklabels=corr.columns.values,
    ...:             yticklabels=corr.columns.values, cmap="copper")
    ...:                              \
Out[152]: <matplotlib.axes._subplots.AxesSubplot at 0x1124d90b8>
<matplotlib.figure.Figure at 0x1124d9908>
```

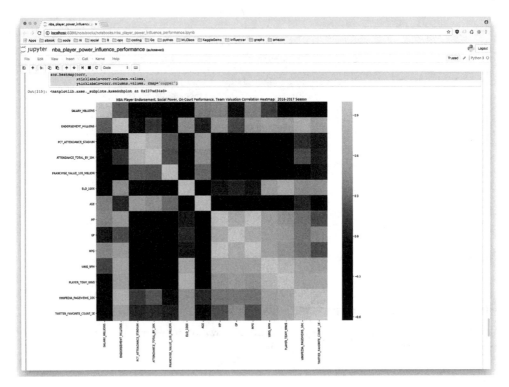

Figure 6.13   Endorsements Correlation Heatmap

Next, in an accent plot, the totality of the work is showcased in Figure 6.14. The code for that is

```
In [153]: from matplotlib.colors import LogNorm
     ...: plt.subplots(figsize=(20,15))
     ...: pd.set_option('display.float_format', lambda x: '%.3f' % x)
     ...: norm = LogNorm()
     ...: ax = plt.axes()
     ...: grid = endorsements.select_dtypes([np.number])
     ...: ax.set_title("NBA Player Endorsement,\
 Social Power, On-Court Performance,\
 Team Valuation Heatmap:  2016-2017 Season")
     ...: sns.heatmap(grid,annot=True,
 yticklabels=endorsements["PLAYER"],fmt='g',
 cmap="Accent", cbar=False, norm=norm)
     ...:
Out[153]: <matplotlib.axes._subplots.AxesSubplot at 0x114902cc0>
<matplotlib.figure.Figure at 0x114902048>
```

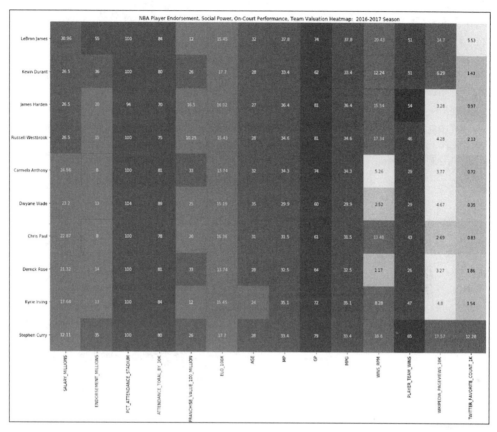

Figure 6.14   Endorsements for Players, Accent Plot

Note that a huge part of making the accent plot readable is converting the colors to LogNorm. This allows relative changes to be the catalyst for boundaries between cells.

Further Pragmatic Steps and Learnings

One of the key reasons for this book to exist is to show how to create complete working solutions deployable to production. One way to get this solution out of a notebook would be to explore some of the solutions in other chapters that go over techniques to get projects shipped into production, for example, creating an NBA Team Valuation prediction API, or an API that showed the social power of NBA superstars. A Y combinator (YC) pitch deck might be just a few more lines of code away.

In addition to that, a Kaggle notebook can be forked (https://www.kaggle.com/noahgift/social-power-nba), and that could be starting point for even more exploration. Finally, a video and slides on this topic can be found on the Strata Data Conference 2018 San Jose schedule: https://conferences.oreilly.com/strata/strata-ca/public/schedule/detail/63606.

Summary

This chapter looked at a real-world ML problem, starting with questions and then moving into techniques on how to collect data from all over the internet. Many of the smaller data sets were cut and pasted from web sites that may or may not have been friendly to their collection. The larger data sources Wikipedia and Twitter required a different approach—a more software engineering–centric approach.

Next, the data was explored in both a statistical fashion and using unsupervised ML and data visualization. In the final section, several solutions were created using cloud providers, including a scalable API, a serverless application, and a data visualization framework (Shiny).

Creating an Intelligent Slackbot on AWS

The man who can drive himself further once the effort gets painful is the man who will win.

Roger Bannister

It has long been a dream to create "artificial life." One of the most common ways to accomplish this has been to create bots. Bots are increasingly becoming part of our everyday life, especially with the rise of Apple's Siri and Amazon's Alexa. In this chapter, the mysteries of how to create bots are revealed.

Creating a Bot

To create a bot, use the Python Slack library (https://github.com/slackapi/python-slackclient). To do anything with Slack, a token first needs to be generated. Generally, a good idea for dealing with tokens like this is to export an environmental variable. I often do this inside of a virtualenv; that way, when it is sourced, I automatically have access to it. This is accomplished by "hacking" the virtualenv by editing the activate script.

To edit the virtualenv with the Slack variable, it would look like this if you edit the activate script in `~/.env/bin/activate`.

Just for reference, there is a new Python official recommended env management tool (https://github.com/pypa/pipenv) on the market, if you want to cover the latest.

```
_OLD_VIRTUAL_PATH="$PATH"
PATH="$VIRTUAL_ENV/bin:$PATH"
export PATH
SLACK_API_TOKEN=<Your Token Here>
export SLACK_API_TOKEN
```

A good way to check whether the environmental variable is set is to use the `printenv` command on OS X or Linux. Next, to test sending a message, the following short script should work.

```
import os
from slackclient import SlackClient

slack_token = os.environ["SLACK_API_TOKEN"]
sc = SlackClient(slack_token)

sc.api_call(
  "chat.postMessage",
  channel="#general",
  text="Hello from my bot! :tada:"
)
```

It is also worth noting that pipenv is a recommended solution that can combine both pip and virtualenv as one component. In addition, it has become a new standard, so it is also worth exploring for package management.

Converting the Library into a Command-Line Tool

Often, as in other examples in this book, it is a great idea to convert this code into a command-line utility so it is easy to iterate on ideas. It is worth pointing out that many new developers are often opposed to command-line tools in lieu of other solutions like simply working in Jupyter Notebook. To play devil's advocate for a second, a question might come from a reader such as, "Why do we want to introduce command-line tools to a Jupyter Notebook–based project? Isn't the point of Jupyter Notebook to eliminate the need to use the shell and command-line?" The nice thing about adding a command-line tool to your project, however, is it gives you the ability to quickly iterate on concepts with "alternative inputs." Jupyter Notebook code blocks don't take input, so in a sense they are hard-coded scripts.

There is a reason why both GCP and AWS have extensive command-line tools throughout their platforms: they add flexibility and power that GUIs just cannot match. A great essay on the subject written by the science fiction author Neal Stephenson is called, "In the Beginning...Was the Command Line." In it, Stephenson states, "GUIs tend to impose a large overhead on every single piece of software, even the smallest, and this overhead completely changes the programming environment." He finishes the essay with the statement, "[L]ife is a very hard and complicated thing; that no interface can change that; that anyone who believes otherwise is a sucker..." Pretty harsh, but in my experience it's true. Life is better with the command-line. If you give it a try, you won't look back.

To accomplish this, the click framework is used, as shown, and the new interface makes it straightforward to send new messages.

```
./clibot.py send --message "from cli"
sending message from cli to #general
```

Figure 7.1 shows the default value set and a customized message from the cli utility.

```
#!/usr/bin/env python
```

```python
import os
import click
from slackclient import SlackClient

SLACK_TOKEN = os.environ["SLACK_API_TOKEN"]

def send_message(channel="#general",
                 message="Hello from my bot!"):
    """Send a message to a channel"""

    slack_client = SlackClient(SLACK_TOKEN)
    res = slack_client.api_call(
      "chat.postMessage",
      channel=channel,
      text=message
    )
    return res

@click.group()
@click.version_option("0.1")
def cli():
    """
    Command line utility for slackbots
    """

@cli.command("send")
@click.option("--message", default="Hello from my bot!",
              help="text of message")
@click.option("--channel", default="#general",
              help="general channel")
def send(channel, message):
    click.echo(f"sending message {message} to {channel}")
    send_message(channel, message=message)

if __name__ == '__main__':
    cli()
```

Figure 7.1   Slackbot Command-Line Tool

Taking the Bot to the Next Level with AWS Step Functions

With the communication pathways created to send messages to Slack, you can take this code to the next level by running it on a schedule and making it do something useful. AWS Step Functions are a powerful way to accomplish this. In the next section, the Slackbot will perform the following actions: scrape Yahoo! sports pages of NBA players, fetch their birthplaces, and then send the information to Slack.

Figure 7.2 shows the finished step function in action. The first step is to fetch URLs of NBA player profiles, and the second step is use Beautiful Soup to find the birthplaces of each player. When this step function is finished, it will then be triggered to send the results to Slack.

AWS Lambda and chalice can be used to coordinate the individual portions of work inside the step function. Lambda (https://aws.amazon.com/lambda/) allows a user to run functions in AWS, and chalice (http://chalice.readthedocs.io/en/latest/) is a framework for building serverless applications in Python. Some prerequisites to get started are as follows.

- The user must have an AWS account.

- The user needs API credentials.

- The Lambda role (that chalice creates) must have a policy associated with privileges necessary to call appropriate AWS services, such as S3.

Getting IAM Credentials Set Up

For detailed instructions on setting up AWS credentials, go to http://boto3.readthedocs.io/en/latest/guide/configuration.html. For details about exporting AWS variables on Windows and Linux, visit https://docs.aws.amazon.com/amazonswf/latest/awsrbflowguide/set-up-creds.html. There are many ways configure credentials, but for users of virtualenv, one trick is to put your AWS credentials into your local virtualenv inside /bin/activate.

```
#Add AWS Keys
AWS_DEFAULT_REGION=us-east-1
AWS_ACCESS_KEY_ID=xxxxxxxx
AWS_SESSION_TOKEN=xxxxxxxx

#export Keys
export AWS_DEFAULT_REGION
export AWS_ACCESS_KEY_ID
export AWS_DEFAULT_REGION
```

Working with Chalice

Chalice has a command-line tool that has many subcommands, as shown.

```
Usage: chalice [OPTIONS] COMMAND [ARGS]...
```

```
Options:
  --version              Show the version and exit.
  --project-dir TEXT     The project directory.  Defaults to CWD
  --debug / --no-debug   Print debug logs to stderr.
  --help                 Show this message and exit.

Commands:
  delete
  deploy
  gen-policy
  generate-pipeline  Generate a cloudformation template for a...
  generate-sdk
  local
  logs
  new-project
  package
  url
```

Inside of the skeleton app.py file, code will be replaced with several Lambda functions. One of the nice things about AWS Chalice is that it not only handles creating web services, but it allows for the creation of "standalone" Lambda functions. This functionality will allow for the creation of multiple Lambda functions that can be associated with the step function and plugged together like LEGO blocks.

For example, to create timed Lambda that does something, it is straightforward.

```
@app.schedule(Rate(1, unit=Rate.MINUTES))
def every_minute(event):
    """Scheduled event that runs every minute"""

    #send message to slackbot here
```

To wire up the web-scraping bot, you need to create a few functions. At the top of the file, some imports are created along with a few variables.

```
import logging
import csv
from io import StringIO

import boto3
from bs4 import BeautifulSoup
import requests
from chalice import (Chalice, Rate)

APP_NAME = 'scrape-yahoo'
app = Chalice(app_name=APP_NAME)
app.log.setLevel(logging.DEBUG)
```

It might be useful for the bot to store some data in S3. This function uses Boto to store the results into a CSV file.

```
def create_s3_file(data, name="birthplaces.csv"):

    csv_buffer = StringIO()
    app.log.info(f"Creating file with {data} for name")
    writer = csv.writer(csv_buffer)
    for key, value in data.items():
        writer.writerow([key,value])
    s3 = boto3.resource('s3')
    res = s3.Bucket('aiwebscraping').\
        put_object(Key=name, Body=csv_buffer.getvalue())
    return res
```

The Fetch page function uses Beautiful Soup (https://www.crummy.com/software/BeautifulSoup) to parse the NBA stats URL and return a soup object.

```
def fetch_page(url="https://sports.yahoo.com/nba/stats/"):
    """Fetchs Yahoo URL"""

    #Download the page and convert it into a beautiful soup object
    app.log.info(f"Fetching urls from {url}")
    res = requests.get(url)
    soup = BeautifulSoup(res.content, 'html.parser')
    return soup
```

The get_player_links function and the fetch_player_urls function grab links to player profile URLs.

```
def get_player_links(soup):
    """Gets links from player urls

    Finds urls in page via the 'a' tag and
filter for nba/players in urls
    """

    nba_player_urls = []
    for link in soup.find_all('a'):
        link_url = link.get('href')
        #Discard "None"
        if link_url:
            if "nba/players" in link_url:
                print(link_url)
                nba_player_urls.append(link_url)
    return nba_player_urls


def fetch_player_urls():
    """Returns player urls"""

    soup = fetch_page()
    urls = get_player_links(soup)
    return urls
```

Next, birthplaces are extracted from the URLs in the find_birthplaces function.

```python
def find_birthplaces(urls):
    """Get the Birthplaces From Yahoo Profile NBA Pages"""

    birthplaces = {}
    for url in urls:
        profile = requests.get(url)
        profile_url = BeautifulSoup(profile.content, 'html.parser')
        lines = profile_url.text
        res2 = lines.split(",")
        key_line = []
        for line in res2:
            if "Birth" in line:
                #print(line)
                key_line.append(line)
        try:
            birth_place = key_line[0].split(":")[-1].strip()
            app.log.info(f"birth_place: {birth_place}")
        except IndexError:
            app.log.info(f"skipping {url}")
            continue
        birthplaces[url] = birth_place
        app.log.info(birth_place)
    return birthplaces
```

The next section gets into the chalice functions. Note that chalice requires that a default route be created.

```python
#These can be called via HTTP Requests
@app.route('/')
def index():
    """Root URL"""

    app.log.info(f"/ Route: for {APP_NAME}")
    return {'app_name': APP_NAME}
```

The next Lambda is a route that wires up an HTTP URL with the function written earlier.

```python
@app.route('/player_urls')
def player_urls():
    """Fetches player urls"""

    app.log.info(f"/player_urls Route: for {APP_NAME}")
    urls = fetch_player_urls()
    return {"nba_player_urls": urls}
```

The following Lambdas are "standalone" Lambdas, which can be called within the step function.

```python
#This a standalone lambda
@app.lambda_function()
def return_player_urls(event, context):
    """Standalone lambda that returns player urls"""
```

```
    app.log.info(f"standalone lambda 'return_players_urls'\
 {APP_NAME} with {event} and {context}")
    urls = fetch_player_urls()
    return {"urls": urls}

#This a standalone lambda
@app.lambda_function()
def birthplace_from_urls(event, context):
    """Finds birthplaces"""

    app.log.info(f"standalone lambda 'birthplace_from_urls'\
 {APP_NAME} with {event} and {context}")
    payload = event["urls"]
    birthplaces = find_birthplaces(payload)
    return birthplaces

#This a standalone lambda
@app.lambda_function()
def create_s3_file_from_json(event, context):
    """Create an S3 file from json data"""

    app.log.info(f"Creating s3 file with event data {event}\
 and context {context}")
    print(type(event))
    res = create_s3_file(data=event)
    app.log.info(f"response of putting file: {res}")
    return True
```

Running the chalice app locally shows the following output.

```
→  scrape-yahoo git:(master) ✗ chalice local
Serving on 127.0.0.1:8000
scrape-yahoo - INFO - / Route: for scrape-yahoo
127.0.0.1 - - [12/Dec/2017 03:25:42] "GET / HTTP/1.1" 200 -
127.0.0.1 - - [12/Dec/2017 03:25:42] "GET /favicon.ico"
scrape-yahoo - INFO - / Route: for scrape-yahoo
127.0.0.1 - - [12/Dec/2017 03:25:45] "GET / HTTP/1.1" 200 -
127.0.0.1 - - [12/Dec/2017 03:25:45] "GET /favicon.ico"
scrape-yahoo - INFO - /player_urls Route: for scrape-yahoo
scrape-yahoo - INFO - https://sports.yahoo.com/nba/stats/
https://sports.yahoo.com/nba/players/4563/
https://sports.yahoo.com/nba/players/5185/
https://sports.yahoo.com/nba/players/3704/
https://sports.yahoo.com/nba/players/5012/
https://sports.yahoo.com/nba/players/4612/
https://sports.yahoo.com/nba/players/5015/
https://sports.yahoo.com/nba/players/4497/
https://sports.yahoo.com/nba/players/4720/
https://sports.yahoo.com/nba/players/3818/
https://sports.yahoo.com/nba/players/5432/
https://sports.yahoo.com/nba/players/5471/
```

```
https://sports.yahoo.com/nba/players/4244/
https://sports.yahoo.com/nba/players/5464/
https://sports.yahoo.com/nba/players/5294/
https://sports.yahoo.com/nba/players/5336/
https://sports.yahoo.com/nba/players/4390/
https://sports.yahoo.com/nba/players/4563/
https://sports.yahoo.com/nba/players/3704/
https://sports.yahoo.com/nba/players/5600/
https://sports.yahoo.com/nba/players/4624/
127.0.0.1 - - [12/Dec/2017 03:25:53] "GET /player_urls"
127.0.0.1 - - [12/Dec/2017 03:25:53] "GET /favicon.ico"
```

To deploy the app, run `chalice deploy`.

```
➜  scrape-yahoo git:(master) ✗ chalice deploy
Creating role: scrape-yahoo-dev
Creating deployment package.
Creating lambda function: scrape-yahoo-dev
Initiating first time deployment.
Deploying to API Gateway stage: api
https://bt98uzs1cc.execute-api.us-east-1.amazonaws.com/api/
```

Using the HTTP CLI (https://github.com/jakubroztocil/httpie), the HTTP route is now called from AWS to retrieve the links available at /api/player_urls.

```
➜  scrape-yahoo git:(master) ✗ http \
https://<a lambda route>.amazonaws.com/api/player_urls
HTTP/1.1 200 OK
Connection: keep-alive
Content-Length: 941
Content-Type: application/json
Date: Tue, 12 Dec 2017 11:48:41 GMT
Via: 1.1 ba90f9bd20de9ac04075a8309c165ab1.cloudfront.net (CloudFront)
X-Amz-Cf-Id: ViZswjo4UeHYwrc9e-5vMVTDhV_IcOdhVIGOBrDdtYqd5KWcAuZKKQ==
X-Amzn-Trace-Id: sampled=0;root=1-5a2fc217-07cc12d50a4d38a59a688f5c
X-Cache: Miss from cloudfront
x-amzn-RequestId: 64f24fcd-df32-11e7-a81a-2b511652b4f6


{
    "nba_player_urls": [
        "https://sports.yahoo.com/nba/players/4563/",
        "https://sports.yahoo.com/nba/players/5185/",
        "https://sports.yahoo.com/nba/players/3704/",
        "https://sports.yahoo.com/nba/players/5012/",
        "https://sports.yahoo.com/nba/players/4612/",
        "https://sports.yahoo.com/nba/players/5015/",
        "https://sports.yahoo.com/nba/players/4497/",
        "https://sports.yahoo.com/nba/players/4720/",
        "https://sports.yahoo.com/nba/players/3818/",
        "https://sports.yahoo.com/nba/players/5432/",
        "https://sports.yahoo.com/nba/players/5471/",
        "https://sports.yahoo.com/nba/players/4244/",
```

```
                "https://sports.yahoo.com/nba/players/5464/",
                "https://sports.yahoo.com/nba/players/5294/",
                "https://sports.yahoo.com/nba/players/5336/",
                "https://sports.yahoo.com/nba/players/4390/",
                "https://sports.yahoo.com/nba/players/4563/",
                "https://sports.yahoo.com/nba/players/3704/",
                "https://sports.yahoo.com/nba/players/5600/",
                "https://sports.yahoo.com/nba/players/4624/"
        ]
}
```

Another convenient way to interact with the Lambda functions is to call it directly via click and the Python Boto library. A new command-line tool can be created called wscli.py (short for "web-scraping command-line interface"). The first part of the code sets up logging and imports the libraries.

```
#!/usr/bin/env python


import logging
import json

import boto3
import click
from pythonjsonlogger import jsonlogger

#intialize logging
log = logging.getLogger(__name__)
log.setLevel(logging.INFO)
LOGHANDLER = logging.StreamHandler()
FORMMATTER = jsonlogger.JsonFormatter()
LOGHANDLER.setFormatter(FORMMATTER)
log.addHandler(LOGHANDLER)
```

Next, the three functions are used to connect to the Lambda function via invoke_lambda.

```
### Lambda Boto API Calls
def lambda_connection(region_name="us-east-1"):
    """Create Lambda Connection"""

    lambda_conn = boto3.client("lambda", region_name=region_name)
    extra_msg = {"region_name": region_name, "aws_service": "lambda"}
    log.info("instantiate lambda client", extra=extra_msg)
    return lambda_conn


def parse_lambda_result(response):
    """Gets the results from a boto json response"""

    body = response['Payload']
    json_result = body.read()
    lambda_return_value = json.loads(json_result)
    return lambda_return_value
```

```python
def invoke_lambda(func_name, lambda_conn, payload=None,
                  invocation_type="RequestResponse"):
    """Calls a lambda function"""


    extra_msg = {"function_name": func_name, "aws_service": "lambda",
            "payload":payload}
    log.info("Calling lambda function", extra=extra_msg)
    if not payload:
        payload = json.dumps({"payload":"None"})

    response = lambda_conn.invoke(FunctionName=func_name,
                    InvocationType=invocation_type,
                    Payload=payload
    )
    log.info(response, extra=extra_msg)
    lambda_return_value = parse_lambda_result(response)
    return lambda_return_value
```

This Lambda invoke function is then wrapped up by the click command-line tool framework. Note, the –func option is defaulted to use the Lambda function deployed earlier.

```python
@click.group()
@click.version_option("1.0")
def cli():
    """Commandline Utility to Assist in Web Scraping"""

@cli.command("lambda")
@click.option("--func",
        default="scrape-yahoo-dev-return_player_urls",
        help="name of execution")
@click.option("--payload", default='{"cli":"invoke"}',
        help="name of payload")
def call_lambda(func, payload):
    """invokes lambda function

    ./wscli.py lambda
    """
    click.echo(click.style("Lambda Function invoked from cli:",
        bg='blue', fg='white'))
    conn = lambda_connection()
    lambda_return_value = invoke_lambda(func_name=func,
        lambda_conn=conn,
        payload=payload)
    formatted_json = json.dumps(lambda_return_value,
         sort_keys=True, indent=4)
    click.echo(click.style(
        "Lambda Return Value Below:", bg='blue', fg='white'))
    click.echo(click.style(formatted_json,fg="red"))
```

```
if __name__ == "__main__":
    cli()
```

The output of the command-line tool shows the same net output as calling the HTTP interface.

```
➜  ✗ ./wscli.py lambda \
--func=scrape-yahoo-dev-birthplace_from_urls\
--payload '{"url":["https://sports.yahoo.com/nba/players/4624/",\
"https://sports.yahoo.com/nba/players/5185/"]}'
Lambda Function invoked from cli:
{"message": "instantiate lambda client",
"region_name": "us-east-1", "aws_service": "lambda"}
{"message": "Calling lambda function",
"function_name": "scrape-yahoo-dev-birthplace_from_urls",
 "aws_service": "lambda", "payload":
"{\"url\":[\"https://sports.yahoo.com/nba/players/4624/\",
 \"https://sports.yahoo.com/nba/players/5185/\"]}"}
{"message": null, "ResponseMetadata":
{"RequestId": "a6049115-df59-11e7-935d-bb1de9c0649d",
"HTTPStatusCode": 200, "HTTPHeaders":
{"date": "Tue, 12 Dec 2017 16:29:43 GMT", "content-type":
 "application/json", "content-length": "118", "connection":
"keep-alive", "x-amzn-requestid":
"a6049115-df59-11e7-935d-bb1de9c0649d",
"x-amzn-remapped-content-length": "0", "x-amz-executed-version":
 "$LATEST", "x-amzn-trace-id":
"root=1-5a3003f2-2583679b2456022568ed0682;sampled=0"},
"RetryAttempts": 0}, "StatusCode": 200,
"ExecutedVersion": "$LATEST", "Payload":
"<botocore.response.StreamingBody object at 0x10ee37dd8>",
"function_name": "scrape-yahoo-dev-birthplace_from_urls",
 "aws_service": "lambda", "payload":
"{\"url\":[\"https://sports.yahoo.com/nba/players/4624/\",
\"https://sports.yahoo.com/nba/players/5185/\"]}"}
Lambda Return Value Below:
{
    "https://sports.yahoo.com/nba/players/4624/": "Indianapolis",
    "https://sports.yahoo.com/nba/players/5185/": "Athens"
}
```

Building Out the Step Function

The final step to get the step function wired up, as described in the documentation from AWS (https://docs.aws.amazon.com/step-functions/latest/dg/tutorial-creating-activity-state-machine.html), is to create the state machine structure in JavaScript Object Notation (JSON) using the web UI. The following code shows how this pipeline goes from the initial Lambda functions, which scrape Yahoo!, to storing the data in S3, and then finally sending the payload to Slack.

```
{
    "Comment": "Fetch Player Urls",
    "StartAt": "FetchUrls",
```

```
      "States": {
        "FetchUrls": {
          "Type": "Task",
          "Resource": \
"arn:aws:lambda:us-east-1:561744971673:\
function:scrape-yahoo-dev-return_player_urls",
          "Next": "FetchBirthplaces"
        },
        "FetchBirthplaces": {
          "Type": "Task",
          "Resource": \
"arn:aws:lambda:us-east-1:561744971673:\
function:scrape-yahoo-dev-birthplace_from_urls",
          "Next": "WriteToS3"
        },
        "WriteToS3": {
          "Type": "Task",
          "Resource": "arn:aws:lambda:us-east-1:\
561744971673:function:scrape-yahoo-dev-create_s3_file_from_json",
          "Next": "SendToSlack"
        },
        "SendToSlack": {
          "Type": "Task",
          "Resource": "arn:aws:lambda:us-east-1:561744971673:\
function:send_message",
          "Next": "Finish"
        },

        "Finish": {
          "Type": "Pass",
          "Result": "Finished",
          "End": true
        }
      }
}
```

In Figure 7.2, the first portion of the pipeline is shown executing. As shown, one incredibly helpful feature is the ability to see intermediate output in the state machine. Additionally, the monitoring in real time of each portion of the state machine is great for debugging.

Figure 7.3 shows the complete pipeline with the addition of the steps of writing out to S3 and sending payloads to Slack. The final step would be to decide how to run this scraper: on an interval or perhaps in response to an event.

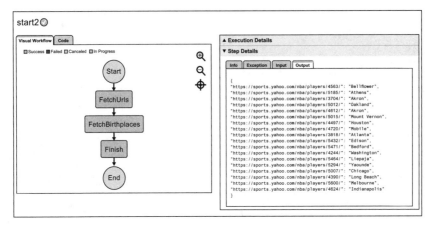

Figure 7.2　Representation of a Slackbot Command Line Tool Initial Pipeline

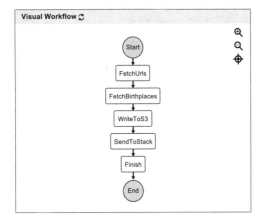

Figure 7.3　Representation of a Slackbot Command Line Tool Final Pipeline

Summary

This chapter unleashed many powerful concepts for building AI applications. A Slackbot was created, a web scraper was created, and then they were glued together with serverless services from AWS. More could be added to this initial skeleton—potentially, a Natural Language-processing Lambda that reads web pages and summarizes them or an unsupervised clustering algorithm that clusters new NBA players by arbitrary attributes.

Finding Project Management Insights from a GitHub Organization

Jiu Jitsu is perfect. It's humans who make errors.

Rickson Gracie

This chapter covers two fascinating problems: how to use data science to investigate project management around software engineering and how to publish a data science tool to the Python Package Index. Data science as a discipline is exploding, and there are many articles on the ins and outs of what algorithm to use, but there are few articles about how to collect data, create a project structure, and then ultimately publish your software to the Python Package Index. This chapter aims to solve this issue with hands-on explicit instructions on both topics. The source code for this can be found on GitHub: https://github.com/noahgift/devml.

Overview of the Problems in Software Project Management

Despite the fact that the software industry has been around for decades, it is still plagued by lingering issues of late delivery and poor quality. Further problems lie in evaluating the performance of teams and individual developers. Often the software industry is at the forefront of new technological changes to work relationships. A current trend in the software industry is to use freelance employees or contract teams to supplement or replace some parts of the development of software. This then brings up an obvious problem: How can a company evaluate this talent?

Further, motivated professional software developers want to find a way to get better. What patterns can they emulate from the best software developers in the world? Fortunately, developers do create behavioral logs that can create signals that can be used to help answer these questions. Every time a developer does a commit to a repository, he is creating a signal.

It only takes minutes of a discussion about analyzing source code metadata for a clever developer to say, "Oh, this doesn't mean anything, I can just game the system." This is a fair point to consider, and it is not hard to visually look at a developer's GitHub profile and see something truly heroic, like 3,000 commits in a year, which equates to around 10 commits a day, every day. In looking further, these commits maybe an automated script that someone created to make her profile look busy, or they could be "fake" commits that add a line to a README file.

The counterpoint to this argument is that the same could be said for math exams: "Oh, you can just cheat on those, that is easy." Measuring a student's performance or measuring a worker's performance can absolutely be gamed, but this doesn't mean everyone should automatically be given an A grade in Calculus or that exams and quizzes should be gotten rid of. Instead, thinking like a true data scientist, this just makes the problem more fun to solve. Ways to remove fake data and noise will need to be considered to accurately measure the performance of teams and developers.

Exploratory Questions to Consider

Here is a partial list of initial questions to consider.

- What are characteristics of a good software developer?
- What are characteristics of an inexperienced or poor software developer?
- What are the characteristics of a good software team?
- Are there signals that can predict faulty software?
- Can a manager of a software project be given a signal that allows him to take immediate correct active to turn around a troubled software project?
- Is there a difference between looking at open-source and closed-source projects?
- Are there signals that predict a developer who is "gaming" the system?
- What are the signals that, across all software languages, predict good developers?
- What are the signals across a project in a specific language?
- How can you measure an apples-to-apples comparison of what the best developers are doing since each repo is spread all over the place? It is easy to "hide."
- How can you find developers at your company and in GitHub who are like your best developers?
- Do you have "flakes," i.e., people who are not reliable? One of the ways to determine this is the probability that a given developer is committing code Monday through Friday. Some of the research I have found in the past several years is poor developers often have large gaps and/or frequent gaps in committing. The best developers—say, a developer with 10-20 years' experience—are often committing code at about 80 to 90 percent of the time on a Monday through Friday (even when they are tutoring or helping people).

- Is there a problem with a new project manager, manager, or CEO that is destroying the productivity of developers through endless hours of meetings?

- Do you have a "bad" unicorn developer? Someone who incredibly prolific...at making code that is unreliable?

Creating an Initial Data Science Project Skeleton

An often-overlooked part of developing a new data science solution is the initial structure of the project. Before work is started, a best practice is to create a layout that will facilitate high-quality work and a logical organization. There are probably quite a few ways to lay out a project structure, but this is one recommendation. You can see the exact output of an ls command in Listing 8.1 and a description of the purpose of each item below.

- **.circleci directory:** This holds the configuration necessary to build the project using CircleCI SaaS build service. There are many similar services that work with open-source software. Alternately, an open-source tool like Jenkins could be used.

- **.gitignore:** It is very important to ignore files that are not part of the project. This is a common misstep.

- **CODE_OF_CONDUCT.md:** It's a good idea to put in your project some information about how you expect contributors to behave.

- **CONTRIBUTING.MD:** Explicit instructions about how you will accept contributions is very helpful in recruiting help and avoiding potentially turning away valuable contributors.

- **LICENSE:** Having a license such as MIT or BSD is helpful. In some cases, a company may not be able to contribute if you don't have a license.

- **Makefile:** A Makefile is a common standard for building projects that has been around for decades. It is a great tool for running tests and deploying and setting up an environment.

- **README.md:** A good README.md should answer basic questions like how a user builds the project and what the project does. Additionally, it can often be helpful to include "badges" that show the quality of the project, such as a passing build—that is, `[![CircleCI] (https://circleci.com/gh/noahgift/devml.svg?style=svg)]`. (See https://circleci.com/gh/noahgift/devml.)

- **Command-line tool:** In this example, there is a `dml` command-line tool. Having a cli interface is very helpful in both exploring your library and creating an interface for testing.

- **Library directory with a __init__.py:** At the root of a project, a library directory should be created with a __init__.py to indicate it is importable. In this example, the library is called devml.

- **ext directory:** This is a good place for things like a config.json or a config.yml file. It is much better to put non-code in a place where it can be centrally referred to. A data subdirectory might be necessary as well to create some local, truncated samples to explore.

- **notebooks directory:** A specific folder for holding Jupyter Notebooks makes it easy to centralize the development of notebook-related code. Additionally, it makes setting up automated testing of notebooks easier.

- **requirements.txt:** This file holds a list of packages necessary for the project.

- **setup.py:** This configuration file sets up the way a Python package is deployed. This can also be used to deploy to the Python Package Index.

- **tests directory:** This is a directory where tests can be placed.

Listing 8.1 **Project Structure**

```
(.devml) ➜  devml git:(master) ✗ ls -la
drwxr-xr-x    3 noahgift  staff     96 Oct 14 15:22 .circleci
-rw-r--r--    1 noahgift  staff   1241 Oct 21 13:38 .gitignore
-rw-r--r--    1 noahgift  staff   3216 Oct 15 11:44 CODE_OF_CONDUCT.md
-rw-r--r--    1 noahgift  staff    357 Oct 15 11:44 CONTRIBUTING.md
-rw-r--r--    1 noahgift  staff   1066 Oct 14 14:10 LICENSE
-rw-r--r--    1 noahgift  staff    464 Oct 21 14:17 Makefile
-rw-r--r--    1 noahgift  staff  13015 Oct 21 19:59 README.md
-rwxr-xr-x    1 noahgift  staff   9326 Oct 21 11:53 dml
drwxr-xr-x    4 noahgift  staff    128 Oct 20 15:20 ext
drwxr-xr-x    7 noahgift  staff    224 Oct 22 11:25 notebooks
-rw-r--r--    1 noahgift  staff    117 Oct 18 19:16 requirements.txt
-rw-r--r--    1 noahgift  staff   1197 Oct 21 14:07 setup.py
drwxr-xr-x   12 noahgift  staff    384 Oct 18 10:46 tests
```

Collecting and Transforming the Data

As usual, the worst part of the problem is figuring out how to collect and transform the data into something useful. There are several parts of this problem to solve. The first is how to collect a single repository and create a Pandas DataFrame from it. In order to do this, a new module is created inside the devml directory, called mkdata.py, to address the issues around converting a Git repository's metadata to a Pandas DataFrame.

A selected portion of the module can be found in its entirety here: https://github.com/noahgift/ devml/blob/master/devml/mkdata.py. The log_to_dict function takes a path to a single Git checkout on disk and then converts the output of a Git command.

```
def log_to_dict(path):
    """Converts Git Log To A Python Dict"""

    os.chdir(path) #change directory to process git log
    repo_name = generate_repo_name()
    p = Popen(GIT_LOG_CMD, shell=True, stdout=PIPE)
    (git_log, _) = p.communicate()
    try:
        git_log = git_log.decode('utf8').\
        strip('\n\x1e').split("\x1e")
```

```
    except UnicodeDecodeError:
        log.exception("utf8 encoding is incorrect,
         trying ISO-8859-1")
        git_log = git_log.decode('ISO-8859-1').\
        strip('\n\x1e').split("\x1e")

    git_log = [row.strip().split("\x1f") for row in git_log]
    git_log = [dict(list(zip(GIT_COMMIT_FIELDS, row)))\
        for row in git_log]
    for dictionary in git_log:
        dictionary["repo"]=repo_name
    repo_msg = "Found %s Messages For Repo: %s" %\
        (len(git_log), repo_name)
    log.info(repo_msg)
    return git_log
```

Finally, in the next two functions, a path on disk is used to call the function above. Note that logs are stored as items in a list, and then this is used to create a DataFrame in Pandas.

```
def create_org_df(path):
    """Returns a Pandas Dataframe of an Org"""

    original_cwd = os.getcwd()
    logs = create_org_logs(path)
    org_df = pd.DataFrame.from_dict(logs)
    #convert date to datetime format
    datetime_converted_df = convert_datetime(org_df)
    #Add A Date Index
    converted_df = date_index(datetime_converted_df)
    new_cwd = os.getcwd()
    cd_msg = "Changing back to original cwd: %s from %s" %\
        (original_cwd, new_cwd)
    log.info(cd_msg)
    os.chdir(original_cwd)
    return converted_df

def create_org_logs(path):
    """Iterate through all paths in current working directory,
    make log dict"""

    combined_log = []
    for sdir in subdirs(path):
        repo_msg = "Processing Repo: %s" % sdir
        log.info(repo_msg)
        combined_log += log_to_dict(sdir)
    log_entry_msg = "Found a total log entries: %s" %\
        len(combined_log)
    log.info(log_entry_msg)
    return combined_log
```

In action, the code looks like this when run without collecting into a DataFrame.

```
In [5]: res = create_org_logs("/Users/noahgift/src/flask")
2017-10-22 17:36:02,380 - devml.mkdata - INFO - Found repo:\
 /Users/noahgift/src/flask/flask
In [11]: res[0]
Out[11]:
{'author_email': 'rgerganov@gmail.com',
 'author_name': 'Radoslav Gerganov',
 'date': 'Fri Oct 13 04:53:50 2017',
 'id': '9291ead32e2fc8b13cef825186c968944e9ff344',
 'message': 'Fix typo in logging.rst (#2492)',
 'repo': b'flask'}
```

The second section that makes the DataFrame looks like this.

```
res = create_org_df("/Users/noahgift/src/flask")
In [14]: res.describe()
Out[14]:
         commits
count    9552.0
mean        1.0
std         0.0
min         1.0
25%         1.0
50%         1.0
75%         1.0
max         1.0
```

At a high level, this is a pattern to get ad hoc data from a third party like a Git log. To dig into this in more detail, it would be a good idea to look at the source code in its entirety.

Talking to an Entire GitHub Organization

With the code in place that transforms Git repositories on disk into DataFrames in place, a natural next step is to collect multiple repositories, that is, all of the repositories for an organization. One of the key issues in analyzing just one repository is that it is an incomplete portion of the data to analyze in the context of a company. One way to fix this is to talk to the GitHub API and programmatically pull down the repositories. The entire source for this can be found here: https://github.com/noahgift/devml/blob/master/devml/fetch_repo.py. The highlights are

```
def clone_org_repos(oath_token, org, dest, branch="master"):
    """Clone All Organizations Repositories and Return Instances of Repos.
    """

    if not validate_checkout_root(dest):
        return False

    repo_instances = []
    repos = org_repo_names(oath_token, org)
```

```
count = 0
for name, url in list(repos.items()):
    count += 1
    log_msg = "Cloning Repo # %s REPO NAME: %s , URL: %s " %\
                    (count, name, url)
    log.info(log_msg)
    try:
        repo = clone_remote_repo(name, url, dest, branch=branch)
        repo_instances.append(repo)
    except GitCommandError:
        log.exception("NO MASTER BRANCH...SKIPPING")
return repo_instances
```

Both the PyGithub and the gitpython packages are used to do much of the heavy lifting. When this code is run, it iteratively finds each repo from the API, then clones it. The previous code can then be used to create a combined DataFrame.

Creating Domain-specific Stats

All of this work was done for one reason: to explore the data collected and to create domain-specific stats. To do that, a stats.py file is created; you can see the entire contents here: https://github.com/noahgift/devml/blob/master/devml/stats.py.

The most relevant portion to show is a function called author_unique_active_days. This function determines how many days a developer was active for the records in the DataFrame. This is a unique, domain-specific statistic that is rarely mentioned in discussions about statistics about source code repositories.

The main function is shown below.

```
def author_unique_active_days(df, sort_by="active_days"):
    """DataFrame of Unique Active Days
        by Author With Descending Order

    author_name  unique_days
    46   Armin Ronacher     271
    260 Markus Unterwaditzer     145
    """

    author_list = []
    count_list = []
    duration_active_list = []
    ad = author_active_days(df)
    for author in ad.index:
        author_list.append(author)
        vals = ad.loc[author]
        vals.dropna(inplace=True)
        vals.drop_duplicates(inplace=True)
        vals.sort_values(axis=0,inplace=True)
```

```
                vals.reset_index(drop=True, inplace=True)
                count_list.append(vals.count())
                duration_active_list.append(vals[len(vals)-1]-vals[0])
        df_author_ud = DataFrame()
        df_author_ud["author_name"] = author_list
        df_author_ud["active_days"] = count_list
        df_author_ud["active_duration"] = duration_active_list
        df_author_ud["active_ratio"] = \
            round(df_author_ud["active_days"]/\
            df_author_ud["active_duration"].dt.days, 2)
        df_author_ud = df_author_ud.iloc[1:] #first row is =
        df_author_ud = df_author_ud.sort_values(\
            by=sort_by, ascending=False)
        return df_author_ud
```

When it is used from IPython, it generates the following output.

```
In [18]: from devml.stats import author_unique_active_days

In [19]: active_days = author_unique_active_days(df)

In [20]: active_days.head()
Out[20]:
                   author_name  active_days active_duration  active_ratio
46              Armin Ronacher          241       2490 days          0.10
260   Markus Unterwaditzer           71       1672 days          0.04
119                 David Lord           58        710 days          0.08
352                Ron DuPlain           47        785 days          0.06
107          Daniel Neuhäuser           19        435 days          0.04
```

The statistics create a ratio, called the active_ratio, which is the percentage of time from the start to the last time they worked on the project for which they were actively committing code. One of the interesting things about a metric like this is it does show engagement, and with the best open-source developers there are some fascinating parallels. In the next section, these core components will be hooked into a command-line tool and two different open-source projects will be compared using the code that was created.

Wiring a Data Science Project into a CLI

In the first part of this chapter, the components were created to get to the point at which an analysis could be run. In this section, they will be wired into a flexible command-line tool that uses the click framework. The entire source code for dml is found here: https://github.com/noahgift/devml/blob/master/dml. The pieces that are important are shown below.

First the library is imported along with the click framework.

```
#!/usr/bin/env python
import os
```

```
import click

from devml import state
from devml import fetch_repo
from devml import __version__
from devml import mkdata
from devml import stats
from devml import org_stats
from devml import post_processing
```

Then the previous code is wired in, and it only takes a couple of lines to hook it into the tool.

```
@gstats.command("activity")
@click.option("--path", default=CHECKOUT_DIR, help="path to org")
@click.option("--sort", default="active_days",
    help="can sort by:  active_days, active_ratio, active_duration")
def activity(path, sort):
    """Creates Activity Stats

    Example is run after checkout:
    python dml.py gstats activity –path\
        /Users/noah/src/wulio/checkout
    """

    org_df = mkdata.create_org_df(path)
    activity_counts = stats.author_unique_active_days(\
        org_df, sort_by=sort)
    click.echo(activity_counts)
```

To use this tool, it looks like this from the command line.

```
# Linux Development Active Ratio
dml gstats activity --path /Users/noahgift/src/linux\
 --sort active_days
```

author_name	active_days	active_duration	active_ratio
Takashi Iwai	1677	4590 days	0.370000
Eric Dumazet	1460	4504 days	0.320000
David S. Miller	1428	4513 days	0.320000
Johannes Berg	1329	4328 days	0.310000
Linus Torvalds	1281	4565 days	0.280000
Al Viro	1249	4562 days	0.270000
Mauro Carvalho Chehab	1227	4464 days	0.270000
Mark Brown	1198	4187 days	0.290000
Dan Carpenter	1158	3972 days	0.290000
Russell King	1141	4602 days	0.250000
Axel Lin	1040	2720 days	0.380000
Alex Deucher	1036	3497 days	0.300000

```
# CPython Development Active Ratio
```

	author_name	active_days	active_duration	active_ratio
146	Guido van Rossum	2256	9673 days	0.230000
301	Raymond Hettinger	1361	5635 days	0.240000
128	Fred Drake	1239	5335 days	0.230000
47	Benjamin Peterson	1234	3494 days	0.350000
132	Georg Brandl	1080	4091 days	0.260000
375	Victor Stinner	980	2818 days	0.350000
235	Martin v. Löwis	958	5266 days	0.180000
36	Antoine Pitrou	883	3376 days	0.260000
362	Tim Peters	869	5060 days	0.170000
164	Jack Jansen	800	4998 days	0.160000
24	Andrew M. Kuchling	743	4632 days	0.160000
330	Serhiy Storchaka	720	1759 days	0.410000
44	Barry Warsaw	696	8485 days	0.080000
52	Brett Cannon	681	5278 days	0.130000
262	Neal Norwitz	559	2573 days	0.220000

In this analysis, Guido of Python has a 23-percent probability of working on a given day, and "Linus" of Linux has a 28-percent chance. What is fascinating about this particular form of analysis is that it shows behavior over a long period of time. In the case of CPython, many of these authors also had full-time jobs, so the output is even more incredible to observe. Another analysis that would be fascinating is to look at the history of developers at a company (combining all of the available repositories). I have noticed that in some cases very senior developers can output code at around an 85-percent active ratio if they are fully employed.

Using Jupyter Notebook to Explore a GitHub Organization

Pallets GitHub Project

One of the issues with looking at a single repository is that it is only part of the data. The earlier code created the ability to clone an entire organization and analyze it. A popular GitHub organization is the Pallets Projects (https://github.com/pallets). It has multiple popular projects like click and Flask. The Jupyter Notebook for this analysis can be found here: https://github.com/noahgift/devml/blob/master/notebooks/github_data_exploration.ipynb.

To start Jupyter, from the command-line type in "jupyter notebook". Then import libraries that will be used.

```
In [3]: import sys;sys.path.append("..")
   ...: import pandas as pd
   ...: from pandas import DataFrame
   ...: import seaborn as sns
   ...: import matplotlib.pyplot as plt
   ...: from sklearn.cluster import KMeans
   ...: %matplotlib inline
```

```
    ...: from IPython.core.display import display, HTML
    ...: display(HTML("<style>.container {\
 width:100% !important; }</style>"))
```

Next, the code to download an organization is used.

```
In [4]: from devml import (mkdata, stats, state, fetch_repo, ts)

In [5]: dest, token, org = state.get_project_metadata(\
        "../project/config.json")

In [6]: fetch_repo.clone_org_repos(token, org,
    ...:            dest, branch="master")

Out[6]:
[<git.Repo "/tmp/checkout/flask/.git">,
 <git.Repo "/tmp/checkout/pallets-sphinx-themes/.git">,
 <git.Repo "/tmp/checkout/markupsafe/.git">,
 <git.Repo "/tmp/checkout/jinja/.git">,
 <git.Repo "/tmp/checkout/werkzeug/.git">,
 <git.Repo "/tmp/checkout/itsdangerous/.git">,
 <git.Repo "/tmp/checkout/flask-website/.git">,
 <git.Repo "/tmp/checkout/click/.git">,
 <git.Repo "/tmp/checkout/flask-snippets/.git">,
 <git.Repo "/tmp/checkout/flask-docs/.git">,
 <git.Repo "/tmp/checkout/flask-ext-migrate/.git">,
 <git.Repo "/tmp/checkout/pocoo-sphinx-themes/.git">,
 <git.Repo "/tmp/checkout/website/.git">,
 <git.Repo "/tmp/checkout/meta/.git">]
```

With the code living on disk, it can be converted into a Pandas DataFrame.

```
In [7]: df = mkdata.create_org_df(path="/tmp/checkout")
In [9]: df.describe()
Out[9]:
        commits
count   8315.0
mean       1.0
std        0.0
min        1.0
25%        1.0
50%        1.0
75%        1.0
max        1.0
```

Next, active days can be calculated.

```
In [10]: df_author_ud = stats.author_unique_active_days(df)
    ...:
In [11]: df_author_ud.head(10)
Out[11]:
```

	author_name	active_days	active_duration	active_ratio
86	Armin Ronacher	941	3817 days	0.25
499	Markus Unterwaditzer	238	1767 days	0.13
216	David Lord	94	710 days	0.13
663	Ron DuPlain	56	854 days	0.07
297	Georg Brandl	41	1337 days	0.03
196	Daniel Neuhäuser	36	435 days	0.08
169	Christopher Grebs	27	1515 days	0.02
665	Ronny Pfannschmidt	23	2913 days	0.01
448	Keyan Pishdadian	21	882 days	0.02
712	Simon Sapin	21	793 days	0.03

Finally, this can be turned into a Seaborn plot by using sns.barplot, as shown in Figure 8.1, to plot the top 10 contributors to the organization by days they are active in the project, that is, days they actually checked in code. It is no surprise the main author of the many of the projects is almost three times more active than any other contributor.

Perhaps some similar observations could be extrapolated for closed-source projects across all the repositories in a company. Active days could be a useful metric to show engagement, and it could be part of many metrics used to measure the effectiveness of teams and projects.

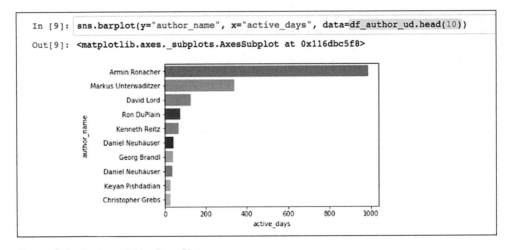

Figure 8.1 Seaborn Active-Days Plot

Looking at File Metadata in the CPython Project

The next Jupyter Notebook we'll examine is an exploration of the metadata around the CPython project found here: https://github.com/noahgift/devml/blob/master/notebooks/repo_file_exploration.ipynb. The CPython project can be found here: https://github.com/python/cpython, and it is the repository used to develop the Python language.

One of the metrics that will be generated is called relative churn, and it can be read about more in this paper from Microsoft Research: https://www.microsoft.com/en-us/research/wp-content/uploads/2016/02/icse05churn.pdf. It states that "an increase in relative code churn measures is accompanied by an increase in system defect density." This can be extrapolated into meaning that too many changes in a file predict defect.

This new notebook will again import the modules needed for the rest of the exploration.

```
In [1]: import sys;sys.path.append("..")
   ...: import pandas as pd
   ...: from pandas import DataFrame
   ...: import seaborn as sns
   ...: import matplotlib.pyplot as plt
   ...: from sklearn.cluster import KMeans
   ...: %matplotlib inline
   ...: from IPython.core.display import display, HTML
   ...: display(HTML("<style>.container \
{ width:100% !important; }</style>"))
```

Next, churn metrics will be generated.

```
In [2]: from devml.post_processing import (
        git_churn_df, file_len, git_populate_file_metadata)

In [3]: df = git_churn_df(path="/Users/noahgift/src/cpython")
2017-10-23 06:51:00,256 - devml.post_processing - INFO –
        Running churn cmd: [git log --name-only
        --pretty=format:] at path [/Users/noahgift/src/cpython]

In [4]: df.head()
Out[4]:
                                       files   churn_count
0                  b'Lib/test/test_struct.py'           178
1               b'Lib/test/test_zipimport.py'            78
2                     b'Misc/NEWS.d/next/Core'           351
3                                     b'and'           351
4   b'Builtins/2017-10-13-20-01-47.bpo-31781.cXE9S...             1
```

A few filters in Pandas can then be used to figure out the top relative churn files with the Python extension. The output is scene in Figure 8.2.

```
In [14]: metadata_df = git_populate_file_metadata(df)

In [15]: python_files_df =\
 metadata_df[metadata_df.extension == ".py"]
    ...: line_python =\
 python_files_df[python_files_df.line_count> 40]
    ...: line_python.sort_values(
by="relative_churn", ascending=False).head(15)
    ...:
```

```
In· [22]:   python_files_df = metadata_df[metadata_df.extension == ".py"]
            line_python = python_files_df[python_files_df.line_count> 40]
            line_python.sort_values(by="relative_churn", ascending=False).head(15)
```

Out[22]:

	files	churn_count	line_count	extension	relative_churn
15	b'Lib/test/regrtest.py'	627	50.0	.py	12.54
196	b'Lib/test/test_datetime.py'	165	57.0	.py	2.89
197	b'Lib/io.py'	165	99.0	.py	1.67
430	b'Lib/test/test_sundry.py'	91	56.0	.py	1.62
269	b'Lib/test/test___all__.py'	128	109.0	.py	1.17
1120	b'Lib/test/test_userstring.py'	40	44.0	.py	0.91
827	b'Lib/email/__init__.py'	52	62.0	.py	0.84
85	b'Lib/test/test_support.py'	262	461.0	.py	0.57
1006	b'Lib/test/test_select.py'	44	82.0	.py	0.54
1474	b'Lib/lib2to3/fixes/fix_itertools_imports.py'	30	57.0	.py	0.53
346	b'Doc/conf.py'	106	206.0	.py	0.51
222	b'Lib/string.py'	151	305.0	.py	0.50
804	b'Lib/test/test_normalization.py'	53	108.0	.py	0.49
592	b'Lib/test/test_fcntl.py'	68	152.0	.py	0.45
602	b'Lib/test/test_winsound.py'	67	148.0	.py	0.45

Figure 8.2   Top Relative Churn in CPython .py Files

One observation from this query is that tests have a lot of churn, which might be worth exploring more. Does this mean that the tests themselves also contain bugs? That might be fascinating to explore in more detail. Also, there are couple of Python modules that have extremely high relative churn, like the string.py module: https://github.com/python/cpython/blob/master/Lib/string.py. In looking through the source code for that file, it does look very complex for its size, and it contains metaclasses. It is possible the complexity has made it prone to bugs. This seems like a module worth further data science exploration on.

Next, some descriptive statistics can be run to look for the median values across the project. It shows, for the couple of decades and 100,000-plus commits the project has been around, that a median file is about 146 lines, it is changed 5 times, and it has a relative churn of 10 percent. This leads to a conclusion that the ideal type of file to be created is small and has a few changes over the years.

```
In [16]: metadata_df.median()
Out[16]:
churn_count       5.0
line_count      146.0
relative_churn    0.1
dtype: float64
```

Generating a Seaborn plot for the relative churn makes the patterns even more clear.

```
In [18]: import matplotlib.pyplot as plt
    ...: plt.figure(figsize=(10,10))
    ...: python_files_df =\
 metadata_df[metadata_df.extension == ".py"]
    ...: line_python =\
```

```
python_files_df[python_files_df.line_count> 40]
    ...: line_python_sorted =\
line_python.sort_values(by="relative_churn",
        ascending=False).head(15)
    ...: sns.barplot(
y="files", x="relative_churn",data=line_python_sorted)
    ...: plt.title('Top 15 CPython Absolute and Relative Churn')
    ...: plt.show()
```

In Figure 8.3, the regtest.py module sticks out quite a bit as the most modified file, and again, it makes sense why it is changed so much. Although it is a small file, typically a regression test can be very complicated. This also may be a hot spot in the code that may need to be looked at: https://github.com/python/cpython/blob/master/Lib/test/regrtest.py.

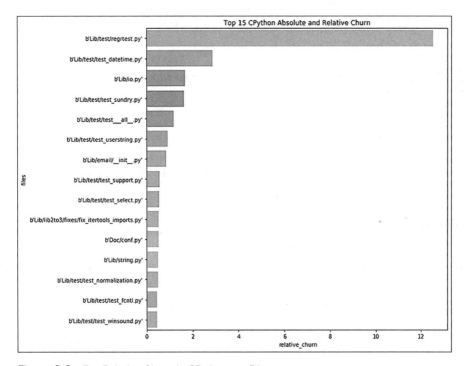

Figure 8.3   Top Relative Churn in CPython .py File

Looking at Deleted Files in the CPython Project

Another area of exploration is files that were deleted throughout the history of a project. There are many directions of research that could be derived from this exploration, like predicting that a file would later be deleted if, say, the relative churn was too high, etc. To look at the deleted files, another function is first created in the post-processing directory: https://github.com/noahgift/devml/blob/master/devml/post_processing.py.

```
FILES_DELETED_CMD=\
    'git log --diff-filter=D --summary | grep delete'

def files_deleted_match(output):
    """Retrieves files from output from subprocess

    i.e:
    wcase/templates/hello.html\n delete mode 100644
    Throws away everything but path to file
    """

    files = []
    integers_match_pattern = '^[-+]?[0-9]+$'
    for line in output.split():
        if line == b"delete":
            continue
        elif line == b"mode":
            continue
        elif re.match(integers_match_pattern, line.decode("utf-8")):
            continue
        else:
            files.append(line)
    return files
```

This function looks for delete messages in the Git log, does some pattern matching, and extracts the files to a list so a Pandas DataFrame can be created. Next, it can be used in a Jupyter Notebook.

```
In [19]: from devml.post_processing import git_deleted_files
    ...: deletion_counts = git_deleted_files(
"/Users/noahgift/src/cpython")
```

To inspect some of the files that have been deleted, the last few records are viewed.

```
In [21]: deletion_counts.tail()
Out[21]:
                            files     ext
8812   b'Mac/mwerks/mwerksglue.c'      .c
8813         b'Modules/version.c'      .c
8814      b'Modules/Setup.irix5'   .irix5
8815      b'Modules/Setup.guido'   .guido
8816      b'Modules/Setup.minix'   .minix
```

Next, see whether there is a pattern that appears with deleted files versus files that are kept. To do that, the deleted files' DataFrame will need to be joined.

```
In [22]: all_files = metadata_df['files']
    ...: deleted_files = deletion_counts['files']
    ...: membership = all_files.isin(deleted_files)
    ...:

In [23]: metadata_df["deleted_files"] = membership
```

```
In [24]: metadata_df.loc[metadata_df["deleted_files"] ==\
 True].median()
Out[24]:
churn_count        4.000
line_count        91.500
relative_churn     0.145
deleted_files      1.000
dtype: float64

In [25]: metadata_df.loc[metadata_df["deleted_files"] ==\
 False].median()
Out[25]:
churn_count        9.0
line_count       149.0
relative_churn     0.1
deleted_files      0.0
dtype: float64
```

In looking at the median values of the deleted files versus the files that are still in the repository, there are some differences, mainly in that the relative churn number is higher for the deleted files. Perhaps the files that were problems were deleted? It is unknown without more investigation. Next, a correlation heatmap is created in Seaborn on this DataFrame.

```
In [26]: sns.heatmap(metadata_df.corr(), annot=True)
```

This can be seen in Figure 8.4. It shows that there is a correlation, a very small positive one, between relative churn and deleted files. This signal might be included in an ML model to predict the likelihood of a file being deleted.

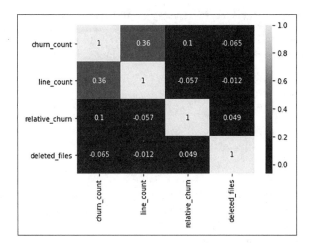

Figure 8.4   Files-Deleted Correlation Heatmap

Next, one final scatterplot shows some differences between deleted files and files that have remained in the repository.

```
In [27]: sns.lmplot(x="churn_count", y="line_count",
 hue="deleted_files", data=metadata_df)
```

Figure 8.5 shows three dimensions: line counts, churn counts, and the category of True/False for a deleted file.

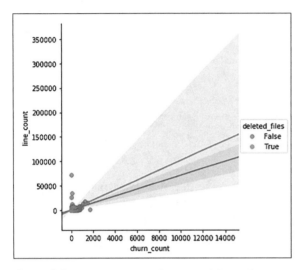

Figure 8.5   Scatterplot Line Counts and Churn Count

Deploying a Project to the Python Package Index

With all of the hard work performed in creating a library and command-line tool, it makes sense to share the project with other people by submitting it to the Python Package Index. There are only a few steps to do this.

1. Create an account on https://pypi.python.org/pypi.

2. Install twine: pip install twine.

3. Create a setup.py file.

4. Add a deploy step in the Makefile.

Starting at step 3, here is the output of the setup.py file. The two parts that are the most important are the packages section, which ensures the library is installed, and the scripts section. The scripts includes the dml script that was used throughout the article. You can see the entire script here: https://github.com/noahgift/devml/blob/master/setup.py.

```
import sys
if sys.version_info < (3,6):
    sys.exit('Sorry, Python < 3.6 is not supported')
import os
```

```
from setuptools import setup

from devml import __version__

if os.path.exists('README.rst'):
    LONG = open('README.rst').read()

setup(
    name='devml',
    version=__version__,
    url='https://github.com/noahgift/devml',
    license='MIT',
    author='Noah Gift',
    author_email='consulting@noahgift.com',
    description="""Machine Learning, Statistics
        and Utilities around Developer Productivity,
        Company Productivity and Project Productivity""",
    long_description=LONG,
    packages=['devml'],
    include_package_data=True,
    zip_safe=False,
    platforms='any',
    install_requires=[
        'pandas',
        'click',
        'PyGithub',
        'gitpython',
        'sensible',
        'scipy',
        'numpy',
    ],
    classifiers=[
        'Development Status :: 4 - Beta',
        'Intended Audience :: Developers',
        'License :: OSI Approved :: MIT License',
        'Programming Language :: Python',
        'Programming Language :: Python :: 3.6',
        'Topic :: Software Development \
        :: Libraries :: Python Modules'
    ],
    scripts=["dml"],
)
```

The scripts directive will then install the dml tool into the path of all users who pip install the module.

The final section is to configure is the Makefile, and this is what it looks like.

```
deploy-pypi:
    pandoc --from=markdown --to=rst README.md -o README.rst
```

```
python setup.py check --restructuredtext --strict --metadata
rm -rf dist
python setup.py sdist
twine upload dist/*
rm -f README.rst
```

The entire contents of the Makefile can be found here in GitHub: https://github.com/noahgift/devml/blob/master/Makefile.

Finally, to deploy, the process looks like this.

```
(.devml) ➜  devml git:(master) ✗ make deploy-pypi
pandoc --from=markdown --to=rst README.md -o README.rst
python setup.py check --restructuredtext --strict --metadata
running check
rm -rf dist
python setup.py sdist
running sdist
running egg_info
writing devml.egg-info/PKG-INFO
writing dependency_links to devml.egg-info/dependency_links.txt
....
running check
creating devml-0.5.1
creating devml-0.5.1/devml
creating devml-0.5.1/devml.egg-info
copying files to devml-0.5.1...
....
Writing devml-0.5.1/setup.cfg
creating dist
Creating tar archive
removing 'devml-0.5.1' (and everything under it)
twine upload dist/*
Uploading distributions to https://upload.pypi.org/legacy/
Enter your username:
```

Summary

A basic data science skeleton was created and the parts were explained in the first part of this chapter. In the second half, a deep dive on exploring the CPython GitHub project was performed in Jupyter Notebook. Finally, the data science command-line tool project, DEVML, was packed up to be deployed to the Python Package Index. This chapter should be a good building block to study for other data science developers who want to build solutions that can be delivered as a Python library and a command-line tool.

Just like other chapters in this book, this is just the start of what could be a company or AI application inside a company. Using techniques exposed in other chapters of this book, APIs written in Flask or chalice and data pipelines could be created to ship this into production.

## 9

Dynamically Optimizing EC2 Instances on AWS

Jiu-Jitsu is a race, and if you make a mistake against someone better than you, you will never catch up [paraphrase].

Luis "Limao" Heredia (5-Time Pan American Brazilian Jiu-Jitsu Champion)

A common problem with production ML is needing to manage jobs. Examples could be as diverse as scraping the contents of a web site to generating descriptive statistics on a large CSV file to programmatically updating a supervised ML model. Managing jobs is one of the most complex problems in computer science, and there are many ways to do it. In addition, running jobs can get very expensive very quickly. In this section, several different AWS technologies will be covered, and examples will be given for each.

Running Jobs on AWS

Spot Instances

Having a strong understanding of Spot instances is essential for both production machine learning systems and for experimentation. Going through the official spot tutorial video at AWS (https://aws.amazon.com/ec2/spot/spot-tutorials/) is useful and may help with some of the content covered. Here is a little background on spot instances.

- Typically, between 50 to 60 percent cheaper than reserved instances
- Useful in many industries and use cases
  - Scientific research
  - Financial services
  - Video/imaging-processing companies
  - Web crawling/data processing

        ▫ Functional testing and load testing

        ▫ Deep learning and machine learning

- There are four common architectures.

        ▫ Hadoop/Elastic Map Reduce (EMR)

        ▫ Check pointing (writing out results as they are processed out to disk)

        ▫ Grid (e.g., StarCluster, http://star.mit.edu/cluster/docs/latest/index.html)

        ▫ Queue-based

Spot Instances Theory and Pricing History

There is a bit of a learning curve in understanding how to reason about spot pricing. Some of the obstacles at the beginning are understanding what type of instance your jobs actually need. Even this is fraught with difficulty because, depending on the type of Spot architecture, there will be different bottlenecks: network in some, disk I/O or CPU in others. Additionally, to the jobs framework, the way the code is architected is itself an issue.

Amdahl's law is best described as shown in Figure 9.1, which shows the limits of real-world parallelization. It states that speedup is limited by serial parts of the program. For example, the overhead in distributing the job may contain serial components. Perhaps the best example is to consider a job that takes 100 seconds, yet contains 5 seconds of a `time.sleep()` that a developer forgot about. When a job like this gets distributed, the theoretical maximum speedup would be 20 times. In the case of hidden sleep (it does happen), even a faster CPU or disk won't do anything to improve the performance of that hidden sleep.

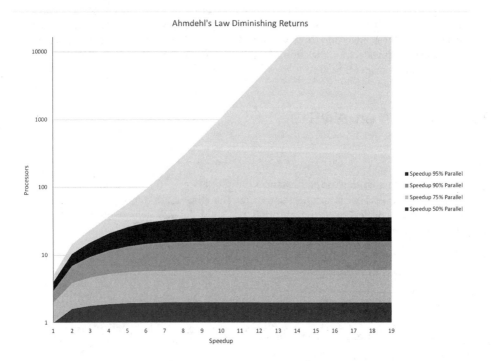

Figure 9.1 Amdahl's Law

In Equation 9.1, the following are described:

- $S_{latency}$ (s) is the total speedup.

- s is the speedup of the parallel portion.

- p is the proportion of execution time that the part benefiting from improved resources originally used.

Equation 9.1   **Amdahl's Law Equation**

$$S_{latency}(s) = \frac{1}{(1-p)+\dfrac{p}{s}}$$

If the serial component of the job is uncompressing something, then a faster CPU and higher disk I/O may help. Ultimately, theory aside, distributed jobs are hard, and the best way to figure out what types of Spot instances and architectures to use requires experimentation and instrumentation. Run a job, look at the metrics of the individual nodes, and consider the time it took to execute. Then experiment with different architectures and configurations, like EFS versus striped Elastic Block Storage (EBS) volumes shared out via Network File System (NFS).

I spent many years working in the film industry, and there is an argument to be made that film is the first "Big Data" industry. Film has been running distributed jobs frameworks for many more years before Hadoop, Big Data, ML, and AI were being discussed in jobs frameworks. Some things I discovered in film that are applicable to Big Data are that things always go wrong in distributed systems. Having incredible discipline about keeping jobs as simple as possible, while maintaining incredible instrumentation, is a key takeaway.

Coming full circle back to the topic of Spot pricing, it pays to know there are many ways to optimize the performance of distributed jobs. At first, the low-hanging fruit may be to just find cheap, high-powered instances, but thinking about other configurations and how to test them is critical for long-term success in developing jobs that work at the production level.

A great resource for comparing Spot prices with on-demand prices and looking at machine capabilities is at http://www.ec2instances.info/. The source code is also available in GitHub (https://github.com/powdahound/ec2instances.info). The authors scrape the AWS site, then compare Spot prices with reserved prices in one handy web page. This data was formatted and put into a CSV file for easy import into Jupyter Notebook.

Creating an ML-Based Spot Instances Pricing Tool and Notebook

Creating ML solutions that make it into production is a major focus of this book. The Unix philosophy embraces the concept of small tools that do one thing well. With production systems, it is often about not just the system, but the small tools developed along the way that enable the system to work. In the spirit of that philosophy, we'll demonstrate a tool that finds Spot pricing in a region and also uses ML to recommend choices in the same cluster. To start, a new Jupyter Notebook is initialized with common boilerplate.

```
In [1]: import pandas as pd
   ...: import seaborn as sns
   ...: import matplotlib.pyplot as plt
   ...: from sklearn.cluster import KMeans
   ...: %matplotlib inline
   ...: from IPython.core.display import display, HTML
   ...: display(HTML("<style>.container \
{ width:100% !important; }</style>"))
   ...: import boto3
```

Next, an initial CSV file is loaded with some information grabbed from http://www.ec2instances
.info/, and formatted slightly first in Excel.

```
In [2]: pricing_df = pd.read_csv("../data/ec2-prices.csv")
   ...: pricing_df['price_per_ecu_on_demand'] =\
       pricing_df['linux_on_demand_cost_hourly']/\
       pricing_df['compute_units_ecu']
   ...: pricing_df.head()
   ...:
Out[2]:
                 Name InstanceType  memory_gb  compute_units_ecu  \
R3 High-Memory Large    r3.large      15.25                6.5
M4 Large      m4.large       8.00                6.5
R4 High-Memory Large    r4.large      15.25                7.0
C4 High-CPU Large     c4.large       3.75                8.0
GPU Extra Large     p2.xlarge      61.00               12.0

vcpu  gpus  fpga enhanced_networking  linux_on_demand_cost_hourly  \
2     0     0               Yes                     0.17
2     0     0               Yes                     0.10
2     0     0               Yes                     0.13
2     0     0               Yes                     0.10
4     1     0               Yes                     0.90

    price_per_ecu_on_demand
0                  0.026154
1                  0.015385
2                  0.018571
3                  0.012500
4                  0.075000
```

The instance names from this data set are passed into the Boto API to grab Spot instance pricing
history.

```
In [3]: names = pricing_df["InstanceType"].to_dict()
In [6]: client = boto3.client('ec2')
   ...: response =client.describe_spot_price_history(\
```

```
           InstanceTypes = list(names.values()),
      ...:           ProductDescriptions = ["Linux/UNIX"])
In [7]: spot_price_history = response['SpotPriceHistory']
   ...: spot_history_df = pd.DataFrame(spot_price_history)
   ...: spot_history_df.SpotPrice =\
 spot_history_df.SpotPrice.astype(float)
   ...:
```

The information that comes back from the API that is the most useful is the *SpotPrice* value, which can be used as the basis for both recommending similar instances and finding the best price per Elastic Compute Unit (ECU) and memory. Also, the results, which come back as JSON, are imported into a Pandas DataFrame. The SpotPrice column is then converted to a float to allow for later numerical manipulation.

```
In [8]: spot_history_df.head()
Out[8]:
  AvailabilityZone InstanceType ProductDescription  SpotPrice  \
0        us-west-2c    r4.8xlarge         Linux/UNIX     0.9000
1        us-west-2c     p2.xlarge         Linux/UNIX     0.2763
2        us-west-2c    m3.2xlarge         Linux/UNIX     0.0948
3        us-west-2c     c4.xlarge         Linux/UNIX     0.0573
4        us-west-2a     m3.xlarge         Linux/UNIX     0.0447

                  Timestamp
0 2017-09-11 15:22:59+00:00
1 2017-09-11 15:22:39+00:00
2 2017-09-11 15:22:39+00:00
3 2017-09-11 15:22:38+00:00
4 2017-09-11 15:22:38+00:00
```

Two DataFrames are merged, and new columns are created that are the SpotPrice over the memory and ECU (compute units). A describe operation in Pandas over three of the columns shows the characteristics of the newly created DataFrame.

```
In [16]: df = spot_history_df.merge(\
pricing_df, how="inner", on="InstanceType")
    ...: df['price_memory_spot'] =\
 df['SpotPrice']/df['memory_gb']
    ...: df['price_ecu_spot'] =\
 df['SpotPrice']/df['compute_units_ecu']
    ...: df[["price_ecu_spot", "SpotPrice",\
 "price_memory_spot"]].describe()
    ...:
Out[16]:
        price_ecu_spot     SpotPrice  price_memory_spot
count    1000.000000  1000.000000         1000.000000
mean        0.007443     0.693629            0.005041
std         0.029698     6.369657            0.006676
```

min	0.002259	0.009300	0.000683
25%	0.003471	0.097900	0.002690
50%	0.004250	0.243800	0.003230
75%	0.006440	0.556300	0.006264
max	0.765957	133.380000	0.147541

Visualizing the data will make things more clear. Doing a groupby operation by AWS InstanceType allows for a median to be performed for each InstanceType.

```
In [17]: df_median = df.groupby("InstanceType").median()
    ...: df_median["InstanceType"] = df_median.index
    ...: df_median["price_ecu_spot"] =\
 df_median.price_ecu_spot.round(3)
    ...: df_median["divide_SpotPrice"] = df_median.SpotPrice/100
    ...: df_median.sort_values("price_ecu_spot", inplace=True)
```

A *Seaborn* bar plot is created that overlays two plots on top of each other. This is an excellent technique to show the contrast of two related columns. The price_ecu_spot, the ratio of spot price versus compute units compares against the raw SpotPrice. This is shown in Figure 9.2, and the sorted DataFrame allows a clear pattern to emerge; there are some great values for thrifty distributed computing users. In this particular region, us-west-2, the r4.large style instances are the best deal if only ECU is considered and both the Spot price and the Spot price, ECU ratio is considered. One trick to improve visibility was to divide the SpotPrice by 100.

```
    ...: plt.subplots(figsize=(20,15))
    ...: ax = plt.axes()
    ...: sns.set_color_codes("muted")
    ...: sns.barplot(x="price_ecu_spot",\
 y="InstanceType", data=df_median,
    ...:              label="Spot Price Per ECU", color="b")
    ...: sns.set_color_codes("pastel")
    ...: sns.barplot(x="divide_SpotPrice",\
 y="InstanceType", data=df_median,
    ...:              label="Spot Price/100", color="b")
    ...:
    ...: # Add a legend and informative axis label
    ...: ax.legend(ncol=2, loc="lower right", frameon=True)
    ...: ax.set(xlim=(0, .1), ylabel="",
    ...:        xlabel="AWS Spot Pricing by Compute Units (ECU)")
    ...: sns.despine(left=True, bottom=True)
    ...:
<matplotlib.figure.Figure at 0x11383ef98>
```

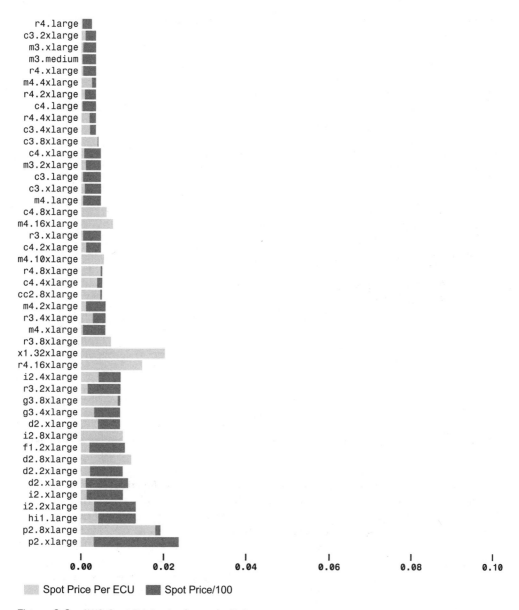

Figure 9.2   AWS Spot Pricing by Compute Units

There is enough information here that it makes sense to turn this into a command-line tool that will be useful in making decisions about what type of Spot instances to provision. To create a new command-line tool, a new module is created in the paws directory, and the previous code is wrapped up into functions.

```python
def cluster(combined_spot_history_df, sort_by="price_ecu_spot"):
    """Clusters Spot Instances"""

    df_median = combined_spot_history_df.\
groupby("InstanceType").median()
    df_median["InstanceType"] = df_median.index
    df_median["price_ecu_spot"] = df_median.price_ecu_spot.round(3)
    df_median.sort_values(sort_by, inplace=True)
    numerical_df = df_median.loc[:,\
["price_ecu_spot", "price_memory_spot", "SpotPrice"]]
    scaler = MinMaxScaler()
    scaler.fit(numerical_df)
    scaler.transform(numerical_df)
    k_means = KMeans(n_clusters=3)
    kmeans = k_means.fit(scaler.transform(numerical_df))
    df_median["cluster"]=kmeans.labels_
    return df_median

def recommend_cluster(df_cluster, instance_type):
    """Takes a instance_type and finds
a recommendation of other instances similar"""


    vals = df_cluster.loc[df_cluster['InstanceType'] ==\
 instance_type]
    cluster_res = vals['cluster'].to_dict()
    cluster_num = cluster_res[instance_type]
    cluster_members = df_cluster.loc[df_cluster["cluster"] ==\
 cluster_num]
    return cluster_members
```

There is a cluster function, which scales the data and takes the price_ecu_spot, price_memory_spot, and SpotPrice and makes three clusters. The recommend cluster function works under the assumption that instances in the same cluster are a likely substitute. A brief peak at the data, in Jupyter, shows there do appear to be three distinct clusters. Cluster 1 has an almost ridiculous amount of memory and a corresponding high SpotPrice; there is only 1 member in this cluster. Cluster 2 has the lowest memory, and 11 instances in it. Cluster 1 has the most members at 33 and is marginally more expensive, but has double the memory on average. These assumptions can now be turned into a useful command-line tool that allows a user to pick whether she wants low, medium, or high memory Spot instances, and shows her how much she would pay.

```python
In [25]: df_median[["price_ecu_spot", "SpotPrice",\
  "price_memory_spot", "memory_gb","cluster"]].\
groupby("cluster").median()
Out[25]:
```

cluster	price_ecu_spot	SpotPrice	price_memory_spot	memory_gb
0	0.005	0.2430	0.002817	61.0
1	0.766	72.0000	0.147541	488.0
2	0.004	0.1741	0.007147	30.0

```
In [27]: df_median[["price_ecu_spot", "SpotPrice",\
 "price_memory_spot", "memory_gb","cluster"]].\
groupby("cluster").count()
Out[27]:
         price_ecu_spot  SpotPrice  price_memory_spot  memory_gb
cluster
0                   33         33                 33         33
1                    1          1                  1          1
2                   11         11                 11         11
```

The last step to create the command-line tool is to use the same pattern shown in the chapter: import the library, use the click framework to manage options, and use click.echo to give back the results. The recommend command takes a –instance flag, which then returns results for all members of that cluster.

```
@cli.command("recommend")
@click.option('--instance', help='Instance Type')
def recommend(instance):
    """Recommends similar spot instances uses kNN clustering

    Example usage:

    ./spot-price-ml.py recommend --instance c3.8xlarge

    """
    pd.set_option('display.float_format', lambda x: '%.3f' % x)
    pricing_df = setup_spot_data("data/ec2-prices.csv")
    names = pricing_df["InstanceType"].to_dict()
    spot_history_df = get_spot_pricing_history(names,
        product_description="Linux/UNIX")
    df = combined_spot_df(spot_history_df, pricing_df)
    df_cluster = cluster(df, sort_by="price_ecu_spot")
    df_cluster_members = recommend_cluster(df_cluster, instance)
    click.echo(df_cluster_members[["SpotPrice",\
 "price_ecu_spot", "cluster", "price_memory_spot"]])
```

In action, the output looks like this.

```
➜ ✗ ./spot-price-ml.py recommend --instance c3.8xlarge
             SpotPrice  price_ecu_spot  cluster  price_memory_spot
InstanceType
c3.2xlarge       0.098           0.003        0              0.007
c3.4xlarge       0.176           0.003        0              0.006
c3.8xlarge       0.370           0.003        0              0.006
c4.4xlarge       0.265           0.004        0              0.009
cc2.8xlarge      0.356           0.004        0              0.006
c3.large         0.027           0.004        0              0.007
c3.xlarge        0.053           0.004        0              0.007
c4.2xlarge       0.125           0.004        0              0.008
```

c4.8xlarge	0.557	0.004	0	0.009
c4.xlarge	0.060	0.004	0	0.008
hi1.4xlarge	0.370	0.011	0	0.006

Writing a Spot Instance Launcher

There are many levels to working with Spot instances. This section will tackle a few of the layers, starting with an easy example and working forward from there. Spot instances are the life's blood of ML on AWS. Understanding how to use them correctly can make or break a company, a project, or a hobby. A recommended best practice is to create self-expiring Spot instances that terminate automatically before an hour is up. This is the hello world of launching Spot instances—at least, the recommended hello world.

In this first section, the click library is imported along with Boto and the Base64 library. The user data that gets sent to AWS needs to be Base64 encoded, and this will be shown in a further snippet. Note that if the line with boto.set_stream_logger is uncommented, there will be very verbose logging messages (that can be very helpful when trying out options).

```python
#!/usr/bin/env python
"""Launches a test spot instance"""

import click
import boto3
import base64

from sensible.loginit import logger
log = logger(__name__)

#Tell Boto3 To Enable Debug Logging
#boto3.set_stream_logger(name='botocore')
```

In the next section, the command-line tool is set up and the user data options are configured with an automatic termination. This is a great trick that Eric Hammond (https://www.linkedin.com/in/ehammond/) invented. Essentially, right when the machine launches, a job is set up using the "at" facility, which terminates the instance. This trick is expanded in this command-line tool, which allows a user to set the duration if he wants to change the default of 55 minutes.

```python
@click.group()
def cli():
    """Spot Launcher"""


def user_data_cmds(duration):
    """Initial cmds to run, takes duration for halt cmd"""

    cmds = """
        #cloud-config
        runcmd:
         - echo "halt" | at now + {duration} min
    """.format(duration=duration)
    return cmds
```

In the following options, everything is set as a default, which only requires the user to specify the launch command. The options are then passed into the Spot request API call to the Boto3 client.

```python
@cli.command("launch")
@click.option('--instance', default="r4.large", help='Instance Type')
@click.option('--duration', default="55", help='Duration')
@click.option('--keyname', default="pragai", help='Key Name')
@click.option('--profile',\
        default="arn:aws:iam::561744971673:instance-profile/admin",
                    help='IamInstanceProfile')
@click.option('--securitygroup',\
        default="sg-61706e07", help='Key Name')
@click.option('--ami', default="ami-6df1e514", help='Key Name')
def request_spot_instance(duration, instance, keyname,
                          profile, securitygroup, ami):
    """Request spot instance"""


    user_data = user_data_cmds(duration)
    LaunchSpecifications = {
            "ImageId": ami,
            "InstanceType": instance,
            "KeyName": keyname,
            "IamInstanceProfile": {
                "Arn": profile
            },
            "UserData": base64.b64encode(user_data.encode("ascii")).\
                decode('ascii'),
            "BlockDeviceMappings": [
                {
                    "DeviceName": "/dev/xvda",
                    "Ebs": {
                        "DeleteOnTermination": True,
                        "VolumeType": "gp2",
                        "VolumeSize": 8,
                    }
                }
            ],
            "SecurityGroupIds": [securitygroup]
        }

    run_args = {
            'SpotPrice'            : "0.8",
            'Type'                 : "one-time",
            'InstanceCount'        : 1,
            'LaunchSpecification'  : LaunchSpecifications
        }
```

```
    msg_user_data = "SPOT REQUEST DATA: %s" % run_args
    log.info(msg_user_data)

    client = boto3.client('ec2', "us-west-2")
    reservation = client.request_spot_instances(**run_args)
    return reservation

if __name__ == '__main__':
    cli()
```

When the command-line tool is run with help, the output shows the options that can be changed. Note that there isn't an option for price, for a couple of reasons. First, the Spot price is market driven, so the request will always use the lowest price. Second, this can easily be added using the same technique shown.

```
➜ ./spot_launcher.py launch --help
Usage: spot_launcher.py launch [OPTIONS]

  Request spot instance

Options:
  --instance TEXT       Instance Type
  --duration TEXT       Duration
  --keyname TEXT        Key Name
  --profile TEXT        IamInstanceProfile
  --securitygroup TEXT  Key Name
  --ami TEXT            Key Name
  --help                Show this message and exit.
```

When launching a Spot instance with a new duration, say, 1 hour 55 minutes, it can be modified by setting the --duration option.

```
➜✗ ./spot_launcher.py launch --duration 115
2017-09-20 06:46:53,046 - __main__ - INFO –
SPOT REQUEST DATA: {'SpotPrice': '0.8', 'Type':
'one-time', 'InstanceCount': 1, 'LaunchSpecification':
 {'ImageId': 'ami-6df1e514', 'InstanceType':
'r4.large', 'KeyName': 'pragai', 'IamInstanceProfile':
 {'Arn': 'arn:aws:iam::561744971673:instance-profile/admin'},
 .....
```

The instance can then be found by going to the EC2 dashboard for the region in which it was launched. For this request, this would be https://us-west-2.console.aws.amazon.com/ec2/v2/home?region=us-west-2#Instances:sort=ipv6Ips in your AWS Console. This is shown in Figure 9.3, where the connection information to ssh into the machine are provided.

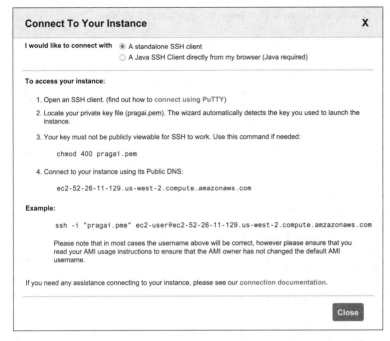

Figure 9.3 Representation of AWS Spot Connect to Instance

Using that information, an ssh connection is created to the Spot instance.

```
➜ ✗ ssh -i "~/.ssh/pragai.pem" ec2-user@52.26.11.129
The authenticity of host '52.26.11.129 (52.26.11.129)'
ECDSA key fingerprint is SHA256:1TaVeVvOL7GE...
Are you sure you want to continue connecting (yes/no)? yes
Warning: Permanently added '52.26.11.129'


       __|  __|_  )
       _|  (     /    Amazon Linux AMI
      ___|\___|___|


https://aws.amazon.com/amazon-linux-ami/2017.03-release-notes/
9 package(s) needed for security, out of 13 available
Run "sudo yum update" to apply all updates.
[ec2-user@ip-172-31-8-237 ~]$
```

From the Amazon Linux shell, the uptime command will inform how long the instance has been running. This instance has been running for 1 hour 31 minutes and will run for a little over 20 more minutes before it terminates.

```
[ec2-user@ip-172-31-8-237 ~]$ uptime
 15:18:52 up  1:31,  1 user,  load average: 0.00, 0.00, 0.00
```

Switching into the root user, the job to halt the machine can be verified.

```
[ec2-user@ip-172-31-8-237 ~]$ sudo su -
[root@ip-172-31-8-237 ~]# at -l
1   2017-09-20 15:42 a root
```

Next, the actual command that will be run at that time in the future can be inspected.

```
#!/bin/sh
# atrun uid=0 gid=0
# mail root 0
umask 22
PATH=/sbin:/usr/sbin:/bin:/usr/bin; export PATH
RUNLEVEL=3; export RUNLEVEL
runlevel=3; export runlevel
PWD=/; export PWD
LANGSH_SOURCED=1; export LANGSH_SOURCED
LANG=en_US.UTF-8; export LANG
PREVLEVEL=N; export PREVLEVEL
previous=N; export previous
CONSOLETYPE=serial; export CONSOLETYPE
SHLVL=4; export SHLVL
UPSTART_INSTANCE=; export UPSTART_INSTANCE
UPSTART_EVENTS=runlevel; export UPSTART_EVENTS
UPSTART_JOB=rc; export UPSTART_JOB
cd / || {
        echo 'Execution directory inaccessible' >&2
        exit 1
}
${SHELL:-/bin/sh} << 'marcinDELIMITER6382915b'
halt
```

There are some exciting changes from Amazon that make this style of research and development even more appealing. As of October 3, 2017, Amazon is offering billing by the second, with 1-minute minimums. This absolutely changes the game for how Spot instances can be used. One of the most obvious changes is that it is now practical to simply use Spot instances to run ad hoc functions, and when they are finished, in say 30 seconds, the instance can be shut down.

The next step to take beyond this simple Spot launcher for many production projects is to get production software deployed onto the instance being launched. There are many ways to accomplish this.

- Passing a shell script to an instance on launch, which is the method just shown. You can see some more complicated examples from the official AWS docs (http://docs.aws.amazon .com/AWSEC2/latest/UserGuide/user-data.html).

- Modifying the AMI itself, then using that snapshot on launch. There are a couple of ways to do this. One is to just launch an instance, configure it, then save it. Another method is to use the AMI Builder Packer (https://www.packer.io/docs/builders/amazon-ebs.html). When the instance is launched, the machine will already have the software needed. This approach could also be used in conjunction with other approaches, say a prebuilt AMI, plus custom shell script.

- Use EFS upon boot to store both data and software and to link binaries and scripts into the environment. This is an approach that was very common in the NFS days of Solaris and other Unix systems, and it is a wonderful way to customize the environment of Spot instances. The EFS volume can be updated via a build server with rsync or a copy.

- Using AWS Batch with Docker containers is also a viable option.

Writing a More Sophisticated Spot Instance Launcher

A more sophisticated Spot launcher would install some software on the system, pull in the source code from a repository, run that source code, and the put the output of the code in, say, S3. To do this, a couple of pieces will need to be changed. First, the `buildspec.yml` file will need to be modified so that it copies the source code to S3. Note that the sync command with `--delete` is useful in that it intelligently syncs just the files that have changed and deletes files that no longer exist.

```
post_build:
  commands:
    - echo "COPY Code TO S3"
    - rm -rf ~/.aws
    - aws s3 sync $CODEBUILD_SRC_DIR \
s3://pragai-aws/master --delete
```

Typically, with build commands like this, I run them locally to make sure I understand what they are doing. Next, Python and a virtual environment will need to be installed as the machine is launching. This can be accomplished by modifying the runcmd's passed to the instance upon boot. The first modified section grabs Python and installs it along with the packages Python needs to install. Note that ensurepip is used because this will allow the Makefile to just work.

```
cmds = """
        #cloud-config
        runcmd:
          - echo "halt" | at now + {duration} min
          - wget https://www.python.org/ftp/\
python/3.6.2/Python-3.6.2.tgz
          - tar zxvf Python-3.6.2.tgz
          - yum install -y gcc readline-devel\
 sqlite-devel zlib-devel openssl-devel
          - cd Python-3.6.2
          - ./configure --with-ensurepip=install && make install
```

Next, the source code that was synced to S3 is pulled down locally, which is a handy way to deploy code to an instance. It is very fast and uses Git ssh keys, and passwords are avoided since the Spot instance has role privileges to communicate with S3. After the S3 data is copied locally, it is sourced using virtualenv and then the ML Spot prices tool is run and the output is sent to S3.

```
          - cd ..
          - aws s3 cp s3://pragai-aws/master master\
 --recursive && cd master
          - make setup
          - source ~/.pragia-aws/bin/activate && make install
          - ~/.pragia-aws/bin/python spot-price-ml.py\
 describe > prices.txt
          - aws s3 cp prices.txt s3://spot-jobs-output
    """.format(duration=duration)
    return cmds
```

A natural next step is to take the prototype and make it more modular so that any arbitrary ML operation could be executed as a script, not just the hard-coded example. In Figure 9.4, a high-level overview of this pipeline shows how this process works in practice.

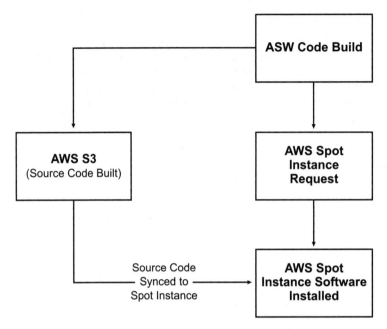

Figure 9.4   AWS Spot Transient Job Lifecycle

Summary

This chapter looked at one of the details of ML that is often neglected—actually running jobs on AWS. Several important concerns were tackled with Spot instances: finding the right instance size, finding out the most economical way to use them, installing software on them, and deploying code.

Recent changes to AWS that allow by-the-second billing and the addition of services like AWS Batch make it a fierce competitor in the war of the clouds. The combination of per-second billing and Spot pricing has never been seen before. Creating ML systems in production on top of infrastructure that AWS has created is a very safe choice, and controlling costs in research and development is easier than ever.

Further directions that could be explored to make this AI solution even more practical would be to trigger the launch of jobs, perhaps on AWS batch, that listen to price signals and use linear optimization in combination with clustering to dynamically figure out the best time and combinations of machines to run on. An even further advancement could be to look at combining this with technologies like Nomad from HashiCorp (https://www.nomadproject.io/) to dynamically run jobs on all clouds in the form of Docker images.

## 10

Real Estate

Once you get on the playing field, it's not about whether you're liked or not liked. All that matters is to play at a high level and do whatever it takes to help your team win. That's what it's about.

LeBron James

Do you know of any good data sets to explore? This is one of the most asked questions I get as a lecturer or when teaching a workshop. One of my go-to answers is the Zillow real estate data sets: https://www.zillow.com/research/data/. The real estate market in the United States is something that every person living in the country has to deal with, and as a result it makes for a great topic of conversation about ML.

Exploring Real Estate Values in the United States

Living in the San Francisco Bay Area makes someone think often and long about housing prices. There is a good reason for that. The median homes prices in the Bay Area are accelerating at shocking rates. From 2010 to 2017, the median price of a single-family home in San Francisco has gone from approximately $775,000 to $1.5 million. This data will be explored with a Jupyter Notebook. The entire project, and its data, can be checked out at https://github.com/noahgift/real_estate_ml.

At the beginning of the notebook, several libraries are imported and Pandas is set to display float versus scientific notation.

```
In [1]: import pandas as pd
   ...: pd.set_option('display.float_format', lambda x: '%.3f' % x)
   ...: import numpy as np
   ...: import statsmodels.api as sm
   ...: import statsmodels.formula.api as smf
   ...: import matplotlib.pyplot as plt
   ...: import seaborn as sns
```

Double import seaborn?

```
...: import seaborn as sns; sns.set(color_codes=True)
...: from sklearn.cluster import KMeans
...: color = sns.color_palette()
...: from IPython.core.display import display, HTML
...: display(HTML("<style>.container \
{ width:100% !important; }</style>"))
...: %matplotlib inline
```

Next, data from Zillow for single-family homes (https://www.zillow.com/research/data/) is imported and described.

```
In [6]: df.head()
In [7]: df.describe()
Out[7]:
        RegionID  RegionName  SizeRank      1996-04      1996-05
count  15282.000   15282.000 15282.000    10843.000    10974.000
mean   80125.483   46295.286  7641.500   123036.189   122971.396
std    30816.445   28934.030  4411.678    78308.265    77822.431
min    58196.000    1001.000     1.000    24400.000    23900.000
25%    66785.250   21087.750  3821.250    75700.000    75900.000
50%    77175.000   44306.500  7641.500   104300.000   104450.000
75%    88700.500   70399.500 11461.750   147100.000   147200.000
max   738092.000   99901.000 15282.000  1769000.000  1768100.000
```

Next, cleanup is done to rename a column and format the column type.

```
In [8]: df.rename(columns={"RegionName":"ZipCode"}, inplace=True)
   ...: df["ZipCode"]=df["ZipCode"].map(lambda x: "{:.0f}".format(x))
   ...: df["RegionID"]=df["RegionID"].map(
             lambda x: "{:.0f}".format(x))
   ...: df.head()
   ...:
Out[8]:
RegionID ZipCode City     State  Metro CountyName  SizeRank
84654    60657   Chicago   IL    Chicago     Cook    1.000
84616    60614   Chicago   IL    Chicago     Cook    2.000
93144    79936   El Paso   TX    El Paso  El Paso    3.000
84640    60640   Chicago   IL    Chicago     Cook    4.000
61807    10467   New York  NY    New York   Bronx    5.000
```

Getting the median values for all of the United States will be helpful for many different types of analysis in this notebook. In the following example, multiple values that match the region or city are aggregated and median calculations are created for them. A new DataFrame is created called df_comparison that will be used with the Plotly library.

```
In [9]: median_prices = df.median()
```

```
In [10]: median_prices.tail()
Out[10]:
2017-05    180600.000
```

```
2017-06   181300.000
2017-07   182000.000
2017-08   182500.000
2017-09   183100.000
dtype: float64

In [11]: marin_df = df[df["CountyName"] == "Marin"].median()
    ...: sf_df = df[df["City"] == "San Francisco"].median()
    ...: palo_alto = df[df["City"] == "Palo Alto"].median()
    ...: df_comparison = pd.concat([marin_df, sf_df,
            palo_alto, median_prices], axis=1)
    ...: df_comparison.columns = ["Marin County",
            "San Francisco", "Palo Alto", "Median USA"]
    ...:
```

Interactive Data Visualization in Python

There are a couple of commonly used interactive data visualization libraries in Python: Plotly (https://github.com/plotly/plotly.py) and Bokeh (https://bokeh.pydata.org/en/latest/). In this chapter, Plotly will be used for data visualization, but Bokeh could also have done similar plots. Plotly is a commercial company that can be used in both offline mode and by exporting to the company web site. Plotly also has an open-source Python framework called Dash (https://plot.ly/products/dash/) that can be used for building analytical web applications. Many of the plots in this chapter can be found at https://plot.ly/~ngift.

In this example, a library called *Cufflinks* (https://plot.ly/ipython-notebooks/cufflinks/) is used to make it trivial to plot directly from a Pandas DataFrame to Plotly. Cufflinks is described as a "productivity tool" for Pandas. One of the major strengths of the library is the capability to plot as an almost native feature of Pandas.

```
In [12]: import cufflinks as cf
    ...: cf.go_offline()
    ...: df_comparison.iplot(title="Bay Area Median\
Single Family Home Prices 1996-2017",
    ...:                     xTitle="Year",
    ...:                     yTitle="Sales Price",
    ...:                     #bestfit=True, bestfit_colors=["pink"],
    ...:                     #subplots=True,
    ...:                     shape=(4,1),
    ...:                     #subplot_titles=True,
    ...:                     fill=True,)
    ...:
```

Figure 10.1 shows a view of the plot without interactions turned on. Palo Alto looks like a truly scary place to be entering the housing market as a buyer.

In Figure 10.2, the mouse is hovering over December 2009, and it shows a point near the bottom of the last housing crash, with the median housing price in Palo Alto at $1.2 million, the median in San Francisco around $750,000, and the median in the entire United States at $170,000.

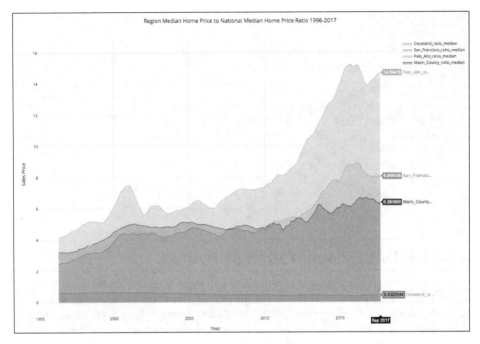

Figure 10.1   Can Palo Alto Grow Exponentially Forever?

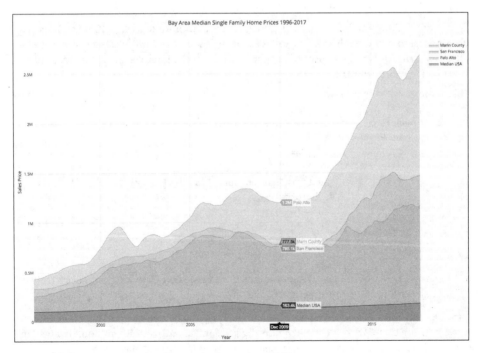

Figure 10.2   Housing Market Bottom in December 2009

By scrolling through the graph, it can be shown that in December 2017, the price in Palo Alto was about $2.7 million, more than double in 8 years. On the other hand, the median home price in rest of the United States has only appreciated about 5 percent. This is definitely worth exploring more.

Clustering on Size Rank and Price

To further explore what is going on, a k-means cluster 3D visualization can be created with both sklearn and Plotly. First, the data is scaled using the MinMaxScaler so outliers don't skew the results of the clustering.

```
In [13]: from sklearn.preprocessing import MinMaxScaler

In [14]: columns_to_drop = ['RegionID', 'ZipCode',
         'City', 'State', 'Metro', 'CountyName']
    ...: df_numerical = df.dropna()
    ...: df_numerical = df_numerical.drop(columns_to_drop, axis=1)
    ...:
```

Next, a quick description is done.

```
In [15]: df_numerical.describe()
Out[15]:
```

	SizeRank	1996-04	1996-05	1996-06	1996-07
count	10015.000	10015.000	10015.000	10015.000	10015.000
mean	6901.275	124233.839	124346.890	124445.791	124517.993
std	4300.338	78083.175	77917.627	77830.951	77776.606
min	1.000	24500.000	24500.000	24800.000	24800.000
25%	3166.500	77200.000	77300.000	77300.000	77300.000
50%	6578.000	105700.000	106100.000	106400.000	106400.000
75%	10462.000	148000.000	148200.000	148500.000	148700.000
max	15281.000	1769000.000	1768100.000	1766900.000	1764200.000

When the cluster is performed after dropping missing values, there are about 10,000 rows.

```
In [16]: scaler = MinMaxScaler()
    ...: scaled_df = scaler.fit_transform(df_numerical)
    ...: kmeans = KMeans(n_clusters=3, random_state=0).fit(scaled_df)
    ...: print(len(kmeans.labels_))
    ...:
10015
```

An appreciation ratio column is added, and the data is cleaned up before visualization.

```
cluster_df = df.copy(deep=True)
cluster_df.dropna(inplace=True)
cluster_df.describe()
cluster_df['cluster'] = kmeans.labels_
```

```
cluster_df['appreciation_ratio'] =\
        round(cluster_df["2017-09"]/cluster_df["1996-04"],2)
cluster_df['CityZipCodeAppRatio'] =\
 cluster_df['City'].map(str) + "-" + cluster_df['ZipCode'] + "-" +
cluster_df["appreciation_ratio"].map(str)
cluster_df.head()
```

Next, Plotly is used in offline mode (i.e., it doesn't get sent to the Plotly servers), and three axes are graphed: *x* is the appreciation ratio, *y* is the year 1996, and *z* is the year 2017. The clusters are shaded. In Figure 10.3, some patterns stick out instantly. Jersey City has appreciated the most in the last 30 years, going from a low of $142,000 to a high of $1.344 million, a 9*x* increase.

Some other visible things are a couple of zip codes in Palo Alto. They have also increased about 6 times in value, which is even more amazing considering how expensive the houses were to begin with. In the last 10 years, the rise of startups in Palo Alto, including Facebook, have caused a distorted elevation of pricing, even factoring in the entire Bay Area.

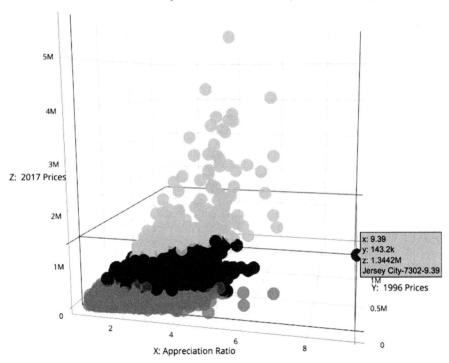

Figure 10.3 What the Heck Is Going on With Jersey City Appreciation?

Another interesting visualization would be the appreciation ratio of these same columns to see whether this trend in Palo Alto can be observed further. The code looks similar to the code for Figure 10.3.

```
In [17]: from sklearn.neighbors import KNeighborsRegressor
    ...: neigh = KNeighborsRegressor(n_neighbors=2)
    ...:


In [19]: #df_comparison.columns = ["Marin County",
        "San Francisco", "Palo Alto", "Median USA"]
    ...: cleveland = df[df["City"] == "Cleveland"].median()
    ...: df_median_compare = pd.DataFrame()
    ...: df_median_compare["Cleveland_ratio_median"] =\
            cleveland/df_comparison["Median USA"]
    ...: df_median_compare["San_Francisco_ratio_median"] =\
            df_comparison["San Francisco"]/df_comparison["Median USA"]
    ...: df_median_compare["Palo_Alto_ratio_median"] =\
            df_comparison["Palo Alto"]/df_comparison["Median USA"]
    ...: df_median_compare["Marin_County_ratio_median"] =\
            df_comparison["Marin County"]/df_comparison["Median USA"]
    ...:


In [20]: import cufflinks as cf
    ...: cf.go_offline()
    ...: df_median_compare.iplot(title="Region Median Home Price to National Median
Home Price Ratio 1996-2017",
    ...:                     xTitle="Year",
    ...:                     yTitle="Ratio to National Median",
    ...:                     #bestfit=True, bestfit_colors=["pink"],
    ...:                     #subplots=True,
    ...:                     shape=(4,1),
    ...:                     #subplot_titles=True,
    ...:                     fill=True,)
    ...:
```

In Figure 10.4, the median appreciation of Palo Alto looks exponential since the housing crash of 2008, yet the rest of the San Francisco Bay Area seems to have be less volatile. A reasonable hypothesis may be that there is a bubble inside the Bay Area, in Palo Alto, that may not be sustainable. Eventually, exponential growth comes to an end.

One more thing to look at would be to look at the rent index and see if there are further patterns to tease out.

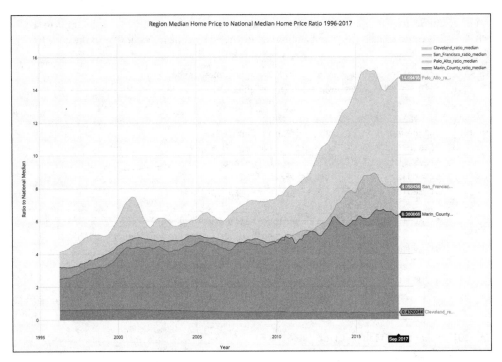

Figure 10.4   Palo Alto Went From Having Home Prices 5 Times Higher Than National Median to 15 Times Higher in About 10 Years

The initial data import is cleaned up and the Metro column is renamed to be a City column.

```
In [21]: df_rent = pd.read_csv(
    ...:     "../data/City_MedianRentalPrice_Sfr.csv")
    ...: df_rent.head()
    ...: median_prices_rent = df_rent.median()
    ...: df_rent[df_rent["CountyName"] == "Marin"].median()
    ...: df_rent.columns
    ...:
Out[21]:
Index(['RegionName', 'State', 'Metro',
       'CountyName', 'SizeRank', '2010-01',

In [22]: df_rent.rename(columns={"Metro":"City"}, inplace=True)
    ...: df_rent.head()
    ...:
Out[22]:
```

```
     RegionName State                              City   CountyName
0      New York  NY                          New York      Queens
1   Los Angeles  CA  Los Angeles-Long Beach-Anaheim  Los Angeles
2       Chicago  IL                           Chicago         Cook
3       Houston  TX                           Houston       Harris
4  Philadelphia  PA                      Philadelphia  Philadelphia
```

Next, the medians are created in a new DataFrame.

```
In [23]: median_prices_rent = df_rent.median()
    ...: marin_df = df_rent[df_rent["CountyName"] ==\
                "Marin"].median()
    ...: sf_df = df_rent[df_rent["City"] == "San Francisco"].median()
    ...: cleveland = df_rent[df_rent["City"] == "Cleveland"].median()
    ...: palo_alto = df_rent[df_rent["City"] == "Palo Alto"].median()
    ...: df_comparison_rent = pd.concat([marin_df,
         sf_df, palo_alto, cleveland, median_prices_rent], axis=1)
    ...: df_comparison_rent.columns = ["Marin County",
 "San Francisco", "Palo Alto", "Cleveland", "Median USA"]
    ...:
```

Finally, Cufflinks is used again to plot the median rents.

```
In [24]: import cufflinks as cf
    ...: cf.go_offline()
    ...: df_comparison_rent.iplot(
         title="Median Monthly Rents Single Family Homes",
    ...:                xTitle="Year",
    ...:                yTitle="Monthly",
    ...:                #bestfit=True, bestfit_colors=["pink"],
    ...:                #subplots=True,
    ...:                shape=(4,1),
    ...:                #subplot_titles=True,
    ...:                fill=True,)
    ...:
```

In Figure 10.5, the trends look much less dramatic, partially because the data is spread over a shorter period of time, but this isn't the whole picture. Although Palo Alto isn't in this data set, the other cities in the San Francisco Bay Area look much closer to the median rents, whereas Cleveland, Ohio, appears to be about half of the median rent in the United States.

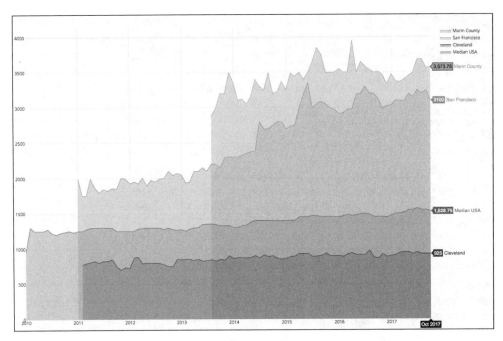

Figure 10.5   Rents in the San Francisco Bay Area since 2011 Have Almost Doubled While the Rest of the US Has Stayed Flat

One final analysis would be to look a similar rent ratio across the United States. In this code, the rent ratio is created with a new empty DataFrame and then inserted into Plotly again.

```
In [25]: df_median_rents_ratio = pd.DataFrame()
    ...: df_median_rents_ratio["Cleveland_ratio_median"] =\
         df_comparison_rent["Cleveland"]/df_comparison_rent["Median USA"]
    ...: df_median_rents_ratio["San_Francisco_ratio_median"] =\
         df_comparison_rent["San Francisco"]/df_comparison_rent["Median USA"]
    ...: df_median_rents_ratio["Palo_Alto_ratio_median"] =\
         df_comparison_rent["Palo Alto"]/df_comparison_rent["Median USA"]
    ...: df_median_rents_ratio["Marin_County_ratio_median"] =\
         df_comparison_rent["Marin County"]/df_comparison_rent["Median USA"]
    ...:

In [26]: import cufflinks as cf
    ...: cf.go_offline()
    ...: df_median_rents_ratio.iplot(title="Median Monthly Rents Ratios Single Family
         Homes vs National Median",
```

```
...:                        xTitle="Year",
...:                        yTitle="Rent vs Median Rent USA",
...:                        #bestfit=True, bestfit_colors=["pink"],
...:                        #subplots=True,
...:                        shape=(4,1),
...:                         #subplot_titles=True,
...:                         fill=True,)
...:
```

Figure 10.6 shows a different story from the appreciation ratio. In San Francisco, the median rent is still double the median of the rest of the United States, but nowhere near the 8✗ increase of the median home price. In looking at the rental data, it may pay to double-check before buying a home in 2018, especially in the Palo Alto area. Renting, even though it is high, may be a much better deal.

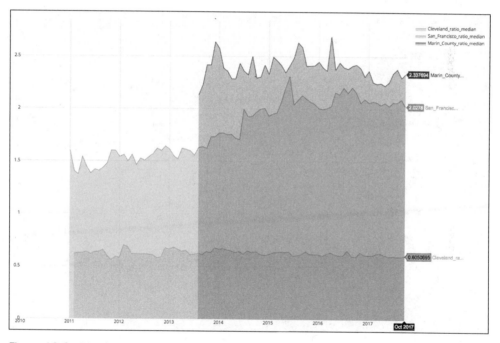

Figure 10.6   Monthly Rents in the San Francisco Bay Area Versus National Median Have Exploded

Summary

In this chapter, a data exploration was performed on a public Zillow data set. The Plotly library was used to create interactive data visualizations in Python. k-means clustering and 3D visualization were used to tease out more information from a relatively simple data set. The findings included the idea that there may have been a housing bubble in the San Francisco Bay Area, specifically Palo Alto, in 2017. It may pay to do further exploration on this data set by creating a classification model of when to sell and when to buy for each region of the United States.

Other future directions to take this sample project is to look at higher-level APIs like ones that House Canary (https://api-docs.housecanary.com/#getting-started) provides. It may be that your organization can build an AI application by using their prediction models as a base, and then layering other AI and ML techniques on top. Another direction might be to use AWS SageMaker to create a deep learning prediction and then to deploy a model internally into your organization that is used to make business decisions.

Production AI for User-Generated Content

The man who can drive himself further once the effort gets painful is the man who will win.

Roger Bannister

What do Russian trolls, Facebook, and U.S. elections have to do with ML? Recommendation engines are at the heart of the central feedback loop of social networks and the user-generated content (UGC) they create. Users join the network and are recommended users and content with which to engage. Recommendation engines can be gamed because they amplify the effects of thought bubbles. The 2016 U.S. presidential election showed how important it is to understand how recommendation engines work and the limitations and strengths they offer.

AI-based systems aren't a panacea that only creates good things; rather, they offer a set of capabilities. It can be incredibly useful to get an appropriate product recommendation on a shopping site, but it can be equally frustrating to get recommended content that later turns out to be fake (perhaps generated by a foreign power motivated to sow discord in your country).

This chapter covers recommendation engines and natural-language processing (NLP), both from a high level and a coding level. It also gives examples of how to use frameworks, such as the Python-based recommendation engine, Surprise, as well as instructions how to build your own. Some of the topics covered including the Netflix prize, singular-value decomposition (SVD), collaborative filtering, real-world problems with recommendation engines, NLP, and production sentiment analysis using cloud APIs.

The Netflix Prize Wasn't Implemented in Production

Before "data science" was a common term and Kaggle was around, the Netflix prize caught the world by storm. The Netflix prize was a contest created to improve the recommendation of new movies. Many of the original ideas from the contest later turned into inspiration for other companies and products. Creating a $1 million data science contest back in 2006 sparked excitement that would foreshadow the current age of AI. In 2006, ironically, the age of cloud computing also began, with the launch of Amazon EC2.

The cloud and the dawn of widespread AI have been intertwined. Netflix also has been one of the biggest users of the public cloud via AWS. Despite all these interesting historical footnotes, the Netflix prize-winning algorithm was never implemented into production. The winners in 2009, the "BellKor's Pragmatic Chaos" team, achieved a greater than 10-percent improvement with a Test RMS of 0.867 (https://netflixprize.com/index.html). The team's paper (https://www.netflixprize.com/assets/ProgressPrize2008_BellKor.pdf) describes that the solution is a linear blend of over 100 results. A quote in the paper that is particularly relevant is "A lesson here is that having lots of models is useful for the incremental results needed to win competitions, but practically, excellent systems can be built with just a few well-selected models."

The winning approach for the Netflix competition was not implemented in production at Netflix because the engineering complexity was deemed too great when compared with the gains produced. A core algorithm used in recommendations, SVD, as noted in "Fast SVD for Large-Scale Matrices" (http://sysrun.haifa.il.ibm.com/hrl/bigml/files/Holmes.pdf), "though feasible for small datasets or offline processing, many modern applications involve real-time learning and/or massive dataset dimensionality and size." In practice, this is one of huge challenges of production ML—the time and computational resources necessary to produce results.

I had a similar experience building recommendation engines at companies. When an algorithm is run in a batch manner, and it is simple, it can generate useful recommendations. But if a more complex approach is taken, or if the requirements go from batch to real time, the complexity of putting it into production and/or maintaining it explodes. The lesson here is that simpler is better: choosing to do batch-based ML versus real-time. Or choosing a simple model versus an ensemble of multiple techniques. Also, deciding whether it may make sense to call a recommendation engine API versus creating the solution yourself.

Key Concepts in Recommendation Systems

Figure 11.1 shows a social network recommendation feedback loop. The more users a system has, the more content it creates. The more content that is created, the more recommendations it creates for new content. This feedback loop, in turn, drives more users and more content. As mentioned at the beginning of this chapter, these capabilities can be used for both positive and negative features of a platform.

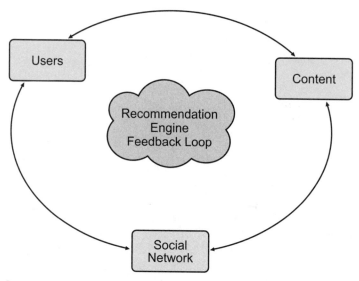

Figure 11.1   Social Network Recommendation Feedback Loop

Using the Surprise Framework in Python

One way to explore the concepts behind recommendation engines is to use the Surprise framework (http://surpriselib.com/). A few of the handy things about the framework are that it has built-in data sets: MovieLens (https://grouplens.org/datasets/movielens/) and Jester, and it includes SVD and other common algorithms including similarity measures. It also includes tools to evaluate the performance of recommendations in the form of root mean squared error (RMSE) and mean absolute error (MAE), as well as the time it took to train the model.

Here is an example of how it can be used in a pseudo production situation by tweaking one of the provided examples.

First are the necessary imports to get the library loaded.

```
In [2]: import io
   ...: from surprise import KNNBaseline
   ...: from surprise import Dataset
   ...: from surprise import get_dataset_dir
   ...: import pandas as pd
```

A helper function is created to convert IDs to names.

```
In [3]: def read_item_names():
   ...:       """Read the u.item file from MovieLens
         100-k dataset and return two
   ...:       mappings to convert raw ids
         into movie names and movie names into raw ids.
   ...:       """
   ...:
```

```
...:         file_name = get_dataset_dir() + '/ml-100k/ml-100k/u.item'
...:         rid_to_name = {}
...:         name_to_rid = {}
...:         with io.open(file_name, 'r', encoding='ISO-8859-1') as f:
...:             for line in f:
...:                 line = line.split('|')
...:                 rid_to_name[line[0]] = line[1]
...:                 name_to_rid[line[1]] = line[0]
...:
...:         return rid_to_name, name_to_rid
```

Similarities are computed between items.

```
In [4]: # First, train the algorithm
        # to compute the similarities between items
   ...: data = Dataset.load_builtin('ml-100k')
   ...: trainset = data.build_full_trainset()
   ...: sim_options = {'name': 'pearson_baseline',
        'user_based': False}
   ...: algo = KNNBaseline(sim_options=sim_options)
   ...: algo.fit(trainset)
   ...:
   ...:

Estimating biases using als...
Computing the pearson_baseline similarity matrix...
Done computing similarity matrix.
Out[4]: <surprise.prediction_algorithms.knns.KNNBaseline>
```

Finally, "10 recommendations" are provided, which are similar to another example in this chapter.

```
In [5]: # Read the mappings raw id <-> movie name
   ...: rid_to_name, name_to_rid = read_item_names()
   ...:
   ...: # Retrieve inner id of the movie Toy Story
   ...: toy_story_raw_id = name_to_rid['Toy Story (1995)']
   ...: toy_story_inner_id = algo.trainset.to_inner_iid(
        toy_story_raw_id)
   ...:
   ...: # Retrieve inner ids of the nearest neighbors of Toy Story.
   ...: toy_story_neighbors = algo.get_neighbors(
        toy_story_inner_id, k=10)
   ...:
   ...: # Convert inner ids of the neighbors into names.
   ...: toy_story_neighbors = (algo.trainset.to_raw_iid(inner_id)
                               for inner_id in toy_story_neighbors)
   ...: toy_story_neighbors = (rid_to_name[rid]
                               for rid in toy_story_neighbors)
   ...:
   ...: print('The 10 nearest neighbors of Toy Story are:')
```

```
...: for movie in toy_story_neighbors:
...:     print(movie)
...:
The 10 nearest neighbors of Toy Story are:
Beauty and the Beast (1991)
Raiders of the Lost Ark (1981)
That Thing You Do! (1996)
Lion King, The (1994)
Craft, The (1996)
Liar Liar (1997)
Aladdin (1992)
Cool Hand Luke (1967)
Winnie the Pooh and the Blustery Day (1968)
Indiana Jones and the Last Crusade (1989)
```

In exploring this example, consider the real-world issues with implementing this in production. Here is an example of a pseudocode API function that someone in your company may be asked to produce.

```
def recommendations(movies, rec_count):
    """Your
    return recommendations"""

movies = ["Beauty and the Beast (1991)", "Cool Hand Luke (1967)",.. ]

print(recommendations(movies=movies, rec_count=10))
```

Some questions to ask in implementing this are: What tradeoffs are you making in picking the top from a group of selections versus just a movie? How well will this algorithm perform on a very large data set? There are no right answers, but these are things you should think about as you deploy recommendation engines into production.

Cloud Solutions to Recommendation Systems

The Google Cloud Platform has an example of using ML on Compute Engine to make product recommendations (https://cloud.google.com/solutions/recommendations-using-machine-learning-on-compute-engine) that is worth exploring. In the example, PySpark and the ALS algorithm are used along with proprietary cloud SQL. Amazon also has an example of how to build a recommendation engine using their platform, Spark and Elastic Map Reduce (EMR) (https://aws.amazon.com/blogs/big-data/building-a-recommendation-engine-with-spark-ml-on-amazon-emr-using-zeppelin/).

In both cases, Spark is used to increase the performance of the algorithm by dividing the computation across a cluster of machines. Finally, AWS is heavily pushing SageMaker (https://docs.aws.amazon.com/sagemaker/latest/dg/whatis.html), which can do distributed Spark jobs natively or talk to an EMR cluster.

Real-World Production Issues with Recommendations

Most books and articles on recommendation focus purely on the technical aspects of recommendation systems. This book is about pragmatism, and so there are some issues to talk about when it comes to recommendation systems. A few of these topics are covered in this section: performance, ETL, user experience (UX), and shills/bots.

One of the most popular algorithms as discussed is $O(n\_samples^{\wedge}2 * n\_features)$ or quadratic. This means that it is very difficult to train a model in real time and get an optimum solution. Therefore, training a recommendation system will need to occur as a batch job in most cases, without some tricks like using a greedy heuristic and/or only creating a small subset of recommendations for active users, popular products, etc.

When I created a user follow recommendation system from scratch for a social network, I found many of these issues came front and center. Training the model took hours, so the only realistic solution was to run it nightly. Additionally, I later created an in-memory copy of our training data, so the algorithm was only bound on CPU, not I/O.

Performance is a nontrivial concern in creating a production recommendation system in both the short term and the long term. It is possible that the approach you initially use may not scale as your company grows users and products. Perhaps initially, a Jupyter Notebook, Pandas, and scikit-learn were acceptable when you had 10,000 users on your platform, but it may turn out quickly to not be a scalable solution.

Instead, a PySpark-based support vector machine training algorithm (http://spark.apache.org/docs/2.1.0/api/python/pyspark.mllib.html) may dramatically improve performance and decrease maintenance time. And then later, again, you may need to switch to dedicated ML chips like TPU or the NVIDIA Volta. Having the ability to plan for this capacity while still making initial working solutions is a critical skill to have to implement pragmatic AI solutions that actually make it to production.

Real-World Recommendation Problems: Integration with Production APIs

I found many real-world problems surface in production in startups that build recommendations. These are problems that are not as heavily discussed in ML books. One such problem is the "cold-start problem." In the examples using the Surprise framework, there is already a massive database of "correct answers." In the real world, you have so few users or products it doesn't make sense to train a model. What can you do?

A decent solution is to make the path of the recommendation engine follow three phases. For phase one, take the most popular users, content, or products and serve those out as a recommendation. As more UGC is created on the platform, for phase two, use similarity scoring (without training a model). Here is some "hand-coded" code I have used in production a couple of different times that did just that. First we have a Tanimoto score, or Jaccard distance, by another name.

```
"""Data Science Algorithms"""
```

```
def tanimoto(list1, list2):
    """tanimoto coefficient

    In [2]: list2=['39229', '31995', '32015']
    In [3]: list1=['31936', '35989', '27489',
        '39229', '15468', '31993', '26478']
    In [4]: tanimoto(list1,list2)
    Out[4]: 0.1111111111111111

    Uses intersection of two sets to determine numerical score

    """

    intersection = set(list1).intersection(set(list2))
    return float(len(intersection))/(len(list1)) +\
        len(list2) - len(intersection)
```

Next is HBD: Here Be Dragons. Follower relationships are downloaded and converted in a Pandas DataFrame.

```
import os
import pandas as pd

from .algorithms import tanimoto

def follows_dataframe(path=None):
    """Creates Follows Dataframe"""

    if not path:
        path = os.path.join(os.getenv('PYTHONPATH'),
            'ext', 'follows.csv')

    df = pd.read_csv(path)
    return df

def follower_statistics(df):
    """Returns counts of follower behavior

    In [15]: follow_counts.head()
        Out[15]:
        followerId
        581bea20-962c-11e5-8c10-0242528e2f1b    1558
        74d96701-e82b-11e4-b88d-068394965ab2      94
        d3ea2a10-e81a-11e4-9090-0242528e2f1b      93
        0ed9aef0-f029-11e4-82f0-0aa89fecadc2      88
        55d31000-1b74-11e5-b730-0680a328ea36      64
        Name: followingId, dtype: int64

    """
```

```
        follow_counts = df.groupby(['followerId'])['followingId'].\
            count().sort_values(ascending=False)
        return follow_counts

def follow_metadata_statistics(df):
    """Generates metadata about follower behavior

    In [13]: df_metadata.describe()
        Out[13]:
        count    2145.000000
        mean        3.276923
        std        33.961413
        min         1.000000
        25%         1.000000
        50%         1.000000
        75%         3.000000
        max      1558.000000
        Name: followingId, dtype: float64

    """

    dfs = follower_statistics(df)
    df_metadata = dfs.describe()
    return df_metadata

def follow_relations_df(df):
    """Returns a dataframe of follower with all relations"""

    df = df.groupby('followerId').followingId.apply(list)
    dfr = df.to_frame("follow_relations")
    dfr.reset_index(level=0, inplace=True)
    return dfr

def simple_score(column, followers):
    """Used as an apply function for dataframe"""

    return tanimoto(column, followers)

def get_followers_by_id(dfr, followerId):
    """Returns a list of followers by followerID"""

    followers = dfr.loc[dfr['followerId'] == followerId]
    fr = followers['follow_relations']
    return fr.tolist()[0]

def generate_similarity_scores(dfr, followerId,
            limit=10, threshold=.1):
    """Generates a list of recommendations for a followerID"""
```

```
    followers = get_followers_by_id(dfr, followerId)
    recs = dfr['follow_relations'].\
        apply(simple_score, args=(followers,)).\
            where(dfr>threshold).dropna().sort_values()[-limit:]
    filters_recs = recs.where(recs>threshold)
    return filters_recs

def return_similarity_scores_with_ids(dfr, scores):
    """Returns Scores and FollowerID"""

    dfs = pd.DataFrame(dfr, index=scores.index.tolist())
    dfs['scores'] = scores[dfs.index]
    dfs['following_count'] = dfs['follow_relations'].apply(len)
    return dfs
```

To use this API, you would engage with it by following this sequence.

```
In [1]: follows import *

In [2]: df = follows_dataframe()

In [3]: dfr = follow_relations_df(df)

In [4]: dfr.head()

In [5]: scores = generate_similarity_scores(dfr,
        "00480160-0e6a-11e6-b5a1-06f8ea4c790f")

In [5]: scores
Out[5]:
2144    0.000000
713     0.000000
714     0.000000
715     0.000000
716     0.000000
717     0.000000
712     0.000000
980     0.333333
2057    0.333333
3       1.000000
Name: follow_relations, dtype: float64

In [6]: dfs = return_similarity_scores_with_ids(dfr, scores)

In [6]: dfs
Out[6]:
                              followerId  \
980     76cce300-0e6a-11e6-83e2-0242528e2f1b
2057    f5ccbf50-0e69-11e6-b5a1-06f8ea4c790f
3       00480160-0e6a-11e6-b5a1-06f8ea4c790f
```

```
                              follow_relations    scores  \
980    [f5ccbf50-0e69-11e6-b5a1-06f8ea4c790f, 0048016...  0.333333
2057   [76cce300-0e6a-11e6-83e2-0242528e2f1b, 0048016...  0.333333
3      [f5ccbf50-0e69-11e6-b5a1-06f8ea4c790f, 76cce30...         1

       following_count
980                  2
2057                 2
3                    2
```

This "phase 2" similarity score-based recommendation with the current implementation would need to be run as a batch API. Additionally, Pandas will eventually run into some performance problems at scale. Ditching it at some point for either PySpark or Pandas on Ray (https://rise.cs.berkeley.edu/blog/pandas-on-ray/?twitter=@bigdata) is going to be a good move.

For "phase 3," it is finally time to pull out the big guns and use something like Surprise and/or PySpark to train an SVD-based model and figure out model accuracy. In the first part of your company's history, though, why bother when there is little to no value in doing formal ML model training?

Another production API issue is how to deal with rejected recommendations. There is nothing more irritating to a user than to keep getting recommendations for things you don't want or already have. So, yet another sticky production issue needs to be solved. Ideally, the user is given the ability to click, "do not show again" for a list of recommendations, or quickly your recommendation engine becomes garbage. Additionally, the user is telling you something, so why not take that signal and feed it back into your recommendation engine model?

Cloud NLP and Sentiment Analysis

All three of the dominant cloud providers—AWS, GCP, and Azure—have solid NLP engines that can be called via an API. In this section, NLP examples on all three clouds will be explored. Additionally, a real-world production AI pipeline for NLP pipeline will be created on AWS using serverless technology.

NLP on Azure

Microsoft Cognitive Services have a Text Analytics API that has language detection, key phrase extraction, and sentiment analysis. In Figure 11.2, the endpoint is created so API calls can be made. This example will take a negative collection of movie reviews from the Cornell Computer Science Data Set on Movie Reviews (http://www.cs.cornell.edu/people/pabo/movie-review-data/) and use it to walk through the API.

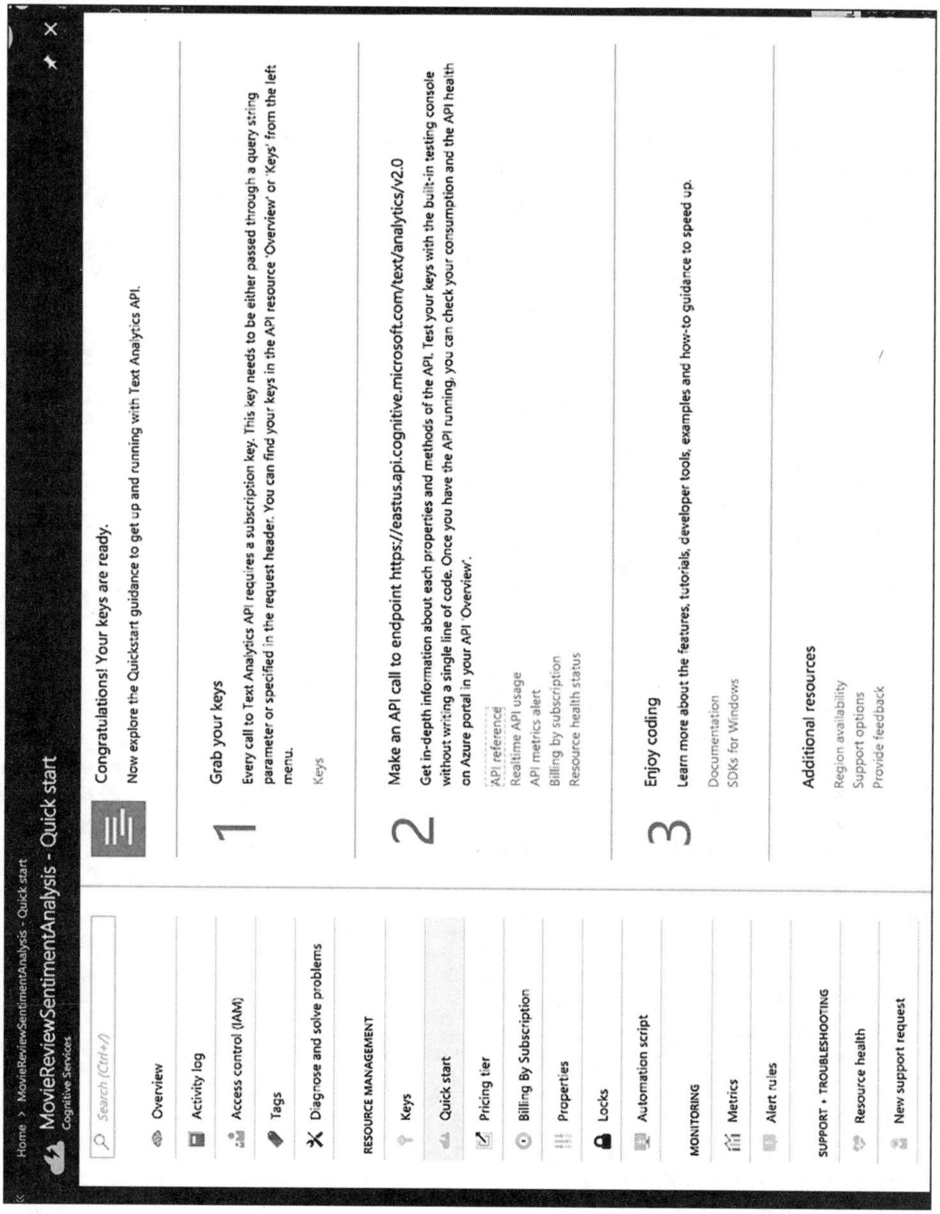

Figure 11.2 Microsoft Azure Cognitive Services API

First, imports are done in this first block in Jupyter Notebook.

```
In [1]: import requests
   ...: import os
   ...: import pandas as pd
   ...: import seaborn as sns
   ...: import matplotlib as plt
   ...:
```

Next, an API key is taken from the environment. This API key was fetched from the console shown in Figure 11.2 under the section keys and was exported as an environmental variable, so it isn't hard-coded into code. Additionally, the text API URL that will be used later is assigned to a variable.

```
In [4]: subscription_key=os.environ.get("AZURE_API_KEY")
In [5]: text_analytics_base_url =\
   ...: https://eastus.api.cognitive.microsoft.com/\
        text/analytics/v2.0/
```

Next, one of the negative reviews is formatted in the way the API expects.

```
In [9]: documents = {"documents":[]}
   ...: path = "../data/review_polarity/\
        txt_sentoken/neg/cv000_29416.txt"
   ...: doc1 = open(path, "r")
   ...: output = doc1.readlines()
   ...: count = 0
   ...: for line in output:
   ...:     count +=1
   ...:     record = {"id": count, "language": "en", "text": line}
   ...:     documents["documents"].append(record)
   ...:
   ...: #print it out
   ...: documents
```

The data structure with the following shape is created.

```
Out[9]:
{'documents': [{'id': 1,
   'language': 'en',
   'text': 'plot : two teen couples go to a\
        church party , drink and then drive . \n'},
  {'id': 2, 'language': 'en',
 'text': 'they get into an accident . \n'},
  {'id': 3,
   'language': 'en',
   'text': 'one of the guys dies ,\
but his girlfriend continues to see him in her life,\
and has nightmares . \n'},
  {'id': 4, 'language': 'en', 'text': "what's the deal ? \n"},
  {'id': 5,
   'language': 'en',
```

Finally, the sentiment analysis API is used to score the individual documents.

```
{'documents': [{'id': '1', 'score': 0.5},
  {'id': '2', 'score': 0.13049307465553284},
  {'id': '3', 'score': 0.09667149186134338},
  {'id': '4', 'score': 0.8442018032073975},
  {'id': '5', 'score': 0.808459997177124
```

At this point, the return scores can be converted into a Pandas DataFrame to do some EDA. It isn't a surprise that the median value of the sentiments for a negative review are 0.23 on a scale of 0 to 1, where 1 is extremely positive and 0 is extremely negative.

```
In [11]: df = pd.DataFrame(sentiments['documents'])

In [12]: df.describe()
Out[12]:
           score
count   35.000000
mean     0.439081
std      0.316936
min      0.037574
25%      0.159229
50%      0.233703
75%      0.803651
max      0.948562
```

This is further explained by doing a density plot. Figure 11.3 shows a majority of highly negative sentiments.

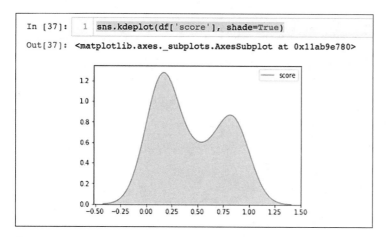

Figure 11.3   Density Plot of Sentiment Scores

NLP on GCP

There is a lot to like about the Google Cloud Natural Language API (https://cloud.google.com/natural-language/docs/how-to). One of the convenient features of the API is that you can use it in two different ways: analyzing sentiment in a string, and also analyzing sentiment from Google Cloud Storage. Google Cloud also has a tremendously powerful command-line tool that makes it easy to explore their API. Finally, it has some fascinating AI APIs, some of which will be explored in this chapter: analyzing sentiment, analyzing entities, analyzing syntax, analyzing entity sentiment, and classifying content.

Exploring the Entity API

Using the command-line gcloud API is a great way to explore what one of the APIs does. In the example, a phrase is sent via the command line about LeBron James and the Cleveland Cavaliers.

```
➔  gcloud ml language analyze-entities --content=\
"LeBron James plays for the Cleveland Cavaliers."
{
  "entities": [
    {
      "mentions": [
        {
          "text": {
            "beginOffset": 0,
            "content": "LeBron James"
          },
          "type": "PROPER"
        }
      ],
      "metadata": {
        "mid": "/m/01jz6d",
        "wikipedia_url": "https://en.wikipedia.org/wiki/LeBron_James"
      },
      "name": "LeBron James",
      "salience": 0.8991045,
      "type": "PERSON"
    },
    {
      "mentions": [
        {
          "text": {
            "beginOffset": 27,
            "content": "Cleveland Cavaliers"
          },
          "type": "PROPER"
        }
      ],
```

```
      "metadata": {
        "mid": "/m/0jm7n",
        "wikipedia_url": "https://en.wikipedia.org/\
wiki/Cleveland_Cavaliers"
      },
      "name": "Cleveland Cavaliers",
      "salience": 0.100895494,
      "type": "ORGANIZATION"
    }
  ],
  "language": "en"
}
```

A second way to explore the API is to use Python. To get an API key and authenticate, you need to follow the instructions (https://cloud.google.com/docs/authentication/getting-started). Then, launch the Jupyter Notebook in the same shell as the GOOGLE_APPLICATION_CREDENTIALS variable is exported:

```
➜  ✗ export GOOGLE_APPLICATION_CREDENTIALS=\
        /Users/noahgift/cloudai-65b4e3299be1.json
➜  ✗ jupyter notebook
```

Once this authentication process is complete, the rest is straightforward. First, the python language api must be imported (This can be installed via pip if it isn't already: `pip install --upgrade google-cloud-language`.)

```
In [1]: # Imports the Google Cloud client library
   ...: from google.cloud import language
   ...: from google.cloud.language import enums
   ...: from google.cloud.language import types
```

Next, a phrase is sent to the API and entity metadata is returned with an analysis.

```
In [2]: text = "LeBron James plays for the Cleveland Cavaliers."
   ...: client = language.LanguageServiceClient()
   ...: document = types.Document(
   ...:         content=text,
   ...:         type=enums.Document.Type.PLAIN_TEXT)
   ...: entities = client.analyze_entities(document).entities
   ...:
```

The output has a similar look and feel to the command-line version, but it comes back as a Python list.

```
[name: "LeBron James"
type: PERSON
metadata {
  key: "mid"
  value: "/m/01jz6d"
}
```

```
metadata {
  key: "wikipedia_url"
  value: "https://en.wikipedia.org/wiki/LeBron_James"
}
salience: 0.8991044759750366
mentions {
  text {
    content: "LeBron James"
    begin_offset: -1
  }
  type: PROPER
}
, name: "Cleveland Cavaliers"
type: ORGANIZATION
metadata {
  key: "mid"
  value: "/m/0jm7n"
}
metadata {
  key: "wikipedia_url"
  value: "https://en.wikipedia.org/wiki/Cleveland_Cavaliers"
}
salience: 0.10089549422264099
mentions {
  text {
    content: "Cleveland Cavaliers"
    begin_offset: -1
  }
  type: PROPER
}
]
```

A few of the takeaways are that this API could be easily merged with some of the other explorations done in Chapter 6, "Predicting Social-Media Influence in the NBA." It wouldn't be hard to imagine creating an AI application that found extensive information about social influencers by using these NLP APIs as a starting point. Another takeaway is that the command line given to you by the GCP Cognitive APIs is quite powerful.

Production Serverless AI Pipeline for NLP on AWS

One thing AWS does well, perhaps better than any of the "big three" clouds, is make it easy to create production applications that are easy to write and manage. One of their "game changer" innovations is AWS Lambda. It is available to both orchestrate pipelines and serve our HTTP endpoints, like in the case of chalice. In Figure 11.4, a real-world production pipeline is described for creating an NLP pipeline.

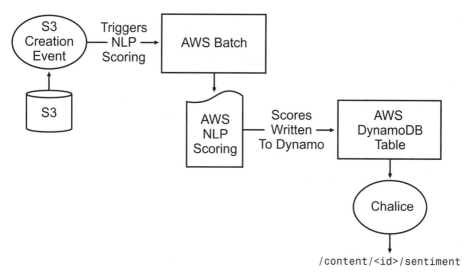

Figure 11.4   Production Serverless NLP Pipeline on AWS

To get started with AWS sentiment analysis, some libraries need to be imported.

```
In [1]: import pandas as pd
   ...: import boto3
   ...: import json
```

Next, a simple test is created.

```
In [5]: comprehend = boto3.client(service_name='comprehend')
   ...: text = "It is raining today in Seattle"
   ...: print('Calling DetectSentiment')
   ...: print(json.dumps(comprehend.detect_sentiment(\
Text=text, LanguageCode='en'), sort_keys=True, indent=4))
   ...:
   ...: print('End of DetectSentiment\n')
   ...:
```

The output shows a "SentimentScore."

```
Calling DetectSentiment
{
    "ResponseMetadata": {
        "HTTPHeaders": {
            "connection": "keep-alive",
            "content-length": "164",
            "content-type": "application/x-amz-json-1.1",
            "date": "Mon, 05 Mar 2018 05:38:53 GMT",
            "x-amzn-requestid":\
```

```
      "7d532149-2037-11e8-b422-3534e4f7cfa2"
            },
            "HTTPStatusCode": 200,
            "RequestId": "7d532149-2037-11e8-b422-3534e4f7cfa2",
            "RetryAttempts": 0
      },
      "Sentiment": "NEUTRAL",
      "SentimentScore": {
            "Mixed": 0.002063251566141844,
            "Negative": 0.013271247036755085,
            "Neutral": 0.9274052977561951,
            "Positive": 0.057260122150182724
      }
}
End of DetectSentiment
```

Now, in a more realistic example, we'll use the previous "negative movie reviews document" from the Azure example. The document is read in.

```
In [6]: path = "/Users/noahgift/Desktop/review_polarity/\
txt_sentoken/neg/cv000_29416.txt"
    ...: doc1 = open(path, "r")
    ...: output = doc1.readlines()
    ...:
```

Next, one of the "documents" (rember each line is a document according to NLP APIs) is scored.

```
In [7]: print(json.dumps(comprehend.detect_sentiment(\
Text=output[2], LanguageCode='en'), sort_keys=True, inden
    ...: t=4))

{
    "ResponseMetadata": {
        "HTTPHeaders": {
            "connection": "keep-alive",
            "content-length": "158",
            "content-type": "application/x-amz-json-1.1",
            "date": "Mon, 05 Mar 2018 05:43:25 GMT",
            "x-amzn-requestid":\
  "1fa0f6e8-2038-11e8-ae6f-9f137b5a61cb"
        },
        "HTTPStatusCode": 200,
        "RequestId": "1fa0f6e8-2038-11e8-ae6f-9f137b5a61cb",
        "RetryAttempts": 0
    },
    "Sentiment": "NEUTRAL",
    "SentimentScore": {
        "Mixed": 0.1490383893251419,
        "Negative": 0.3341641128063202,
```

```
    "Neutral": 0.468740850687027,
    "Positive": 0.04805663228034973
  }
}
```

It's no surprise that that document had a negative sentiment score since it was previously scored this way. Another interesting thing this API can do is to score all of the documents inside as one giant score. Basically, it gives the median sentiment value. Here is what that looks like.

```
In [8]: whole_doc = ', '.join(map(str, output))

In [9]: print(json.dumps(\
comprehend.detect_sentiment(\
Text=whole_doc, LanguageCode='en'), sort_keys=True, inden
   ...: t=4))
{
    "ResponseMetadata": {
        "HTTPHeaders": {
            "connection": "keep-alive",
            "content-length": "158",
            "content-type": "application/x-amz-json-1.1",
            "date": "Mon, 05 Mar 2018 05:46:12 GMT",
            "x-amzn-requestid":\
 "8296fa1a-2038-11e8-a5b9-b5b3e257e796"
        },
    "Sentiment": "MIXED",
    "SentimentScore": {
        "Mixed": 0.48351600766181946,
        "Negative": 0.2868672013282776,
        "Neutral": 0.12633098661899567,
        "Positive": 0.1032857820391655
    }
}='en'), sort_keys=True, inden
   ...: t=4))
```

An interesting takeaway is that the AWS API has some hidden tricks up its sleeve and has a nuisance that is missing from the Azure API. In the previous Azure example, the Seaborn output showed that, indeed, there was a bimodal distribution with a minority of reviews liking the movie and a majority disliking the movie. The way AWS presents the results as "mixed" sums this up quite nicely.

The only things left to do is to create a simple chalice app that will take the scored inputs that are written to Dynamo and serve them out. Here is what that looks like.

```
from uuid import uuid4
import logging
import time

from chalice import Chalice
import boto3
```

```
from boto3.dynamodb.conditions import Key
from pythonjsonlogger import jsonlogger

#APP ENVIRONMENTAL VARIABLES
REGION = "us-east-1"
APP = "nlp-api"
NLP_TABLE = "nlp-table"

#intialize logging
log = logging.getLogger("nlp-api")
LOGHANDLER = logging.StreamHandler()
FORMMATTER = jsonlogger.JsonFormatter()
LOGHANDLER.setFormatter(FORMMATTER)
log.addHandler(LOGHANDLER)
log.setLevel(logging.INFO)

app = Chalice(app_name='nlp-api')
app.debug = True

def dynamodb_client():
    """Create Dynamodb Client"""

    extra_msg = {"region_name": REGION, "aws_service": "dynamodb"}
    client = boto3.client('dynamodb', region_name=REGION)
    log.info("dynamodb CLIENT connection initiated", extra=extra_msg)
    return client

def dynamodb_resource():
    """Create Dynamodb Resource"""

    extra_msg = {"region_name": REGION, "aws_service": "dynamodb"}
    resource = boto3.resource('dynamodb', region_name=REGION)
    log.info("dynamodb RESOURCE connection initiated",\
            extra=extra_msg)
    return resource

def create_nlp_record(score):
    """Creates nlp Table Record

    """

    db = dynamodb_resource()
    pd_table = db.Table(NLP_TABLE)
    guid = str(uuid4())
    res = pd_table.put_item(
        Item={
            'guid': guid,
            'UpdateTime' : time.asctime(),
```

```
                'nlp-score': score
        }
    )
    extra_msg = {"region_name": REGION, "aws_service": "dynamodb"}
    log.info(f"Created NLP Record with result{res}", extra=extra_msg)
    return guid

def query_nlp_record():
    """Scans nlp table and retrieves all records"""

    db = dynamodb_resource()
    extra_msg = {"region_name": REGION, "aws_service": "dynamodb",
        "nlp_table":NLP_TABLE}
    log.info(f"Table Scan of NLP table", extra=extra_msg)
    pd_table = db.Table(NLP_TABLE)
    res = pd_table.scan()
    records = res['Items']
    return records

@app.route('/')
def index():
    """Default Route"""

    return {'hello': 'world'}

@app.route("/nlp/list")
def nlp_list():
    """list nlp scores"""

    extra_msg = {"region_name": REGION,
        "aws_service": "dynamodb",
        "route":"/nlp/list"}
    log.info(f"List NLP Records via route", extra=extra_msg)
    res = query_nlp_record()
    return res
```

Summary

If data is the new oil, then UGC is the sand tar pits. Sand tar pits have been historically difficult to turn into production oil pipelines, but rising energy costs and advances in technology have allowed their mining to become feasible. Similarly, the AI APIs coming out of the "big three" cloud providers have created new technological breakthroughs in sifting through the "sandy data." Also, prices for storage and computation have steadily dropped, making it much more feasible to convert UGC into an asset from which to extract extra value. Another innovation lowering the cost to process UGC is AI accelerators. Massive parallelization improvements by ASIC chips like TPUs, GPUs, and field-programmable graphic arrays (FPGAs) may make some of the scale issues discussed even less of an issue.

This chapter showed many examples of how to extract value from these tar pits, but there are also real tradeoffs and dangers, as with the real sand tar pits. UGC to AI feedback loops can be tricked and exploited in ways that create consequences that are global in scale. Also, on a much more practical level, there are tradeoffs to consider when systems go live. As easy as the cloud and AI APIs make creating solutions, the real tradeoffs cannot be abstracted away, like UX, performance, and the business implications of implemented solutions.

A

AI Accelerators

AI accelerators are a relatively new but rapidly developing technology. There are few different categories: new or bespoke products, GPU-based products, AI co-processors, and R/D products. In the new-products category, TPU has perhaps the most buzz because it allows TensorFlow developers an easy pathway to developing software.

GPU-based products are currently the most common form of AI acceleration. Professor Ian Lane, Carnegie Mellon University, says this about them: "With GPUs, pre-recorded speech or multimedia content can be transcribed much more quickly. Compared to CPU implementation we are able to perform recognition up to 33× faster."

In the category of FPGA, one company to look out for is reconfigure.io (https://reconfigure.io/). Reconfigure.io enables developers to easily use FPGAs to accelerate their solutions, including for AI. Using simple tools, and a powerful cloud build-and-deploy capability, Reconfigure.io gives developers speed, latency, and power previously only available to hardware designers. They provide a Go-based interface that takes Go code, compiles and optimizes it, and deploys it to cloud-based FPGAs on AWS. FPGAs are especially useful for using AI in network situations and where low power is needed, and so they are being heavily used by major cloud providers.

Although both GPUs and FPGAs do offer great performance improvements over CPUs, application-specific integrated circuits (ASICs) like TPUs can best these by a factor of 10. So the main use case in something like FPGAs is the familiarity that comes with being able to use tools like Go to more rapidly develop applications.

Some issues to consider with AI accelerators include the following.

1. What are the application performance requirements and general data center cost structure criteria when deciding whether to implement accelerators for use in an inference application?

2. What are the use cases of a data center inference application being accelerated?

AI accelerators should be on the radar of every company looking to do cutting-edge AI. The reason is the performance. With GPUs and FPGAs getting 30× improvement over CPUs, and then dedicated ASICs getting another 10× improvement on top of that, it is too big a breakthrough to ignore. It could lead the way to developing forms of AI that we haven't fully imagined.

Deciding on Cluster Size

There are many examples of k-means clustering in this book. One of the most commonly asked questions about these is how many clusters should be made. There is no correct answer because clustering is the process of creating labels, and two domain experts may use their judgments differently.

In Figure B.1, I created a cluster of the 2013–2014 NBA season stats, and I labeled the eight clusters by descriptions I thought were useful. Another NBA expert may have created fewer or more clusters.

However, there are some ways to help with deciding how many clusters to create. The scikit-learn documentation has some good examples of how to evaluate clustering performance (http://scikit-learn.org/stable/modules/clustering.html#clustering-performance-evaluation). Two popular techniques discussed are elbow plots and silhouette plots. This would be the recommended starting point at which to dig deeper if the clustering assignments seem like they could be improved.

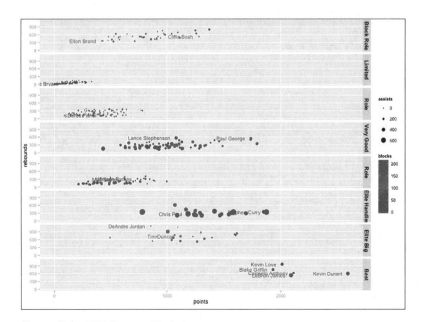

Figure B.1 NBA Season Clustering

Index

E

M

N

X-Y-Z

Credits

Chapter 1: "Don't mistake activity with achievement" John Wooden.

Chapter 2: "We're talking about practice. We're talking about practice. We ain't talking about the game." Allen Iverson.

Chapter 2, Figure 2.1: Based on screenshot of AWS © 2018, Amazon Web Services, Inc.

Chapter 2, Figure 2.2: Based on screenshot of AWS © 2018, Amazon Web Services, Inc.

Chapter 2, Figure 2.3: Based on screenshot of AWS © 2018, Amazon Web Services, Inc.

Chapter 2, Figure 2.4: Based on screenshot of AWS © 2018, Amazon Web Services, Inc.

Chapter 2, Figure 2.5: Based on screenshot of AWS © 2018, Amazon Web Services, Inc.

Chapter 2, Figure 2.6: Based on screenshot of AWS © 2018, Amazon Web Services, Inc.

Chapter 3: "I'm going to go out there and be ridiculous and see what happens. I've got nothing to lose." Wayde Van Niekerk.

Chapter 3, Figure 3.2: Based on screenshot of AWS © 2018, Amazon Web Services, Inc.

Chapter 3, Figure 3.3: Based on screenshot of AWS © 2018, Amazon Web Services, Inc.

Chapter 3, Figure 3.5: Based on screenshot of AWS © 2018, Amazon Web Services, Inc.

Chapter 3, Figure 3.6: Based on screenshot of AWS © 2018, Amazon Web Services, Inc.

Chapter 4: "There are no shortcuts to building a team each season. You build the foundation brick by brick." Bill Belichick.

Chapter 4, Figure 4.1: Screenshot of GCP © Google LLC.

Chapter 4, Figure 4.2: Screenshot of GCP © Google LLC.

Chapter 4, Figure 4.5: Screenshot of GCP © Google LLC.

Chapter 4, Figure 4.6: Screenshot of GCP © Google LLC.

Chapter 4, Figure 4.7: Photo courtesy of Noah Gift.

Chapter 5: "Your love makes me strong. Your hate makes me unstoppable." Cristiano Ronaldo.

Chapter 5, Figure 5.3: Screenshot of Swagger © SmartBear Software.

Chapter 5, Figure 5.4: Screenshot of Swagger © SmartBear Software.

Chapter 6: "Talent wins games, but teamwork and intelligence wins championships." Michael Jordan.

Chapter 6, Figure 6.2: Screenshot of Jupyter Copyright © 2018 Project Jupyter.

Chapter 6, Figure 6.3: Screenshot of Jupyter Copyright © 2018 Project Jupyter.

Chapter 6, Figure 6.4: Screenshot of Jupyter Copyright © 2018 Project Jupyter.

Chapter 6, Figure 6.5: Screenshot of Jupyter Copyright © 2018 Project Jupyter.

Chapter 6, Figure 6.6: Screenshot of Jupyter Copyright © 2018 Project Jupyter.

Chapter 6, Figure 6.7: Screenshot of Jupyter Copyright © 2018 Project Jupyter.

Chapter 6, Figure 6.8: Screenshot of Jupyter Copyright © 2018 Project Jupyter.

Chapter 6, Figure 6.11: Screenshot of Jupyter Copyright © 2018 Project Jupyter.

Chapter 6, Figure 6.13: Screenshot of Jupyter Copyright © 2018 Project Jupyter.

Chapter 6, Figure 6.14: Screenshot of Jupyter Copyright © 2018 Project Jupyter.

Chapter 7: "The man who can . . . is the man who will win" Roger Bannister.

Chapter 7: "GUIs tend to . . . otherwise is a sucker." Neal Stephenson, In the Beginning...was the Command Line, Turtleback Books, 1999.

Chapter 7, Figure 7.1: Screenshot of Slack Copyright © Slack Technologies.

Chapter 7, Figure 7.2: Based on screenshot of AWS © 2018, Amazon Web Services, Inc.

Chapter 7, Figure 7.3: Based on screenshot of AWS © 2018, Amazon Web Services, Inc.

Chapter 8: "Jiu Jitsu is perfect. It's humans who make errors." Rickson Gracie.

Chapter 8: "Increase in relative code . . . in system defect density." Use of Relative Code Churn Measures to Predict System Defect Density by Thomas Ball.

Chapter 9: "Jiu-Jitsu is a race . . . you will never catch up." Luis "Limao" Heredia (5-Time Pan American Brazilian Jiu-Jitsu Champion).

Chapter 10: "Once you get on the . . . . That's what it's about." LeBron James.

Chapter 11: "The man who can drive himself further once the effort gets painful is the man who will win." Roger Bannister.

Chapter 11: "though feasible for . . . dimensionality and size" Michael P. Holmes, Fast SVD for Large-Scale Matrices Approximate PCA, eigenvector methods and more via stratified Monte Carlo.

Chapter 11: "a lesson here is that having lots . . . a few well-selected models." The BellKor 2008 Solution to the Netflix Prize.

Chapter 11: "A lesson here . . . well-selected models." Robert M. Bell, Yehuda Koren, Chris Volinsky, The Bell K or 2008 Solution to the Netflix Prize.

Chapter 11, Figure 11.2: Screenshot of Microsoft Azure © Microsoft 2018.

Appendix A: "With GPUs, pre-recorded speech or . . . recognition up to 33x faster." Professor Ian Lane, Carnegie Mellon University.

Page 253: Photo by wavebreakmedia/Shutterstock.

Page 254: Photo by izusek/gettyimages.

Register Your Product at informit.com/register

Access additional benefits and **save 35%** on your next purchase

- Automatically receive a coupon for 35% off your next purchase, valid for 30 days. Look for your code in your InformIT cart or the Manage Codes section of your account page.

- Download available product updates.

- Access bonus material if available.*

- Check the box to hear from us and receive exclusive offers on new editions and related products.

*Registration benefits vary by product. Benefits will be listed on your account page under Registered Products.

InformIT.com—The Trusted Technology Learning Source

InformIT is the online home of information technology brands at Pearson, the world's foremost education company. At InformIT.com, you can:

- Shop our books, eBooks, software, and video training
- Take advantage of our special offers and promotions (informit.com/promotions)
- Sign up for special offers and content newsletter (informit.com/newsletters)
- Access thousands of free chapters and video lessons

Connect with InformIT—Visit informit.com/community

Addison-Wesley • Adobe Press • Cisco Press • Microsoft Press • Pearson IT Certification • Prentice Hall • Que • Sams • Peachpit Press

 Pearson